A Prayer Strategy
for Jesus' Victory Over Radical Islam
Book I

Discerning the Times
Exposing Satan's Plans in Radical Islam

Zeb Bradford Long

PRMI Exousia Press

DISCERNING THE TIMES:
EXPOSING SATAN'S PLANS IN RADICAL ISLAM
A Prayer Strategy for Jesus' Victory Over Radical Islam Book I
Copyright © 2016 Zeb Bradford Long

PRMI
EXOUSIA
PRESS

Published by PRMI Exousia Press,
a ministry of the Presbyterian-Reformed Ministries
International Dunamis Institute
Black Mountain, North Carolina, USA
www.dunamisinstitute.org

Cover design and graphics by Joe Schlosser, Excellent Adventures Inc.

Scripture quoted by permission. All scripture quotations, unless otherwise indicated, are taken from the NET Bible® copyright ©1996-2016 by Biblical Studies Press, L.L.C. All rights reserved.

Because of the dynamic nature of the Internet, any web addresses or links contained in this book may have changed since publication and may no longer be valid.

ISBN-13: 978-0692716731

Library of Congress Control Number: 2016946100
PRMI EXOUSIA PRESS, Black Mountain, NC

DEDICATION

This book is dedicated to the millions upon millions of unnamed Jews and Christians through all the ages who were martyred for their faith or coerced into Islamic tyranny by the sword and subjugation.

The War

Moses built an altar, and he called it "The LORD is my Banner," for he said, "For a hand was lifted up to the throne of the LORD—that the LORD will have war with Amalek from generation to generation" (Exodus 17:15-16).

For our struggle is not against flesh and blood, but against the rulers, against the powers, against the world rulers of this darkness, against the spiritual forces of evil in the heavens. (Ephesians 6:12)

The Victory

Jesus replied, "I am the way, and the truth, and the life. No one comes to the Father except through me" (John 14:6).

He humbled himself, by becoming obedient to the point of death—even death on a cross! As a result, God exalted him and gave him the name that is above every name, so that at the name of Jesus every knee will bow—in heaven and on earth and under the earth—and every tongue confess that Jesus Christ is Lord to the glory of God the Father (Philippians 2:8-11).

Author's Note
Why I Chose These Graphics

The graphics chosen for the book are the result of discerning the times. These images and colors are a composite based on the images used by the leaders to present their own vision and goals. The dome with the crescent moon and the minaret are universal symbols of Islam. The colors of the billowing clouds of green, yellow and black have symbolic and historical associations with Islam.

The black flag of ISIS needs more explanation for those not versed in the Arabic language and Islamic history. The color black goes back to the banner of Muhammad. Black is particularly significant for ISIS because it was used by the Abbasid Caliphate started in 747.[1] The mission of ISIS is to reestablish the Caliphate. The second meaning of the color black points to ISIS as an apocalyptic cult. "It is also a symbol in Islamic eschatology (heralding the advent of the Mahdi)."[2] The Arabic at the top of the ISIS flag in white is the first part of the "shahada," the Islamic declaration of faith, "There is no God but Allah." The white circle with the Arabic in black contains the second part of the shahada, "Muhammad is the Messenger of Allah." This represents the official seal of the prophet Muhammad.

The armed men and women, who often wear black masks while holding up their weapons, do so as symbols of armed jihad that imposes Islamic hegemony through death and subjugation.

These images are not intended to be sensational but revelatory of the true nature of the gathering storm of Radical Islam.

ACKNOWLEDGMENTS

I could not have discerned Satan's plans in Radical Islam without those who have courageously exposed those plans to the world. They have revealed the truth at the risk of their lives and reputations. So my deepest thanks to the following: Robert Spencer of Jihad Watch, Raymond Ibrahim, the author of *Crucified Again*, Geert Wilders, Dutch Member of Parliament and leader of the Freedom Party, Newt Gingrich who exposed the threat of militant Islam to America, and Israel's Prime Minister Benjamin Netanyahu, who has warned the world of the threat of militant Islam. Barry Rubin and Wolfgang G. Schwanitz, historians and authors of the book *Nazis, Islamists, and the Making of the Modern Middle East* have also played a key role in this exposure by clearly revealing Islam and Nazism as two parallel tracks leading to Radical Islam's ideology of genocide of Jews and Christians.

Also, my appreciation for those intercessors who have joined me in this battle. Thanks to the Presbyterian Reformed Ministries International (PRMI) Board of Directors and ministry staff who have all taken part in the discernment of this work and provided the prayer covering as well as the administrative support for me to do the research and writing for the development of this book.

In addition to the intercessors I have worked closely with the following team who helped directly with the formation of the ideas, writing, and editing of this book, work made immensely more difficult by my own profound learning disability. So, my thanks to Cindy and Steve Strickler, Doug McMurry, and Judy Cook. Thanks to Mary Ellen Conners and Daniele King for layout and review. Thanks to Joe Schlosser who formed the graphics for the book. Without your help this project would never have been completed. Thanks to Steve Aceto for profound discernment into the structures of good and evil.

Above all, glory and praise to God the Father, Son, and Holy Spirit, whose Kingdom of life, truth, and freedom will prevail over Satan's plans for death and tyranny in Radical Islam.

TABLE OF CONTENTS

Preface
By Doug McMurry

The people of God—His royal priesthood—cannot afford to assume that life is what it seems to be on the surface. The Word of God assures us that this world is under the power of the devil—which means that we are under deception. We know this from Genesis 2, where we see Adam coming under deception, and from Revelation 20, where we see Jesus rescuing us from enemy deception at the end of the present age. But we today are in between these two earth-changing events. Implication: we can expect to be under satanic deception, and we must make some attempts to get out from under it.

When I was a kid, secularism was king. We grew up in a world in which the existence of a spiritual realm was scoffed at by most people, even Christians. The possibility that secularism was itself a cloaking device never occurred to us. Pop culture was made aware of cloaking devices by the Star Trek series, which defines a cloaking device as "technology of Romulan origin, first described in 2266, that can generate an energy screen to render a target object—usually a spacecraft—relatively invisible to sensors."

More and more, fiction guides reality. Now we are realizing that cloaking devices are a real strategy that enemies use when drawing near for attack. Brad Long sees this strategy as a very real weapon against us who are in Christ, who are working for the Gospel of the Kingdom. We are opposed by an enemy who is using cloaking devices against us. The problem is that the cloaking devices are hidden from us, because we are deceived, naïve, simple-minded, and secular. Cloaking devices may be real for the galactic battles of the starship Enterprise; but we don't see them at work anywhere around us!

Our popular culture is trying to emerge from secularism and

its massive deception. The film *The Matrix* follows the adventures of a certain millennial named Neo as he discovers that "normal" Western culture is a deceptive web of beliefs promulgated by invisible beings who control and enslave people without their being aware of it. Neo joins a small team of warriors who have devoted themselves to resist this enslavement and bring the truth that will set the human race free.

Anyone who sees this film with their spiritual eyes open will recognize that this is exactly what Jesus, "the One from above," does for us, and for all humanity. He unmasks enemy deception for us, who have been enslaved by it, and gives us the Truth that will set us free. He also enlists us in an army of warriors to fight the Deceiver, and promises absolute victory at the conclusion of history. Furthermore, He empowers us with supernatural weapons in our fight, and allows us the use of his very own iron scepter, that is, his authority over the nations. This is not some fictional movie we are tracing here; this is history itself. His Story. And the Deceiver is a very real enemy, though we rarely get a glimpse of him.

It seems to me that somewhere around 1400 years ago or so, this enemy decided to change his strategy with us. Prior to the seventh century, the dark powers loved to intimidate people with shows of raw power and terror. This was the strategy of all classical warfare in the old days, even among human kings. Put your forces out there in the open, boast of your strength and ferocity and intimidate your opponent into surrendering—for fear of what you will do to them if they don't surrender. This is how they did things in ancient Greece, Assyria and Rome. It is also how the enemy used to do things, too, as we read in the writings of the Desert Fathers, such as Evagrius of Pontus or Anthony the Great.

But in the first centuries of Christian prayer, Satan got bruised and bloodied and pushed into a corner. So, he discovered the benefits of guerilla warfare. Go into hiding, then emerge just when your enemy is most unaware of your existence. Use cloaking devices and occult religions. These give you the element of surprise, which you will need, because you know you are weaker than your enemy and will probably lose the war in the end. Still, you fight on.

Secularism has been an effective cloaking device for this Deceiver. It has convinced Christians that there is no spirit realm (except heaven, where you go after you die), no warfare, no enemy—and no enemy deception. So we don't even try to get ourselves undeceived. We spend no time in our Bibles, thinking that they are full of irrelevant, boring Sunday School stories. We spend no time listening to God—even though Jesus paid the ultimate price to allow us to do this. We assume that our secular culture is more or less right about most things and that the truths God wants us to learn are hopelessly "religious," meaning that they are unrelated to the real world—just things you are supposed to say when you are in church.

The Bible is, instead, a manual for battle. Without it, we cannot hope to be victorious against the darkness arrayed against us. It lays out the battlefield, tells us what the war is about, and gives us a choice as to which side we will join. Jesus is "the One from above," the only one who sees clearly. All the rest of us are "from below," under the matrix of deception.

Brad Long sees this clearer than most. In Book I of this series, he has done an excellent job of opening our eyes to see Islam from the standpoint of Kingdom conflict at a cosmic level. No doubt, this book that Brad has written will get attention because ISIS and Radical Islam are a concern to most people just now. Its main value, however, will be its potential to open our eyes to the broader spiritual conflicts of history. A book like this can help us to wake up from our slumber and enlist for the battle.

Radical Islam is, after all, only one of many deceptions of modern times. Behind such deceptive worldviews is an enemy who is determined to keep Jesus from taking control of Creation as the Son of David, to "restore all things" to God's original intentions.

We look forward to Book II in this series, which will outline the tactics of actual spiritual warfare against the stronghold of Radical Islam. The two-part manual is no mere academic treatise for some ivory tower institution. It comes from years of experience Brad has gained in ground-level spiritual warfare in Asian, African, and Western nations. Brad's voice is a voice that promises to gain much attention in future years.

Douglas McMurry – June 19, 2016

Author's Preface
On the Dangers of Naming One's Enemies

It is crucial that I use precise language in this book so that you do not misconstrue my words or intentions. There are many inherent dangers in naming the enemy.

When I use the term *Islam*, I am referring to the religion born in the Arabian desert of the early 7th century which is still practiced today in a number of forms and places. Although I do conclude that Islam is a false religion, based on the demonic deception of Muhammad, I intend in no way to disparage the character of the majority of Muslims world-wide practicing their religion peacefully.

The terms *Radical Islam*, *Militant Islam*, *Islamic Fascism*, *Apocalyptic Islam*, and *Jihadist Islam* are all terms used to denote terrorist movements bent on world conquest with the intent of imposing Sharia law on all. This brand of Islam is taken from some verses in the Quran which justify the genocide of Jews and Christians, and fellow Muslims considered infidels. Whether these movements represent true Islam or not is not my topic.

There is a great concern that naming our enemy Islamic leads to painting all Muslims with the same brush of terrorism, thus, our sworn enemies. The opposite is the case. The intention of this book is to provide a framework for discerning and naming our true adversaries. This discernment is the necessary precondition for developing the battle plans for winning the victory.

I have studied the many plans put forth for defeating the various expressions of Radical Islam which have declared war on the Western world, Jews, Christians and all our culture based on our Judeo-Christian values. Often these plans fall into two separate, disconnected categories: 1. Those based on human sociological, cultural, and military assumptions. 2. Those based on spiritual assumptions that our warfare is not with flesh and blood but with demonic powers. Neither in isolation are up to the task. The books in this series provide a set of paradigms based on a Christian worldview that unifies these two perspectives.

One of these paradigms is that of "strongholds," which are essentially intermingled human and demonic organizations which give Satan the human means to accomplish his purposes on earth. The necessity of demonic spiritual beings working through human beings and human social organizations is comparable to how God works in the world. From my Reformed theological perspective, God works through common grace structures of governments, legal systems, and economic systems for human well-being. He also works through the Church of Jesus Christ as his means of advancing his Kingdom on earth. Essentially, Satan has usurped for his own evil intentions the means which God has established. Satan is able to build strongholds for great evil out of any religious or philosophical system. This includes Islam and Christianity. By understanding this reality, we are able to discern accurately who our real enemies are—in this case, strongholds based on Islam which are both spiritual and human, and which will require both spiritual and earthly weapons to defeat. This approach allows us to avoid the simplistic notion that all Muslims are our enemies. Rather, by naming our true enemies, we create the context where Jews, Christians, Muslims, secularists, indeed all who love humanity and cherish freedom, diversity and creativity, may make common cause in order to win the war.

This book seeks to outline the unified spiritual and human framework needed for defeating Radical Islam. My starting point, however, is the spiritual perspective which is the only way to understand fully the human dimensions. This book is first and foremost a prayer strategy for Christians who are called to join the Father's plan to overcome the strongholds of Radical Islam and, along the way, take part in the ultimate fulfillment of the Great Commission.

Zeb Bradford Long June 19, 2016

Part I
The Gathering Storm

The Gathering Storm

"The gathering storm" is how Sir Winston Churchill viewed the period between the Great War that was supposed to be the war to end all wars, and the outbreak of the even more disastrous Second World War. We are entering another such period of a gathering storm. In the decades of supposed peace after November 11, 1918, powerful forces were at work which the world would identify as the Great Depression, the Communist Revolution, the rise of a political movement called Nazism, and Japan's quest to establish an empire in Asia.

Only a few people of that day had eyes to see and could "discern the times." [1] Through them the Lord was warning the world—largely in vain—of the impending catastrophe. He spoke in the 1930s through Christians such as Rees Howells, who received a prophetic vision which revealed to him that more than the clash of ideologies was impending. Behind these human social, political, and cultural movements was the reality of demonic strongholds. "The gathering storm" foreboded these spiritual strongholds gaining earthly power and military might to oppose the Kingdom of God and to unleash upon the world Satan's plans for the future.

On September 30, 1938, British Prime Minister Neville

Chamberlain, fresh back from meetings with Hitler and waving the Anglo-German Declaration, announced to a jubilant crowd that he had achieved "peace with honour." Chamberlain said, "I believe it is peace for our time." Those who could see, saw otherwise. Winston Churchill proclaimed the Munich Agreement "a total, unmitigated defeat."[2] Churchill told Neville Chamberlain, "You were given the choice between war and dishonour. You chose dishonour and you will have war."[3]

Rees Howells was called by the Holy Spirit as an intercessor and spiritual warrior. At the Bible College in Wales, Howells, led by the Holy Spirit, was joined by college students during the crisis of Munich to pray nonstop for three weeks for God to "bend Hitler."[4] Howells later celebrated that God had bent Hitler away from seizing the last chance to invade English soil before she armed. When Hitler broke the Locarno Treaty and invaded the Rhineland in 1939, Howells had a prophetic vision of, "France on fire in a day," and a "general European war" breaking out.[5] These predictions all came to pass with the horror of World War II, with the death of millions, the Holocaust, whole cities and nations laid waste, all followed by the mass killings by Stalin in Russia and Mao Tse Tung in China. All this devastation was brought about because the demonic strongholds of atheistic Communism, Nazism, and Japanese imperialism were able to grow unchecked to maturity, unleashing vast and terrible death, suffering, and tyranny in the world.

If only the world had listened to those who were discerning the times, if they had heeded their warnings, and resolved to take action immediately. But the world did not! International leaders could not see. And by the time the true character of the strongholds was obvious to all, Satan had obtained the means of carrying out his intentions. Preventing their total fulfillment would exact a terrible toll.

We are now entering another such time in history, a "gathering storm," in which demonic strongholds are growing in maturity and are obtaining the political, economic, cultural, and military means to unleash Satan's plans on earth. This configuration of political movements, ideology, and individual actors are different from those of the last great outbreak of evil.

This time it is the political/military/religious system of Radical Islam, and the movement in the West of Liberal Progressivism. The demonic strongholds go by different names, but Satan's purposes remain the same as in the last great flowering of his schemes—to annihilate Jews and Christians. Satan's ultimate goal is the complete replacement of Yahweh's way of redemption revealed in the Old and New Testaments through Jesus Christ with the deception of Islam. Satan intends to enslave humanity through Sharia law and other systems of tyranny opposed to the Kingdom of God.

Into the Gap During the Gathering Storm

Our Father has been and is presently raising up many prophetic voices warning that we are in the time of the gathering storm. They are discerning a gathering of demonic powers in the stronghold of Radical Islam preparing to launch Satan's plans. Giving opportunity to Radical Islamic resurgence is the spiritual and cultural weakening taking place in the Western world brought about largely by the prevailing worldview of Liberal Progressivism.

I mention here a few prophetic voices speaking in this second decade of the 21st century. Google search them: Rick Joyner, Chuck Pierce, and Joel Rosenberg. In addition, review the words of secular analysts and leaders such as military historian Victor Davis Hanson and political leaders, most notably Israel's Prime Minister Benjamin Netanyahu. His speeches given before the UN General Assembly and the US Congress in 2014-15 sound like a combination of an Old Testament prophet and Winston Churchill. Take heed to Australia's

Tony Abbott and Egypt's President Abdel Fattah el-Sisi. Listen carefully to US Senators John McCain and Joseph Lieberman, and past New York Mayor Rudy Giuliani. Listen to Newt Gingrich, the former Speaker of the United States House of Representatives. I recommend William McCants's fine, insightful volume, *The Isis Apocalypse*, published in 2015 by St. Martin's Press. View, read, and listen to those writing the editorial pages of the *Wall Street Journal* and to the news broadcast and opinions of Fox News as well as Glenn Beck's *The Blaze*.

These warnings have been given for a long time. In a speech given by Senator Rick Santorum in 2007 entitled "The Gathering Storm of the 21st Century," he warned, "I am here again today talking about this issue because Islamic Fascism continues to rear its ugly head. And because it is being joined by others, becoming a hydra. The war is at our doorsteps, and it is fueled, figuratively and literally, by Islamic fascism, nurtured and bred in Iran."[6]

Pay attention! Listen to them! You will see a growing crescendo of warning from many different perspectives—prophetic, religious, political, military and cultural—that we really are in a period of a gathering storm, and that a tsunami of evil from Radical Islam is about to break upon us.

Assess these prophetic warnings and calls to action yourself as to whether or not they are from the Holy Spirit. But analysis and assessment of the danger is not enough. We must all move to concerted Holy Spirit-led actions to advance the Kingdom of God over Satan's empire of evil.

Discerning the Times

For those who can discern the times through understanding of history, analysis of obvious threats, and prophetic vision, we can see in the rise of Radical Islam and in the global situation, that we have entered a time comparable to the 1930s. The spiritual forces of evil and the human movements are converging to provide the means for Satan to make a second attempt at accomplishing his terrible goals which he previously intended in Nazism, Stalinist Communism and Japanese Imperialism.

Satan's plan from the beginning has been to usurp the one, true God with his own evil reign. His deception of Muhammad lives today in a virulent form of Islam bent upon destroying the Church of Jesus Christ, and upon the deception and bondage of Islam through the "sword and subjugation." The culture, the religion, and the sacred texts of Islam have provided Satan with the building blocks for constructing strongholds as well-honed weapons intent upon destroying the Church of Jesus Christ and blocking the advancement of the Kingdom of God in the world.

The terrifying possibility and indeed looming inevitability is that in building the Caliphate in either its Sunni or Shia form, Islamists give Satan carte blanche to carry out genocide on a global scale. Genocide of millions of human beings is to Satan's advantage in imposing the spiritual and political bondage of Sharia law worldwide. For those who can "discern the times," it is obvious and well documented that these Radical Islamic movements are gaining strength. Unless soon stopped, they pose a clear and present danger not just to the Church of Jesus Christ and to the Jewish people, but to all humanity.

I am called, along with many others, to sound the alarm. Further, the Holy Spirit has pressed upon me to join the battle and to invite you to enlist. Together we are called by Jesus to take part in the Holy Spirit's work of mobilizing, equipping and deploying an international army of intercessors. Not only that. We must understand that while Yahweh is Lord of history, He has called us not as slaves, but rather as friends and coworkers. Jesus has made us free citizens of his eternal Kingdom through His life, death, resurrection and ascension. As such, the Holy Spirit issues the summons for intercessors and spiritual warriors who must respond in faith and obedience to fight for and with Jesus. Unlike Satan's slave armies of captives to Islam, our General, while Lord of heaven and earth, depends on our willingness to join his army not out of coercion but out of love. When we join in the battle, Jesus will gain the victory on earth over Satan's strongholds of Radical Islam. Satan's schemes for death and subjugation of humanity will be defeated, and God's plans of life, freedom and justice revealed in Jesus Christ will prevail on earth. When we march against the gates of hell, the gates of hell cannot prevail. But we must march forward in joyful obedience under the banner of Christ. Let Jesus' Church arise!

Global Strategy of the Father, Son and Holy Spirit

Discerning the times is an essential first step in obtaining the intelligence necessary to know our enemy—Radical Islam. The second step which I cover in the next book is developing the prayer and spiritual warfare strategies needed to defeat our enemy. Both are to enable us to take part in the two interconnected but distinct campaigns King Jesus has launched in the last decades of the 20th and the dawn of the 21st century. These are:

The campaign to advance the Kingdom of God into the entire world. The part of this vast campaign that we are focusing on here is the sending of waves of the Holy Spirit to bring the Muslim world to saving faith in Jesus Christ in fulfillment of the Great Commission.

The campaign to defeat the demonic strongholds of Radical Islam in the world today. These strongholds have been built with the two-fold aim of: A. Preventing the Muslim world from coming to faith in Jesus Christ, and B. The actual replacement and extermination of the Church of Jesus Christ, along with her Jewish roots, through subjugation and extermination through the demonic deception of the culture and religion of Islam.

There are many other campaigns underway for defeating Satan and advancing the Gospel, but our focus here is on these two where Presbyterian Reformed Ministries International (PRMI) and I have been called to make specific contributions to the war effort. This book, *Discerning the Times* and the one following, *Defeating the Demonic Strongholds of ISIS and Radical Islam*, are assets among a number that the Holy Spirit has called us and others to make available to prepare and deploy an international army of intercessors.[7] Jesus Christ is deploying his army of intercessors to provide the prayer support for the spiritual, military, political and cultural battles required for total victory over the jihadist armies and culture of Radical Islam.

Apocalyptic Visions and the Call to Prayer

Why am I working to discern the times so that I can develop this prayer strategy to defeat radical Islam?

It may sound strange to many modern ears, but the truth is that the Holy Spirit caught me up into the presence of the resurrected Jesus Christ, where He clearly spoke to me. Jesus gave me clear warnings as well as marching orders. I am extending this personal call experience to you so that you will understand my motives, passion and urgency to defeat Radical Islam. My prayer is that the Holy Spirit would also call you into Jesus' army of intercessors.

None of what follows is written out of hatred for Muslims, Islamophobia, or a reactionary conservatism to protect Western culture. I am, of course, not immune to such influences, but what drives me is that I have by grace alone been born again into God's Kingdom, and have come to know the Father, Son and Holy Spirit, one God in three persons. There has been ignited in me the fire of the Holy Spirit to follow Jesus Christ, the Lord of the universe, and to offer all of who I am to the great cause of advancing his Kingdom.

In March 2010, I had a very personal encounter with Jesus. This happened during the health care debate in the United States.

All during the debate I had a heavy burden to pray. Over the weekend of March 20, as Congress was moving toward the vote the call grew in intensity. I could not help it; the Holy Spirit continued to pray through me, and I knew I needed to yield to the Spirit. This intercessory prayer work was so intense that I felt that I should not go to Canada for a long-scheduled meeting. I knew I was called by the Father to stay within the territorial boundaries of the United States.

On Sunday morning I fully intended to go to church, but instead the Holy Spirit told me to walk the prayer paths at the Community of the Cross[1] and pray. I walked around the land pausing in different locations, first along the river, and then up the prayer trail, until I finally came to the prayer bench on the ridge with a view overlooking the higher mountains across the valley. It was there that I started to intercede in earnest, mostly in tongues as the Holy Spirit was rushing through me. But from time to time my prayers in the Spirit did take on words. I was praying for the health care debate; I was praying for the US Congress to exercise wisdom.

I had the persistent image of a rope that was being pulled so tight that one-by-one the threads were fraying and snapping. I did not know exactly what that meant, but I kept praying into the vision. As I did, I saw the rope continuing to fray. I kept asking the Father, "Lord, what does this mean?" Over and over I prayed.

Suddenly I was caught up into the heavenly realms and was overwhelmed by apocalyptic visions of mass destruction. It would take pages to write all that I saw, but it was overwhelming and terrifying. As I reflected on this I realized that I was seeing the end of our world as we know it. The destruction seemed to come from two directions. Attacks came against our churches from "within" as biblical faith in Jesus Christ was eroded by the worldview of liberal progressivism. Our systems of government were also assaulted by progressivism, and I saw western society and political systems collapsing. [2] And then I saw massive destruction coming from "without" as Radical Islam unleashed terrorism around the globe.

The vision was graphic and intensely disturbing. Not just visual, but visceral, as actual lived experience. A whole Tom Clancy-like novel would be required to detail the unfolding drama of what I experienced while caught up in the Spirit. I remember thinking to myself as this started to happen, "Lord? I thought you were calling me to pray about the health care debate?" No answer came back, just overwhelming visions.

So, in brief, I saw the massive, unsustainable public debt needed to feed, clothe and house the millions dependent on the social welfare system, collapsing whole economies. The streets of New York, Toronto, and London full of starving people rioting for food. I saw Christians fleeing the Netherlands because of the imposition of Sharia law. I saw the Church persecuted in the UK, Canada, and in America by liberal Christians and by radical Muslims.

This vision happened to me! I did not make it up or imagine something that wasn't truly taking place in the Spirit. I was caught up in the Spirit. And then it all grew more terrible. I saw Islamic jihadist attacks using biological, nuclear, and conventional weapons, first against Israel, then against the United States and the United Kingdom, and in mounting waves of destruction against Canada, Russia and India. Then, the massive attacks were leveled against all the Christian nations and populations of Africa. Australia was under siege. Cities were laid waste, and millions of people were dead or dying. Chaos and anarchy abounded so that the complete breakdown of civil government and society resulted.

In Europe I saw waves of fanatical, reactionary revolutionaries overthrowing Western democratic governments, and in answer to the cries of a desperate population for food, shelter, and order, came the establishment of various forms of Fascist, Communist, and Islamic tyrannies.

I saw a worldwide holocaust, this time not just against Jews, but also against Christians. Christians and Jews were slaughtered in staggering numbers with vast heaps of beheaded bodies in nations wherever the balance of power had tipped in favor of Muslims. Western democracies of the United States, the United Kingdom and Canada were unable to do anything about this new worldwide holocaust because they had been completely destroyed, compromised or subjugated by Islamic hegemony.

Worst of all was the state of the Church in the West. It was depleted as most of its members were dead and the entire formal leadership structures destroyed, with all nominal members having converted to Islam. Yet she was still alive, like a seed in winter driven deep underground with no means of expressing her faith beyond the Holy Spirit within a few faithful hearts. The Church had been rendered helpless to take part in preventing any of these evils. The Church in the West was unable to advance the Gospel of Jesus Christ around the world, and had been stripped of all earthly means to engage Satan's iron veil of Islamic tyranny that was falling over the West.

Then I glimpsed with horror Satan's end game where the strongholds of Islamic terrorism and Liberal Progressivism were but pawns in the grand scheme! The ultimate goal was the complete replacement of the Father's plan of redemption as revealed in the Old and New Testaments with the deception and bondage of the totalitarian system of Islam. Churches and synagogues were either destroyed, empty of people, or converted into flourishing Mosques.

I was overwhelmed and confused about the visionary experiences that, like a monstrous wave, had just washed over me. Actually I felt like Ezekiel who, after seeing his vision and being carried to the exiles at Tel Abib, sat dumbfounded for seven days,[3] though of course my experience was not nearly as long and severe as his. After recovering from the shock of the visionary experience, I asked the Lord, "What is all this? What does it mean?" The Holy

Spirit had taken me way beyond interceding for the health care debate into another prophetic reality.

Intercede So That These Things Do Not Happen!

Then I experienced the Lord speaking to me with the same vividness and urgency of the vision, telling me that He was pouring out His Holy Spirit worldwide, raising up intercessors to pray so that none of these things would come to pass. The Lord said, "I have given you a glimpse of Satan's plans for the world; these are not my plans!" Then there came the reaffirmation of a calling that God has given PRMI: Our mission is to join the Holy Spirit's work of mobilizing, equipping and deploying intercessors through whom the Father is going to remove the blocks to advance the Gospel of Jesus Christ moving worldwide.

I also was aware that there was great blessing in store for the nations as these blocks to the Gospel were removed. I saw millions upon millions of Muslims liberated from the death and tyranny of Islam by Jesus Christ who was welcoming them into His Kingdom of life and freedom. There also came the terrible awareness that this was a call into intense battle against the empire of Satan. And that while the victory would be God's, we still had a critical role. We were to be called into the gap as intercessors like Moses for Israel and Jesus ultimately for His Church. God would indeed defeat Satan's plans and confirm His own. This would be a costly battle to which we were being called, and our prayers, obedience and suffering would all be an essential part of Jesus' victory over the demonic strongholds of Radical Islam. There would be battles and victories over other strongholds as well, but the focus of this call to prayer is Radical Islam.

Then the Lord was saying that I was not to be afraid to name the strongholds Satan is raising up to implement this awful future. I then felt His guidance that I was called into the gap to pray, and that I was to mobilize, equip and deploy other intercessors to step into the gap at this time.

I submitted this mystical experience and call to the PRMI Board of Directors and our ministry team for discernment and clarification.[4] I have since learned that other intercessors were called into the heavenlies at the very same time I was, and were given the same call.

The Holy Spirit is calling an international team of intercessors to take part in the great counter-offensive against Satan's strongholds so that these terrible visions will never come to pass, and the Father's plans for life and freedom will prevail.

A Ten-Year-Old Encountering the Holocaust

While this visionary encounter was an unexpected experience, my call to mobilize prayer to defeat Satan's strongholds of death actually has its beginnings in my childhood. When I was in elementary school, my young soul was seared with pictures from the Holocaust I saw graphically displayed in *Life* magazine. I also found and read my parents' copy of Elie Wiesel's just published book, *Night*. At that time, when I was 10 years old, I was aghast to find there was such evil in the world.

I knew that God was giving me two life assignments. The first assignment was to take the Gospel of Jesus Christ to the whole world as the only way of life and hope. The second assignment was that God would use me in ways I still cannot fully grasp, to defeat the great evil I had seen in *Night*, preventing another holocaust like that from ever happening again.

Both of these callings have had a profound impact on the course of my life. First, I have been driven not only rationally and theologically to understand the Kingdom of God, but to cooperate with the Holy Spirit to advance the Kingdom of God in the world. Second, this early encounter with the radical evil of the Holocaust led me into a lifelong passion to understand how Satan was able to build the demonic stronghold of Nazism to accomplish such evil.

The question that has tormented me for years is, "What could have been done in the human and spiritual realms to prevent the tyranny, human suffering, mass slaughter and destruction due to the Holocaust and World War II?" Sir Winston Churchill has called World War II "the unnecessary war," because "There never was a war more easy to stop than that which has just wrecked what was left of the world from the previous struggle."[5] Churchill further notes his motive for writing the history that has provided one part of the answer to my urgent question. "It is my earnest hope that pondering upon the past may give guidance in days to come, enable a new generation to repair some of the errors of former years and thus govern, in accordance with the needs and glory of man, the awful unfolding scene of the future."[6]

I have taken to heart the lessons gained by such insights that Churchill presented. What I have added to them is their interface with the spiritual realm. Here my teachers start in the Bible, reach back to include the great intercessors of the past, and culminate with Rees Howells whose role in defeating Nazism in the spiritual realm worked in tandem with Churchill in the human realm.

From these teachers, God has given us guidance as to the strategies and tactics of how the spiritual and political leaders of future generations may gain victory over threats to the Church and to humanity. Most importantly, we can learn how to defeat this evil well before Satan's plans reach their terrible flowering as they did in Nazism.

My Worldview Assumptions

I make no apologies for being a Christian. I affirm that Jesus Christ is who He says He is: "I am the way, and the truth, and the life. No one comes to the Father except through me." (John 14:6) I affirm the universal creeds of the Church, the Apostles' and the Nicene.

My biblical worldview has been shaped by the present-day empowering work of the Holy Spirit which is the only way that Christians can take part in fulfilling the Great Commission effectively. I have a Reformed understanding of God sovereignly working in human history which includes us as his friends and coworkers to spread and enlarge the Kingdom of Jesus Christ to the ends of the earth. I am convinced through the biblical witness, 2000 years of Church history, and my own personal experience, that the work of intercessory prayer is the starting point of our cooperation with the Father, Son, and Holy Spirit to grow the Church and to fulfill the Great Commission.

I am the first to admit that the worldview of many Christians, especially in the Western world, cannot accept the fundamental premise of this book, which is that both the Triune God of Grace and the Devil are at work in human history. My purpose here is not to debate these assumptions—certainly some may dismiss my work out of hand. My warning to those who do reject this is that it is only with a biblical worldview that they will be able to understand and do anything about the evil that is growing in the world.

The Method in Preparing this Prayer Strategy

I am not alone in writing this book. I am joined by a prayer and discernment team that includes intercessors from a number of western and non-western nations and cultures. Because of the sensitivity of this topic, those in this team will remain unnamed.

My approach to discerning the times and developing this prayer strategy is to seek primarily to understand Jesus' plans and purposes in the world. My sources are the Bible, rational analysis of history and the present facts, as well as revelation by the Holy Spirit today which is consistent with the witness of the Bible. I am at the same time seeking to understand what Satan is doing in the world and what his evil purposes are.

So, my focus is on both what God is doing and what Satan is doing. The rationale is that our battle, the real war in which we live, is "not against flesh and blood, but against the rulers, against the powers, against the world rulers of this darkness, against the spiritual forces of evil in the heavens." (Ephesians 6:12)

We must not be ignorant of Satan's stratagems and tactics and long-term objectives. This is the primary battlefield on which we as intercessors and spiritual warriors are called to engage.

A necessary but secondary concern is with the "flesh and blood" human beings, the Islamic texts, the cultures, and human organizations that Satan is using to build strongholds. We must engage with these human structures because they are the ways in which the demonic work is expressed in the world of time and space and flesh and blood.

I make the assumption, based on my biblical worldview as well as practical experience, that the spiritual realm—both divine and demonic—interfaces with the human realm and decisively shapes it. My basis for this statement is found in the following words of Jesus recorded in John 14:10-17:

> 10 "Do you not believe that I am in the Father, and the Father is in me? The words that I say to you, I do not speak on my own initiative, but the Father residing in me performs his miraculous deeds. 11 Believe me that I am in the Father, and the Father is in me, but if you do not believe me, believe because of the miraculous deeds themselves. 12 I tell you the solemn truth, the person who believes in me will perform the miraculous deeds that I am doing, and will perform greater deeds than these, because I am going to the Father. 13 And I will do whatever you ask in my name, so that the Father may be glorified in the Son. 14 If you ask me anything in my name, I will do it. 15 If you love me, you will obey my commandments. 16 Then I will ask the Father, and he will give you another Advocate to be with you forever—17 the Spirit of truth, whom the world cannot accept,

because it does not see him or know him. But you know him, because he resides with you and will be in you."

This is foundational to the war with Radical Islam: there exists one God in three persons—Father, Son and Holy Spirit. When we are born again into his Kingdom through faith in Jesus Christ, we become Jesus' friends and coworkers, and are given power and authority by the Holy Spirit to cooperate with the Father in shaping reality—spiritual and material.

Are You Called to Take Part in This War?

If you do not share the basic assumptions of the interface between the spiritual and the human worlds, of the existence of radical evil, of human beings as friends and coworkers with the three Persons of the Trinity enabled to shape reality according to God's vision, then what follows may seem but a distant medieval fantasy. But please give this your attention, because whether you share these assumptions or not, when the evil comes to fruition it will impact all humanity.

If you do not share my spiritual assumptions, then at least make common cause with us on the basis that Radical Islam has made clear its intentions to quench human liberty and creativity by imposing submission to Allah and enslaving humanity in the system of totalitarian control of Sharia law. All who love freedom and cherish diversity and human creativity must join as one to fight against this tyranny.

For you who whisper or shout, "Amen," and feel the confirming witness of the Holy Spirit as you ponder the words of our resurrected Lord Jesus Christ in John 14:10-17, read on! The Lord is calling you, in some fashion, to join this great battle of his truth and life prevailing against Satan's lies and plans for genocide at the dawn of the 21st century.

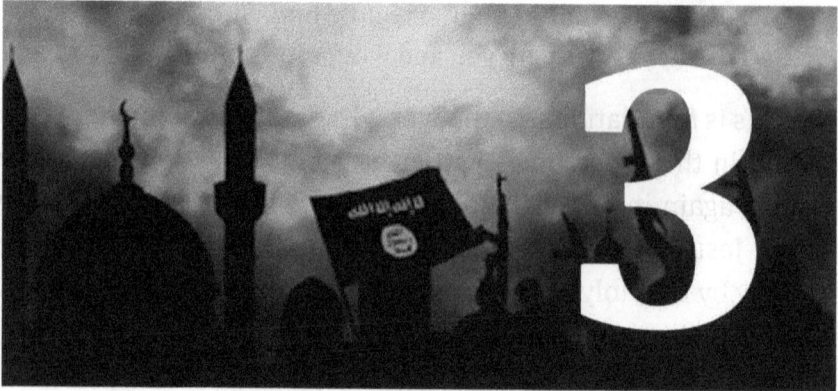

Dangers of Exposing Satan's Plans in Radical Islam

The intelligence I gained from discerning the times and the resulting prayer strategy was originally developed for use by a small circle of trusted, well-equipped intercessors. To provide the basis for these intercessors to engage, I had to provide a clear understanding of our enemy. This led to delving into the origins of Islam where I discovered the lies that Satan planted in the heart of Muhammad which are recorded in the Quran and the Ahadith for building the strongholds of Radical Islam. This was a necessary foundation to developing the prayer strategy. This information exposing the truths about Islam was so inflammatory I kept it limited to this trusted group.

Then I started to receive guidance to present it to as wide an audience as possible. I believe the Father wants to use this to expose Satan's lies and plans in order for intercessors globally to be called and equipped to join Jesus in defeating the demonic stronghold of Radical Islam and to advance the Kingdom of God. In faithfulness to the guidance of the Holy Spirit, this foundational material is made available in this book. The full prayer strategy will be published in the second book.

The decision to give up control of the content by making it available to the public has many inherent dangers. First, the materials might be used by people who are unprepared for the battle and could get hurt. Second, we may reveal too much to our natural and supernatural enemies, who may mount a counter-attack.

However, the danger in *not* sharing the results of our discerning the times and the prayer strategy more broadly is that some whom the Holy Spirit is calling into the battle may miss out for lack of instruction. Therefore, let me address the two concerns more fully.

First Concern
Unprepared Christians May Get Hurt

Some may read about these tactics for engaging demonic powers who are not well prepared or not even called by Jesus to such involvement. If they rush into spiritual battle without preparation and without the call, they may get hurt. A very real danger!

This book is not intended as a complete guide to spiritual warfare. To provide basic training in prayer and spiritual warfare, PRMI offers a complete course, The Dunamis Project, at various locations around the globe. This book is designed for people who are already grounded in these principles. Here are some guidelines to summarize these basics:

1. Confirm that you are born again into the Kingdom of God by faith in Jesus Christ and are growing in a relationship with Him. Without that relationship you will have no authority to engage in this warfare (John 15).

2. Ask Jesus to "baptize," that is, to fill you with the Holy Spirit so you may have the power, spiritual gifts and guidance to

cooperate with him in this form of intercession and spiritual warfare (Acts 1:4-8).

3. Do not do this alone! You must be part of a prayer team whose members can join you in the process of discerning the leading of the Holy Spirit, and can provide spiritual cover for you.

4. In areas where you find yourself over your head, seek further equipping through reading and study. Seek out wise and experienced teachers. PRMI may be able to help with that. Please find our course offerings of the PRMI Dunamis Institute at www.dunamisinstitute.org. The institute attempts to provide instruction even where there is no track of Dunamis Project conferences available.

Above all, make sure that you do not get ahead of what the Holy Spirit is calling you to do. When you start to look deeply at the evil you may find yourself dealing with great anger. Or compassion! But do not be led to action based on powerful emotions alone. You must be led by the Holy Spirit and stay connected to Jesus, our commander. When we are with Jesus and are carrying out His specific commands, we do not need to fear engaging even the most powerful high level demons or Satan himself, for it will not be we, but Jesus Christ in and through us, who leads and does the fighting.

Second Concern
Is it Too Dangerous to Expose Satan's Lies in Islam?

This fear is justified. Radical Muslims have threatened death to those who say anything negative about their prophet. They have in many instances carried out these threats. Counterattacks, both natural and supernatural, can be very real.

For example, as I have been doing the research for this book I have been overcome by waves of fear and despair that Satan has already won the battle in Radical Islam! As I have read passages from the Quran and the Ahadith, I have felt the tendrils of Satan's deceptions probing for weakness in my own foundations in the Word of God. I suspect that many of you may deal with the same fear.

Dutch Member of Parliament Geert Wilders, who exposed the lies and true goals of Islam, must now live in government provided safe houses because of death threats against him.[1] Others have had fatwas of death declared against them. All these facts point to the reality that this is dangerous. Satan, through those whose hearts have been captivated by his deception, may indeed work through them to silence all who would expose his schemes.

So what do we do with such threats? Do we cave in to the fear that comes from Satan and be silenced and hide the truth, both of the evil but also of Jesus Christ the only one who can overcome the evil? Should we not engage this evil and oppose it every way we can?

A Story from My Own Life

As a foretaste of what lies ahead, I report here a significant skirmish in which I had to face very real dangers. This story may also serve as a prelude to the type of high level spiritual warfare in which the Holy Spirit may call us to join him as the Gospel of Jesus Christ is advanced.

Pastor Richard White, his fourteen-year-old daughter Rachel, my sixteen-year-old daughter Rebecca and I were on a mission trip to Uganda. We were part of a mission team headed by Peterson Sozi, the famous Ugandan evangelist who started moving in signs and wonders during the days of Idi Amin, who killed over a million and a half Christians.

In Kampala, not far from Ida Amin's palace, we were to hold an evangelistic service in an Anglican church. As we approached the location, we could hear the worship music that had already started. Just before reaching the church we drove past a large, well-maintained mosque into which were streaming crowds of men in flowing white robes. Then we came to the church, a large, dilapidated brick structure. Just beyond the church was a high, dirty gray wall. Peterson noted that beyond that wall was a village of witch doctors. We all felt the spiritual oppression. This place was inhospitable to the preaching of the Gospel.

When we walked around and into the church, the oppression deepened. It was a large, ramshackle, deserted building. In the back, in a field, the platform was set up for the worship team. Despite an hour or two of worship, no one was there except one severely handicapped man in dirty rags crawling around like a spider making grotesque noises. Whether he was demon possessed or just insane, it was hard to tell. But this wretched distortion of humanity filled me with dread as he embodied the evil and hopelessness of that large, dilapidated, empty church set between the deception of Islam on one side, and black magic on the other.

I was up first to preach. I asked God, "Well Lord, what am I to do? There is no one here." The Holy Spirit said, "I am calling you to preach the Gospel to the demons who have control of this area and in my name to break their power in the strongholds they have built holding people captive here." I shared this with my daughter Rebecca, who with a look of fear and concern said, "Daddy! That sounds dangerous." That named the feeling I was having—a cold dread of death and impending evil. I then shared the guidance with Peterson and the rest of the African team, and they all confirmed that yes, I was to preach to the demons. Peterson encouraged me with the words that Jesus often had led him to deal with the demons first before being able to preach to the people.

So Peterson, wearing a bright red African suit, and I in a bright blue one, stepped up onto the platform. I prayed a desperate prayer for help, and then as the Holy Spirit fell upon me, I found the words to preach—not to the people, as there was no one there—but to the demons in the area. I announced to the powers that they had been defeated on the cross by Jesus Christ. Making sure these were not my words, I quoted Colossians 2:15: "Disarming the rulers and authorities, He has made a public disgrace of them, triumphing over them by the cross." I also used many more words from the Bible.

As Peterson was translating for me into the local African dialect, I looked over at the mosque. From the raised platform we could see directly into their courtyard. All these men in their white robes were highly agitated, like an angry hornets' nest. As I persisted in declaring the victory of Jesus Christ over the Devil's forces, to my horror these agitated men were pointing at us and a few had rifles they were waving in the air. Peterson and I, looking like two tropical birds, were perfect targets up on our platform.

I said to Peterson, "Look, they might shoot us! What do we do?" Without missing a word in translating my sermon to the demons, he said, "All they can do is kill our bodies. We keep preaching Jesus Christ, the way of life. We belong to him! So we are not afraid of the Devil, either." (Matthew 10:28) I had a moment of silent prayer, commending myself and my family to Jesus and resolving to obey and follow Him regardless of the cost, even if it meant being shot down by Muslims enraged by the proclamation of the Gospel. No one else on our team could see what was happening, so they were not alarmed and, with the exception of my daughter Rebecca, were not engaged in intercessory prayer protection for us as we held forth to the empty courtyard.

As I persisted in speaking the Word of God, and as the Holy Spirit kept leading and anointing us, a strange thing happened. We felt a breakthrough. Something in the spiritual realm lifted and a calm settled on the men at the mosque. They put down their weapons.

No sooner had it become quiet on the Muslim side, then from the witch doctor side we were both hit by an invisible wave of evil.

I started to find it hard to breathe, and I felt a strange pressure on my chest. A terrifying thought went through me, "If it is not by a bullet, then Satan will take me out by a heart attack brought on by a demonic death curse." I struggled to breathe and to keep on preaching. I could see that Peterson was having the same physical symptoms. This time I announced Jesus' victory over the demons in the witch doctor village. Suddenly, what I was feeling in the spiritual realm took a physical form.

Acrid white smoke started billowing over the wall and wafting over the platform. Some of the African team members ran up and shouted at Peterson, "Stop preaching! Don't you know what the witch doctors are doing?" Peterson shouted back, "Yes, I know they are cursing us!" With a violent gesture of rejection, he shouted back in English, "NO! We will never stop preaching, even if they send demons of death against us! Jesus will defeat them and we will proclaim the Gospel of Life over them." We persisted, and after a time the evil oppression from the witch doctor village lifted, the pressure on my chest stopped, and I could freely breathe again. The white smoke disappeared. Both Peterson in the local language and I in English announced the victory in Jesus Christ. We were both filled with praise of the Father, Son, and Holy Spirit. We sang those praises in the Spirit to the whole village. Later we would describe the sensation of a chorus of joy in heaven surging through us.

Then, amazingly, the people started pouring into the compound. Richard White had the joy of preaching the Gospel of Jesus Christ to the people. From the platform he turned to the Muslim mosque and said, "I know you seek God. Through Jesus you may know him and receive salvation and eternal life." He turned toward the witch doctor village and announced, "I know you seek power in the spiritual and earthly realm. Jesus Christ is the one who gives us true power for good in the Holy Spirit." Then he preached in the anointing of the Holy Spirit to the people who had gathered. We moved into healing prayer ministry. At the right time Peterson gave them a call to accept Jesus Christ as Lord and Savior. In the next three days of the revival, hundreds came to faith.

Following Jesus Christ is the Only Place of Safety

This encounter is a model for how Jesus may call us to engage with him in defeating the demonic strongholds of Radical Islam so that genocide and bondage may be averted and so that Muslims can come to saving faith in Jesus Christ. The word that Peterson gave me while I stood fearing for my life on that platform is the same word that I believe the Holy Spirit gives us now! We are to follow Jesus Christ in complete obedience and not be afraid of those who can only kill the body or curse us. For if we are in Jesus and are called into the battle with him, we can count on his protection, guidance, and power. Even if we are taken out in this great battle in the service of Jesus, we have the assurance that we have made our contribution to the Father's plan to destroy the works of Satan so His plans of salvation can go forth.

Here is my commitment: by the grace of God, I will not be silenced. I will instead trust Jesus Christ and do battle as he calls and empowers me. I will trust his protection. And all of you who are called into this great spiritual conflict will need to make a similar decision. I am not recommending arrogance, foolishness, or mocking anyone's faith or religion. I am urging a steadfast commitment to the Truth and to radical obedience and trust in the Lord Jesus Christ.

Make a commitment to follow Jesus and trust him totally in life and in death. Go no further with engaging in the book *Discerning the Times*, or implementing this prayer strategy or praying for the advancement of the Kingdom of God over Satan's kingdom until you have made that commitment. It is this commitment to follow Jesus Christ that is the only sure defense against the fear of attacks both from natural as well as supernatural means. Once we are in Jesus

Christ, we will be able to follow Him boldly into the battle that is before us. We are ultimately safe only as we are walking in the love and obedience of the Father, Son, and Holy Spirit.

The War Declared by Satan and Muhammad

All Christians and Jews—and indeed all members and beneficiaries of Western liberal democratic culture—must recognize that Radical Islam has declared war against us all. It is a war of conquest and subjugation, and for many of us, a war of extermination.

All this begins with the Devil who has launched a series of invasions of earth[1] and has declared war on all those who follow God's way of redemption in Jesus Christ (Revelation 12:17). That is the beginning of it all. Moreover, Satan's tools, Islam in general, and—at this time in history—radical, militant Islam in particular, have declared a war of conquest and extermination against Western culture and the people of the one true God, Jews and Christians. It needs to be understood that this war was declared on Jews and Christians by Islam's own prophet Muhammad, and has been waged ever since with varying degrees of intensity down through history.

It is the prophet Muhammad, deceived by Satan in the form of "the angel Gabriel," who gave the commands with which Satan has been able to build the deception of Islam and Radical Islam as the way to wage his war against the Kingdom of God. Satan is adroit at building this system of deception. He first built into it the means of preventing the exposure of his lies by making the Quran to pose as the infallible word of Allah dictated verbatim to Muhammad. This makes the book off limits to human rational analysis and questioning, even by Islamic adherents. Second, Satan has built in the interpretative lens called the doctrine of "abrogation" to ensure that the many contradictory statements in the Quran are interpreted by those who have submitted to Allah in a way most useful for using Islam as a weapon against God's people.

Coptic Christian Raymond Ibrahim, after noting the positive verses in the Quran toward Christians, then explains how Satan can negate this positive tradition, building a religion not of peace, but of war.

> In any case, statements in the Koran have to be read according to the doctrine of "abrogation," which was developed early in Islamic jurisprudence to deal with the Koran's many contradictory statements. Muslims believe that wherever verses contradict each other, the verse from later in Muhammad's career cancels out the verses from earlier. Allah himself justifies abrogation in the Koran: "Whenever we abrogate a verse or cause it to be forgotten, we replace it by a better or similar one. Know you not that Allah has power over all things?" (Koran 2:106; see also 16:101, 13:39, and 17:86). As it happens, the few verses that speak tolerantly of Christians are from early in Muhammad's career, when he had no political power, whereas the hostile verses that name Christians "infidel" enemies occur toward the end, near the height of his career. Thus the later hostile verses cancel out any tolerance for Christians expressed in the earlier verses.[2]

This war of subjugation and extermination that Satan has declared against Christians through Islam, beginning with Muhammad and intensifying in the present, is well documented in history. See Raymond Ibrahim's *Crucified Again* and Rodney Stark's *God's Battalions: The Case for the Crusades* for the full view of this war unfiltered by the lens of political correctness.

The war against the Jewish people is also rooted in the original deceptions spoken to Muhammad. They are more vitriolic and hateful, calling for genocide rather than simply subjugation.

Say (O Muhammad to the people of the Scripture): Shall I inform you of something worse than that, regarding the recompense from Allah: those (Jews) who incurred the Curse of Allah and His Wrath, those of whom (some) He transformed into monkeys and swines,[3] (sic), those who worshipped Taghut (false deities); such are worse in rank (on the Day of Resurrection in the Hellfire), and far more astray from the Right Path (Q 5:60)[4]

There are Ahadith (Arabic plural of Hadith, accepted sayings of Muhammad not found in the Quran) that justify both hating and killing Jews.

Abu Huraira reported Allah's Messenger (may peace be upon him) as saying: The last hour would not come unless the Muslims will fight against the Jews and the Muslims would kill them until the Jews would hide themselves behind a stone or a tree and a stone or a tree would say: Muslim, or the servant of Allah, there is a Jew behind me; come and kill him; but the tree Gharqad would not say, for it is the tree of the Jews. — Sahih Muslim 6985[5]

Raymond Ibrahim summarizes. The war declared on Christians and Jews is indeed based on the sacred texts of Islam now used by Satan to build the demonic stronghold of Radical Islam.[6]

The Koran's final word on the fate of Christians and Jews is found in Koran 9:29. There, Allah commands believers, "Fight those among the People of the Book who do not believe in neither Allah nor the Last Day, nor forbid what Allah and His Messenger have forbidden, nor embrace the religion of truth, until they pay the jizya with willing submission and feel themselves subdued." In Islamic parlance, "People of the Book" is a reference to those pre-Islamic peoples who had their own scriptures—chief among them, Christians and Jews. This verse gives divine sanction to the perpetual subjugation of Christians under Islam. Koran 9:29 and its equally bellicose counterpart Koran 9:5 [7], known as the "Sword Verses," appeared as Muhammad's armies were preparing to invade the Christian territories of the Byzantine Empire.[8]

Radical Islam Has Declared War Against Cultures Arising from the Judeo-Christian Worldview

This is a war that is waged not just against individuals but also against all non-Islamic cultures. The religion of Islam and the resulting culture historically—and especially now through militant Islam—has been vigorously opposed to and aggressively moving against the cultures stemming from biblical Christianity: Western, Orthodox, African, and Latin American. When Muslims chant "death to America and death to Israel," they are revealing that they declared war on our Judeo-Christian heritage, which has produced a culture of freedom, diversity, and liberal democracy.

The reality of the war declared against Jews and Christians and Western culture was presented with total clarity by Prime Minister Benjamin Netanyahu to the joint session of the US Congress on March 3, 2015.[9]

Don't be fooled. The battle between Iran and ISIS doesn't turn Iran into a friend of America. Iran and ISIS are competing for the crown of militant Islam. One calls itself the Islamic Republic. The other calls itself the Islamic State. Both want to impose a militant Islamic empire, first on the region and then on the entire world. They just disagree among themselves who will be the ruler of that empire.

In this deadly game of thrones, there's no place for America or for Israel, no peace for Christians, Jews, or Muslims who don't share the Islamist medieval creed, no rights for women, no freedom for anyone.[10]

Whether we like it or not, we are truly in a war. This is first of all Satan's war against the Church of Jesus Christ, but it is also a war against all of humanity. This is a war with many dimensions: spiritual, demonic, cultural, political and military. In the second decade of the 21st century, we are entering a new and terrible phase in this war. Weapons of mass destruction now make visions of global genocide possible.

As followers of Jesus Christ, we are called by the Holy Spirit to join Jesus' global strategic plans to advance the Kingdom of the Father. This includes defeating the powers of Satan gathering in Radical Islam, and then advancing forward with the Gospel of Jesus Christ who is the way, the truth, and the life, into the entire Muslim world.

Jesus' Call to Spiritual Warfare

The situation is growing desperate. With each passing day the demonic stronghold of Radical Islam in both the Sunni and Shia forms are growing in strength and power. History teaches that the more spiritual and earthly power a stronghold gains, the more deadly and costly it becomes to stop. Truly, the storm clouds of destruction are gathering. It is our calling as Christ's intercessors and spiritual warriors to join the battle to help defeat this growing menace to the Church and humanity.

There is much more that will need to be learned and understood about our adversary and his army, but we are already in the battle, and Jesus is calling us to join Him now before it is too late. Armies are constantly on the move; the arena is constantly changing; a year from now, specifics will differ from the present. For now, I am offering you this prayer strategy as an emergency battlefield manual. The focus will be mostly on the demonic stronghold of ISIS, the Islamic State, or what is also called Da'ash[1], one Sunni expression of Radical Islam. However, by the time this is in your hands that expression may have morphed into something else, consumed itself, or been defeated. Therefore, we will need to adapt the strategies and tactical principles to the situation we are facing then and seek new guidance from the Holy Spirit in how He may be applying these principles to your present situation.

We must also apply these same principles of spiritual warfare to defeating the Shia demonic strongholds expressed in the Islamic Republic of Iran and their proxies. While Sunni and Shia both hate each other and may well destroy each other, Satan is using both to accomplish the very same evil against everyone else.

This is all about Jesus Christ

I have entitled this prayer strategy which will be published in in two books, *A Prayer Strategy for the Victory of Jesus Christ*. This is all about Jesus Christ—the way, and the truth, and the life. No one comes to the Father except through Him (John 14:6). While we must pay urgent attention to the Devil and his schemes of death and bondage through the strongholds of Radical Islam, we must never lose our focus on Jesus Christ. If we do, we will not be able to keep our balance. We must recognize that Jesus loves and died for Muslims, including those in seemingly hopeless bondage to Satan's strongholds intending to exterminate Jews and Christians. We must of necessity join the Holy Spirit to wage war and defeat the works of the Devil so that the Kingdom of God may prevail on the earth.

With those precautions and encouragements, I offer this tactical manual to all whom the Holy Spirit would call, a great army of intercessors through whom Jesus will work to defeat Satan's schemes and thus extend the Gospel to the ends of the earth.

Jesus Christ is Calling His Church
to War Against the Army of Satan

Before launching into this battle, which will involve us in both spiritual and earthly warfare, we must be very certain that it truly is Jesus Christ, the Commander in Chief of Yahweh's armies, who is mobilizing, equipping, and deploying us in this war. To go further without establishing that this is indeed Jesus' war, and that Jesus Christ is calling us to His side may lead us into engagement with Satan alone, leaning on our own wisdom and strength. Outside of the Holy Spirit's guidance and protection, we may not only jeopardize the Father's campaigns, but also put ourselves in grave spiritual and physical danger.

The Bible reveals two glimpses of Jesus as commander of the armies of Heaven and Earth. One is when Israel was fighting for the land of Israel, the other at the final battle when Jesus defeats the armies of Satan and the Beast.

Joshua 5:13-15

13 Now when Joshua was near Jericho, he looked up and saw a man standing in front of him with a drawn sword in his hand. Joshua went up to him and asked, "Are you for us or for our enemies?" 14 "Neither," he replied, "but as commander of the army of the LORD I have now come." Then Joshua fell facedown to the ground in reverence, and asked him, "What message does my Lord have for his servant?" 15 The commander of the LORD's army replied, "Take off your sandals, for the place where you are standing is holy." And Joshua did so.

Revelation 19:11-16

11 Then I saw heaven opened and here came a white horse! The one riding it was called "Faithful" and "True," and with justice he judges and goes to war. 12 His eyes are like a fiery flame and there are many diadem crowns on his head. He has a name written that no one knows except himself. 13 He is dressed in clothing dipped in blood, and he is called the Word of God. 14 The armies that are in heaven, dressed in white, clean, fine linen, were following him on white horses. 15 From his mouth extends a sharp sword, so that with it he can strike the nations. He will rule them with an iron rod, and he stomps the winepress of the

furious wrath of God, the All-Powerful. 16 He has a name written on his clothing and on his thigh: "King of kings and Lord of lords."

Who is the Commander of the LORD's armies with a drawn sword who meets Joshua before the battle of Jericho? In addition, who is the rider on the white horse with a drawn sword, this time coming out of His mouth? Are they connected? What does it mean for us in this present battle to answer the call to defeat Radical Islam?

Asher Intrater in his study "Who Ate Lunch with Abraham: The Appearance of God in the Form of a Man in the Hebrew Scriptures" convinced me that both are Jesus Christ, the Second Person of the Trinity. There is a unity in them both being Jesus, one appearing at the beginning of the conquest of the Promised Land, and the other a prophetic vision at the great last battle where Jesus defeats the Beast and the kings of the earth and their armies. This places us at the particular era after Jesus has come in the flesh but not yet come again in glory.

Until the Last Battle We Are to Join the Lord Jesus to Defeat Radical Islam

Jesus is the commander of both the armies of heaven and earth. At the battle of Jericho, it was God who got the victory, but Joshua and the human army did their part—they marched around the walls day after day blowing the shofar. The victory was always Yahweh's in other battles for the conquest of the land, but there was always human involvement.

Before the Last Battle in Revelation chapter 19:6-7 the saints have prayed and praised the Lord in obedience even unto death.

6 "They were shouting: "Hallelujah! For the Lord our God, the All-Powerful, reigns! 7 Let us rejoice and exult and give him glory,

because the wedding celebration of the Lamb has come, and his bride has made herself ready."

Then we come to the last battle delivered to us in Revelation chapter 19:17-21:

> 17 Then I saw one angel standing in the sun, and he shouted in a loud voice to all the birds flying high in the sky: "Come, gather around for the great banquet of God, 18 to eat your fill of the flesh of kings, the flesh of generals, the flesh of powerful people, the flesh of horses and those who ride them, and the flesh of all people, both free and slave, and small and great!" 19 Then I saw the beast and the kings of the earth and their armies assembled to do battle with the one who rode the horse and with his army. 20 Now the beast was seized, and along with him the false prophet who had performed the signs on his behalf—signs by which he deceived those who had received the mark of the beast and those who worshiped his image. Both of them were thrown alive into the lake of fire burning with sulfur. 21 The others were killed by the sword that extended from the mouth of the one who rode the horse, and all the birds gorged themselves with their flesh.

At the Last Battle there is no reference to any human involvement. Jesus, the Commander in Chief of the armies of heaven, defeats the armies of Satan in his own power. The Beast and the false prophet are both seized and thrown into the lake of fire. The vast human army of Satan was slain by the sword that comes from Commander in Chief Jesus' mouth.

It is possible that in the impending battles with Radical Islam we have entered the end time in which we may count on Jesus' direct action to defeat Satan without His Church. But we do not know for sure, and cannot know for sure, that this is the *End Time* battle until it happens.

So at this point in the history of God's campaign to defeat the

Devil, He is calling us, like Joshua, to take part in the battle. While the battle belongs to Yahweh, until the Last Battle when Jesus returns in glory, he is calling us to join Him in the fight and to be the means through whom He will defeat the demonic stronghold of Radical Islam. We must also press on in obedience to Jesus' call to fulfill the Great Commission. This includes cooperating with the Holy Spirit to extend the Gospel of Jesus Christ into the hearts of those enslaved to the bondage of Islam.

Pietistic waiting on the Lord to protect us or to defeat these vicious enemies of Jesus and humanity is an abdication of our call and equipping as his friends and co-workers given dominion on earth. To all those who have been born again into the Kingdom of God, Jesus issues the çall to join him in the battle to defeat Satan and advance the Kingdom of God.

I, and presumably countless others, are having encounters with the Lord Jesus, the commander of the Lord's armies with the drawn sword, calling us to battle. Just as he called Joshua, He is calling us now through our prayers and obedience to join the Holy Spirit in defeating Satan's plans and the strongholds he has created. Many of you can enlist right here for spiritual warfare. For some of you, this may mean taking up the human weapons of defense and offense in the armed forces.

If you are unsure of your call or your orders for joining the battle, ask the Lord Jesus to reveal himself to you. Keep reading this book! The Holy Spirit may use it to speak to you and bring you into just such an encounter with the Commander-in-Chief.

Actionable Intel for Spiritual Warriors

When Jesus calls us to join him in this war against Satan, we are under his command. But we are not driven into this battle as slaves as Satan's armies are. Rather, we willingly join as Jesus' friends and coworkers.[1] As partners, Jesus reveals to us the Father's overarching strategic plans and wants us to have access to the battlefield intelligence that we need in order to cooperate intelligently and willingly with the Holy Spirit. Jesus, through the Holy Spirit, shares vital actionable intelligence with us. Gathering this intelligence is what I am identifying as "discerning the times." He does this both through revelation and by our natural faculties of reason, observation, and analysis. We must constantly be listening to the Holy Spirit, seeking information from the news media, and doing our own analysis of the facts. We will find that revelations of what is taking place in the spiritual realm will be corroborated by objectively verifiable facts in the human realm. This will provide us with the intelligence we need to engage our human and demonic enemies and to cooperate with the Holy Spirit in advancing the Kingdom of God.

The Problem of Getting Good Intelligence in War

Often as we start to open ourselves to receive this intelligence, we are beset with the problem that there is just too much information available and we have great difficulty in determining what is true and what is false. Almost daily we see on TV, read in the paper, or view on the internet some new atrocity committed by the Islamic jihadists. We also hear reports of them gaining new territory and recruiting new jihadists in their quest for a radical Islamic caliphate. Or we hear of some new attack taking place against Israel, or in Europe, and with increasing frequency in the USA. We also hear reports of Iran getting closer to obtaining a nuclear bomb. Almost daily Christian media report new prophetic words of warning or harbingers of the end times. All of this can be bewildering and overwhelming.

I find Carl von Clausewitz's description of the problem of intelligence on the physical battlefield to be consistent with the spiritual battle in which we are fighting Satan, the master of deception and confusion.

> By "intelligence" we mean every sort of information about the enemy and his country—the basis, in short, of our own plans and operations. If we consider the actual basis of this information, how unreliable and transient it is, we soon realize that war is a flimsy structure that can easily collapse and bury us in its ruins...In short, most intelligence is false, and the effect of fear is to multiply lies and inaccuracies. As a rule, most men would rather believe bad news than good and rather tend to exaggerate the bad news. The dangers that are reported may soon, like waves, subside; but like waves they keep recurring, without apparent reason. The commander must trust his judgment and stand like a rock on which the waves break in vain. It is not an easy thing to do...[2]

Like "waves that keep recurring" is what this has felt like to me as I have been called to engage the stronghold of Radical Islam. How do we stand like a rock? Clausewitz's suggestion seems apt, "If he does not have a buoyant disposition, if experience of war has not trained him and matured his judgment, he had better make it a rule to suppress his personal convictions, and give his hopes and not his fears the benefit of the doubt. Only thus can he preserve a proper balance."[3]

We must Remain in Jesus to Obtain Accurate Intelligence

There is real wisdom in not giving in to our fears. Satan is a master of using fear to blind and to deceive us. However, for the spiritual warrior, the only way to stand like a rock and overcome fear and all the other assaults of Satan is by putting on the armor of God as in Ephesians 6. More succinctly put, we must live moment by moment in vital relationship with the Lord Jesus (John 15).

From the fortress of this relationship with Jesus, in which Jesus assures us that Satan's lies have no power over us, we may receive the gifts of the Holy Spirit and be armed with the full authority of Jesus Christ to engage the demonic.

As we take up the spiritual weapons of our warfare, we must cultivate the gifts of discernment. We must be able to see deeply into the agendas of men as well as those of Satan. That requires both spiritual discernment as well as a commitment to knowing and assessing the actual facts related to the actions, statements, and intentions of Radical Islam. This is no easy matter as we shall later discuss due to the problems of demonic cloaking, in which both Satan and Islamists in collusion with liberal progressives all seem dedicated to hiding the facts related to the true intentions as well as actions of Radical Islam. This collusion is not a formal coalition, as if Islamists and liberal progressives were conspiring together on the telephone to commit terrorist acts. It is much more in line with what John Stormer in *None Dare Call It Treason* refers to as "a conspiracy of shared values." I show this to be the case later in the book, about how their worldviews, while very different, contribute to the same results.[4]

In our present war against Satan's stronghold of Radical Islam, we may take hope and also learn from the example of those who have gone before us who had to fight the deadly strongholds of Nazism and Communism. Our need for discernment that pierces the lies of Satan is actually no different than seeing past the deceptions of those desperately seeking peace in the 1930s. These well-intentioned seekers of peace actively hid or ignored the facts of the German military buildup during the first gathering storm.[5] So did the academics with an idealized view of communism who rejected reports revealing the terrible atrocities and mass murders of Stalinist communist Russia. [6]

To obtain these facts, we can depend on revelation from the Holy Spirit. But we must also establish ways to corroborate or verify divine revelation lest we be deceived about facts on the ground. So let us ask how to obtain information about what is really happening in the growing stronghold of Radical Islam.

Reliable Sources of Information about Islamic Jihad

In my opinion, the mainstream public news media (the *Wall Street Journal* and *Fox News* excepted) are so blinded by their materialistic, liberal progressive worldview that they are unable to discern or to report on the in-depth spiritual and religious dimensions of the demonic stronghold of Radical Islam. Their worldview filters prevent them from seeing, much less reporting the facts. I am fully aware that Fox News, and my favorite, the *Wall Street Journal*, which are owned by the same company, have their own blind spots. However, I know what they are. I also believe that their worldview based on Judeo-Christian values enables them to see more deeply into the nature of reality than other news media that have rejected those values.

I have also turned to other helpful sources of information. The best intelligence and spiritual discernment I have found comes from Robert Spencer, Director of "Jihad Watch."[7] He is a Catholic who has a masterful knowledge of the history and sacred texts of Islam. Another person who is most helpful is the Coptic Christian Raymond Ibrahim, who often writes for "Jihad Watch." His articles are profoundly helpful.[8] The Heritage Foundation[9] and the David Horowitz Freedom Center [10] are also excellent sources of intelligence. Glenn Beck's The Blaze[11] tells the truth about the dual attacks against liberty both from liberal progressivism and Islam. Another prophetic voice who sees with great clarity in this area is Newt Gingrich, the former Speaker of the House. He has written, spoken and done videos on the threat of Radical Islam. See for instance the video, *America at Risk: The War with No Name.*

An intercessor just introduced me to Sam Solomon, who came to embrace Christianity after spending fifteen years training in Sharia law in the Middle East. His decision to follow Jesus led to his arrest, his death sentence, his escape, and now his exile from his homeland. He is very direct and combative against the great evil that he knows well from personal experience.

One website is called Answering Islam.[12] Many of the articles are written by Muslims who have come to saving faith in Jesus Christ. In revealing the teachings of Islam, their obvious intention is to point to Jesus Christ as the true answer to Islam and the only way of salvation.

For very good discernment from the Jewish Messianic perspective, I recommend the web site and articles from the ministry Revive Israel. [13] Also, see the video teaching of Asher Intrater, the director of Revive Israel, and Dr. Daniel Juster. These are the two apostolic leaders of the Jewish Messianic movement with whom I have had personal contacts while I visited Israel in

2016. They are at the epicenter of this spiritual war. The Jewish people have also learned through terrible experience to take with utmost seriousness those who announce that they are planning to kill them. We need to listen to these Jewish voices, as they are able to see what many of us have not had to learn to see. It is the height of folly to ignore their warnings.

For an article that is very insightful on ISIS, which suggests that it is part of what may be called Apocalyptic Islam, I recommend the article in the *Atlantic,* "What ISIS Really Wants" by Graeme Wood, March, 2015. [14] This article clearly shows the religious Islamic roots of ISIS. This, of course, is what Robert Spencer and Raymond Ibrahim have been saying for years, but it is significant that this was published in the *Atlantic* which most often betrays a liberal worldview.

The Gift of Discerning the Times

Before leaving this section, I know that I am taking a risk in actually naming some of these people who may provide us with reliable information about Radical Islam. I am not endorsing everything they are saying about everything. I do, however, believe that the Holy Spirit is using them to reveal to us the true dangers of Radical Islam. We must be careful that we do not fall into Satan's scheme of preventing us from hearing the truth they may be saying about this topic simply because we may disagree with either their actions or words in other arenas. We shall deal more with the problem of Satan preventing us from hearing in chapter seventeen on demonic cloaking.

While the sources listed above are profoundly helpful, we must still discern and evaluate whether they are actually reporting the facts. Also, in the process of discerning beneath the surface to the human and especially to the demonic motivations behind the facts, we still need all the powers of our rational analysis and the spiritual gift of discernment.

So we must ask the Holy Spirit to give each of us discernment and guidance to see beyond information from the news media into the designs and purposes of Satan. Ask also for the Lord to show us his plans and tactics so that we can cooperate with Jesus in each of our own spheres of authority in this present war against Satan.

In Book II, I offer more on the question of discernment so that we can pierce the demonic cloaking. But we must start now in *Discerning the Times* to assess the facts from the sources I name above that provide the basic intelligence for understanding our enemy. Without this foundation of good intelligence, we cannot hope to cooperate with the Holy Spirit's plans to overcome Radical Islam and take the Gospel of our Lord Jesus to the Muslim world.

Exposing Satan's Plans in Islam

In any warfare, whether human or spiritual, we must know what the true intentions of the enemy are in order to prevail. Without this basic intelligence, we will lack an interpretative framework to understand our enemy's actions. Misjudging or misunderstanding the enemy's true intentions and long-term goals results in choosing the wrong strategies and tactics. This will lead to defeat.

Our warfare is not primarily with flesh and blood, but with Satan and his legions. Therefore, we must ask, "What are Satan's goals and long range plans that he is seeking to accomplish through the religion of Islam and the present day strongholds of Radical Islam?" I believe the Holy Spirit has revealed to us that Satan has four basic schemes, which if allowed to come to fruition, will have terrible implications for the Church and humanity.

The purpose of this chapter and the next will be to provide a summary of Satan's goals and battle plans. In this chapter I will ask the larger question, why would Satan seek to accomplish these terrible plans for humanity? Why would he wish to use Radical Islam to launch a genocide of billions of people? Only as we discover Satan's ultimate rationale will we see the logic in this madness. A secondary purpose is to show that in the religion of Islam in general, and in Radical Islam in particular, Satan has raised up accomplices to carry out his terrible plans.

Satan's First Scheme
Replace God's Way of Salvation with the Deception of Islam

Satan's ultimate goal through the religion and cultural system of Islam is the complete replacement of Yahweh's way of redemption with the totalitarian system of militant Islam. From the start, he has sought to:

- Replace the Jewish patriarchs, and prophets, Jesus Christ and the Apostles with the false prophet Muhammad

- Replace the Old and New Testaments with the deception of the Quran and the Ahadith

- Replace the Kingdom of God with the totalitarian spiritual, cultural, and political bondage of Sharia law

- Replace the worship of God in spirit and in truth with submission ("Islam") to Allah

- Replace the true God, Father, Son and Holy Spirit revealed in the Bible, with "Allah,"—Satan himself disguised as the moon god worshiped at Mecca

- Replace the good news (salvation by faith in Jesus), with works righteousness leading to eternal death

- Replace the promise of eternal life with the Father, Son, and Holy Spirit with a hope of eternity with the "houris," the dark-eyed ones (virgins who minister to Allah's warriors).

We do not expect the average person to understand Satan's

scheme to replace God's means of salvation. However, Jews and Christians must understand that replacing God's Kingdom through the spiritual, cultural and political system of Islam is Satan's primary purpose.

Satan's Second Scheme
Exterminate Jews and Christians in order to Replace Yahweh's Covenants

Islam has always been a tool for Satan to subjugate Jews and replace the Church of Jesus Christ. Go to Jerusalem today and you will notice that virtually every holy Jewish or Christian site, cherished by the Lord's covenant people, has a mosque built directly on top of it or next to it. The purpose is not to establish "another religion." It is to *replace* Yahweh's covenant people by either absorbing them into Satan's new system, or getting rid of them. Now, as Satan realizes that his time is short, a new assault has come to kill Jews and Christians and thus to nullify Yahweh's covenant by exterminating His covenant people.

In chapters fourteen to sixteen I trace the most recent history of this genocidal thrust in the twentieth century. The terrible danger the world faces in the near future, unless stopped, is that these strongholds are increasingly providing Satan with the means of modern weapons of mass destruction, and the social, political, and military communication systems to accomplish these terrible purposes. The extermination of billions of people is now a real and dreadful possibility in the 21st century, with nuclear and biological weapons and modern means of delivery anywhere on earth. Satan is planning a new and terrible holocaust of God's covenant people. Let us wake up, people of God!

But why? Why would Satan want to destroy billions of innocent people? The answer? Satan must destroy the covenant basis for the way our God the Creator has decided to work on earth.

His goal is to replace God and his anointed Messiah and to retain absolute control of this earth. And since the fulfillment of God's covenant plan is at hand, Satan is turning to desperate measures, manifesting the true evil of his nature. The gloves have come off!

Messianic Jewish biblical scholar Asher Intrater[1] exposes the deep motive of Satan, which helps us understand the genocidal purposes in the strongholds of Nazism and Radical Islam. After reflecting on Romans 15:8-9 and Jeremiah 31:25-37, Intrater makes this profound statement:

> There is a triangular covenant here. The New Covenant connects the forgiveness of sins to the preservation of the nation of Israel, which is in turn connected to the preservation of natural creation. The creation of the world was made by covenant; the chosenness of the nation of Israel was made by covenant; and eternal salvation to all believers was made by covenant. These three are linked together by covenant.
>
> Covenant demands that either all three be true, or none of them. This is the *secret spiritual root as to why both the Nazis and the Islamic Jihad set a goal to exterminate the Jewish people*. If they had succeeded in destroying our people, then the New Covenant and the created order would have been in jeopardy.[2]

Satan's plans are more audacious and sinister than merely replacing the faith of Jews and Christians with the deception of Islam. He intends to replace God! To achieve that goal true to his nature as a murderer from the beginning, Satan is willing to murder millions, even billions, of human beings.

Satan's Third Scheme
Strangle the Winds of the Holy Spirit
Blowing in the House of Islam

The Holy Spirit is bringing more Muslims to faith in Jesus

Christ than at any other time in history.[3] This movement is well documented in *A Wind in the House of Islam: How God is Drawing Muslims around the World to Faith in Jesus Christ* by David Garrison.

From a speech by Abdel Fattah el-Sisi, President of Egypt, it is apparent that many voices of reform and moderation within Islam reject the radical Islamic doctrines of death and subjugation. Is this a gust of this wind of the Holy Spirit to open Muslim hearts and minds to Jesus Christ? While hopeful, we must also be aware that these tendencies toward moderation and reinterpretation may just represent a cloaking device. How shall we evaluate this?

Some aspects of the Islamic faith and their sacred texts will be redeemed as the Holy Spirit blows in the house of Islam. God's vision is that Muslims everywhere will be set free from the demonic deception of Islam by Jesus, for, "...there is no other name under heaven given among people by which we must be saved..."[4] (Acts 4:11-12).

In any event, at this point in 2016, Satan seems intent on using the demonic stronghold of Radical Islam both to restrain the Holy Spirit from drawing Muslims to Christ and to choke movements toward moderation. Satan is using the sword and all means of social-political coercion to enforce the Wahhabis' interpretative framework of the sacred texts of Islam and the tyrannical rule of Sharia law. The Wahhabis are shouting at the top of their lungs; the moderates are barely speaking in whispers. The former justify the murder of all Muslims deemed "kefir" (infidel) who do not measure up to their level of "purity." The Muslim world accepts death as the appropriate punishment for anyone who leaves Islam for another religion.[5] This includes Al-Sisi's Egypt, where terrible things are happening to Christians year after year. Islam's social, political, religious and military structure of oppression insures bondage of the mind, soul, and spirit to Satan's deceptions first planted in the heart of Muhammad.

Satan's Fourth Scheme
Establish a Radical Islamic Caliphate from which to Wage Offensive Jihad

The Caliphate is the full, mature expression towards which the demonic stronghold of Radical Islam is—unless stopped—inexorably growing.

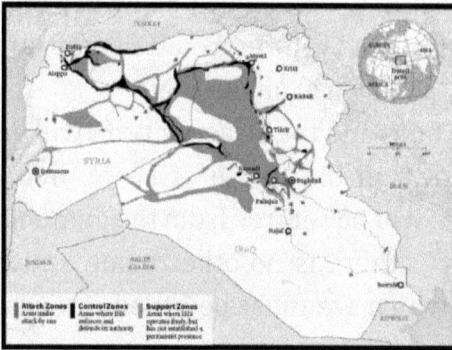

The caliphate's control as of January 15, 2015 along with areas it has attacked.

[http://www.theatlantic.com/features/archive/2015/02/what-isis-really-wants/384980/

The Caliphate in Islamic culture demands the allegiance and obedience of every Muslim on earth. This explains why jihadist groups like Boko Haram in Nigeria rushed to align with ISIS when they declared the restoration of the Caliphate. [6] It explains why it is not just vain talk or propaganda, but a serious threat when ISIS calls for "lone wolves" to attack U.S. soldiers. Or gives orders for jihadists to find service members' addresses online and then "show up and slaughter them." [7] The Caliphate gives Satan a highly effective command and control system to implement his commands.

The Caliphate gives Satan the human, spiritual, cultural, political, economic, and above all the military means to replace God's covenant people with Satan's slave army and slave state. Satan uses a number of strategies to establish the Caliphate:

The first is conquering and holding land. The Caliphate must have land! The Sunni ISIS is on a rampage of death to conquer and hold land. The Shia expression is found in Iran's expanded reach through its proxies. Both ISIS and Iran are currently stepping into the vacuum left by President Obama's retreat from leadership in the world. Spiritually and culturally, Islam is making gains over hearts and minds wherever the Church of Jesus Christ has departed from its biblical foundations, from the empowering, vitalizing work of the Holy Spirit, and from the faith that Jesus Christ is the only way of salvation.

The second strategy in extending the Caliphate (whether of the Sunni or Shia approach) is to stir up as much death and chaos as possible in order to hasten the coming of the Mahdi, and with his coming, the worldwide hegemony of Radical Islam.

The third strategy in the Sunni ISIS version is a last apocalyptic battle in Jerusalem of Islamic warriors against the world. In the Shiite 12th Imam Iranian version of this deception, it includes "wiping Israel off the map" and destroying America. The intent to destroy Israel is not just a crazy idea of a few radicals like the past President Ahmadinejad, but the formal policy aim of the Iranian government.[8] Even on the eve of working toward a deal on nuclear weapons in July 2015, the annual ritual of Quds Day of announcing "Death to America" and "Death to Israel" went unabated. "Reportedly, President Hassan Rouhani attended a rally in Tehran and was treated to posters of Prime Minister Netanyahu, President Obama, and King Salman of Saudi Arabia being burned. He did not protest."[9]

The fourth strategy in Satan's plans in the rise of the Caliphate is a specific focus on destroying through subversion or military means those nations that have the power to block the advance of a worldwide Islamic Caliphate. The nations targeted are America, Canada, the United Kingdom, Europe, and Russia—with domination by the Caliphate of the rest of the world to follow. In the minds of the Islamists, these are the "nations of the Cross." [10] Because Islamists carry a special hatred of the Jewish people, whether in the state of Israel or in New York, they are targeted for annihilation. To achieve their ends, Radical Islamist jihadist groups, whether Shia or

Sunni, desire to obtain the weapons of mass destruction needed to carry out genocide on the vast scale both they and Satan have imagined.

Satan's Battle Plans Revealed
in ISIS's Apocalyptic Expectations

When the Holy Spirit pierces the demonic cloaking, these four schemes and Satan's battle plans for implementing them are exposed to us. For a long time, however, I did not understand what these plans were. I knew that they had to be written down somewhere and spoken for Satan's enslaved human and demonic agents to follow. But where? Where was Radical Islam's equivalent to Adolph Hitler's *Mein Kampf*? I prayed that the Holy Spirit would reveal to me Satan's over-all battle plans. Then the answer came.

I was on the interstate driving in pouring rain to a meeting when I received a strong nudge to turn on the radio and listen to the Glenn Beck radio show. I did not even know where to find the station, so I called my wife. She told me the number and said, "You have got to listen to this! It is all about a new video that ISIS just released full of their apocalyptic expectations of the end of the world. Glenn Beck is calling for, "breaking the chain of events leading to the fulfillment of these prophecies." I then listened to the program and realized the Holy Spirit was revealing Satan's over-all battle plan. The following summary from his blog is what Glenn Beck was saying on the radio about the ISIS video.[11]

> Some wonder if we are in the end times. Some wonder if Islam is the religion of the Anti-Christ and ISIS is the army of the beast. IT DOESNT MATTER IF YOU AND I BELIEVE THAT TO BE NONSENSE. They believe it to be true. They are fighting the end times battle. Every American needs to see this video. It does NOT include beheadings etc. It is the latest message from ISIS. The reason you should see it, is because you will understand

why they fight and how our politicians are either lying to you or fools. Why they fight is clear. It IS about Islam. What you will see is the fulfillment of their end times prophecy. It happens to be a direct reflection of our end times prophecy as well. (As you will see in the video–one world government, Gog and Magog = Russia and Iran alliance).[12]

Besides Glenn Beck, there are a number of other prophetic voices exposing the apocalyptic dimensions of the twin demonic strongholds of the Islamic State and the Islamic Republic of Iran. A good starting place for understanding this complicated topic is Joel Rosenberg's article, "What is 'Apocalyptic Islam' and why is it so dangerous? The research behind my remarks to the Jerusalem Leaders' Summit," November 5, 2015"[13]

He is not alone in this assessment and points to two other authors. They are Graeme Wood, "What ISIS Really Wants," *The Atlantic* magazine, March 2015 issue.[14] Another book that has come out in 2015 is *The ISIS Apocalypse: The History, Strategy & Doomsday Vision of the Islamic State* by Brookings Institution scholar William McCants.

These sources give the full research into the background and present expressions of Islamic eschatology that constitute Satan's present war plans. Whether ISIS or Iran, they are following the script provided by Satan embedded in the Quran and the Ahadith and in the Islamic visions of the End Times.

At the Jerusalem Leaders' Summit on November 3-4, 2015,[15] Joel Rosenberg summarizes these apocalyptic beliefs. He explains why "Apocalyptic Islam" is even more of a threat than Radical Islam.

I argued at this Summit that the evidence strongly indicates that we are dealing with "true believers" in Iran and ISIS, men who believe deeply—passionately—in a cause few Westerners even comprehend, much less accept. Indeed, for the first time in human history, the top leaders of not just one nation state but two—Iran and the Islamic State—are being driven by Islamic eschatology, or End Times theology. Their particular brands of Shia and Sunni eschatology are driving them towards genocide. Why? Because they believe:

- that the End of Days has arrived;

- that the Islamic messiah known as the "Mahdi" will appear at any moment;

- that when the Mahdi appears, he will rule the entire Earth;

- that Jesus will also return to Earth, but not as the Messiah, Savior, or Son of God, but as the deputy to the Mahdi;

- that Jesus will force all Jews, Christians and other so-called "infidels" to convert to Islam or be executed;

- that the way to hasten the arrival and full establishment of the global Islamic kingdom or "caliphate" is to annihilate Jews and Christians, and specifically to annihilate Israel (which they call the "Little Satan" in their eschatology), and the United States (which they call the "Great Satan.");

- that time is very short, and they must move decisively because soon each Muslim will face the Mahdi face to face and be brought into judgment if they have not faithfully followed the Mahdi's orders.[16]

These end times beliefs, along with the means of genocide, are the new and terrible elements that Satan has added to the stronghold of Radical Islam, providing the theological basis and the practical battle plan to implement these four schemes. It is of critical strategic importance that we turn this information into actionable intelligence.

The strategy suggested by Glenn Beck (breaking the chains of events leading to the fulfillment of Satan's battle plans) is one that the Holy Spirit has already led us to. We shall discuss strategy for defeating these in more details in Book II. The Holy Spirit has given a prayer strategy for us intercessors to prevent the fulfillment of the Islamic prophesies.

However, before we move further into the strategies and tactics for defeating these plans, we must address whether we can be sure beyond a shadow of doubt that Satan is committed to these four terrible schemes and is actually carrying them out through Radical Islam. That is the question to be addressed in the next chapter. If we are called to engage in this war, we had better be sure that these threats are real.

Confirming Satan's Four Schemes

Do we doubt that these horrendous objectives reflect Satan's plans in the demonic stronghold of Radical Islam? The extermination of millions, even billions of people, is so morally repulsive that it is easy to dismiss it all as the ravings of madmen or the paranoid delusions of hateful Islamophobes.

Once before in recent history Satan's plans were explicitly written down and spoken publicly by one of his demonized servants—Adolf Hitler. Visions of world domination and the extermination of whole races were viewed as impossible in our civilized societies. The price for not discerning the true roots of these nightmare visions in the stronghold of Nazism, was incalculable human suffering and the death of millions.

Satan's plans in Radical Islam are nearly identical to those of Nazism. These have been exposed to us, and now we must act upon this vital intelligence. But before we do, we must discern whether these really are Satan's plans. The next question becomes, "Is Satan actually making preparations through Radical Islam to accomplish these plans?" We must discern whether or not these threats are real.

The Rules of Discernment of Spirits as the Basic Presuppositions Leading to the Following Conclusions

Before providing the conclusions of my discernment process which confirms that these are Satan's plans, let me describe the rules of discernment that I am bringing to this project. Making such determinations grows out of a long rich tradition within the Christian Church (both Catholic and Protestant) of the discernment of spirits. This tradition, based on a biblical worldview, assumes that there are different sources of inspiration informing human ideas of what is real and imaginary, good and evil, and true and false. These various sources are 1) God and the angelic, 2) Satan and evil spirits, 3) the human mind, spirit and emotions, 4) culture and social ethos, 5) the awesomeness of the created order, 6) or some combination of the above.

This Christian process of discernment also assumes the very real likelihood that Satan is actively working to deceive us. This assumption is based on the following warnings of Jesus and Paul. Jesus warns us, "Watch out that no one deceives you. For many will come in my name, claiming, 'I am the Christ,' and will deceive many" (Matthew 24:4-5). Jesus tells us that not all signs, wonders and miracles come from the Holy Spirit. "For false Christs and false prophets will appear and perform great signs and miracles to deceive even the elect—if that were possible" (Matthew 24:24). Paul tells us not to be deceived by those people not serving Jesus Christ. *For such people are not serving our Lord Christ, but their own appetites. By smooth talk and flattery, they deceive the minds of naïve people* (Romans 16:18). Paul affirms that Satan is behind the people who in their words or actions may be deceiving us. *For such men are false apostles, deceitful workmen, masquerading as apostles of Christ. And no wonder, for Satan himself masquerades as an angel of light. It is not surprising then, if his servants masquerade as servants of righteousness. Their end will be what their actions deserve* (2

Corinthians 11:13-15).

Finally, the first thing Jesus promises when he returns at the end of the age is to bind Satan "to keep him from deceiving the nations anymore..." (Rev. 20:3) Jesus makes this a priority because He sees clearly how effective Satan is at deceiving the entire human race. Therefore, the solution he offers fits the diagnosis of the problem. The best way to avoid being deceived is to take seriously these warnings about satanic deception. We need Jesus not only because He saves us from hell, but because he is "the one from above," (Jn. 8:23) who sees things clearly and truthfully, while all the rest of us are "from below"—and we do not. Christian discernment grows out of a desperate reliance on Jesus to show us the truth from his point of view.

Discernment is a process involving human reason and observation in which words or behaviors may be measured against the standard of Scripture. However, it is the eye-opening work of the Holy Spirit that reveals the source of some word or behavior. Discernment is an art that may be cultivated through experience as the Holy Spirit helps us detect truth from falsehood.

A summary of this process may be reduced to four discernment questions we may ask concerning any word, idea, or action. The four questions are as follows:

1. Does it give glory to Jesus Christ? (John 14:26, 16:13-14)

2. Is it consistent with the intentions and character of God as revealed in the Old and New Testaments? (John 2:22, II Timothy 3:14-17)

3. Do other born again, Spirit-filled Christians have a confirming witness? (I Corinthians 2:14-16, 14:29)

4. Is there confirmation in objectively verifiable events or facts? (Deuteronomy 18:21-22, Matthew 7:15-20)

There is a great deal more that could be said about this basic process of discernment. [1] The task before us, however, is to move beyond these foundations to give the following guidelines about discerning whether these schemes of Satan in Radical Islam are actually being carried out. Or, to put it another way, are we justified in interpreting current events in the Islamic world as a Satanic scheme to destroy God's covenant people?

First Confirmation
These Four Schemes Are Consistent
with the Nature of Satan as both Deceiver and Murderer

We must go right to the top of Hell's organizational chart to Satan or the devil. We need to listen to what Jesus says about Satan's true nature and the behaviors that we can expect to be reflected in the people and organizations that Satan is working through.

In John 8 there are some pointed exchanges between Jesus and some unbelieving Jews.

John 8:39-41, 44

39 They answered him, "Abraham is our father!" Jesus replied, "If you are Abraham's children, you would be doing the deeds of Abraham. 40 But now you are trying to kill me, a man who has told you the truth I heard from God. Abraham did not do this! 41 You people are doing the deeds of your father."

44 "You people are from your father the devil, and you want to do what your father desires. He was a murderer from the beginning, and does not uphold the truth, because there is no truth in him. Whenever he lies, he speaks according to his own nature, because he is a liar and the father of lies."

In these few remarkable verses in John, Jesus describes the nature of Satan, reveals his goals and uncovers the nature of the relationship he enjoys with those through whom he implements his plans.

If this conversation were taking place today, a conversation led by Jesus with Islamists , I believe Jesus would address Islamists in a way akin to how he spoke to the unbelieving, namely "children of Satan, those reflecting Satan's nature and doing his will. They have fallen for Satan's lies spoken through Muhammad, that the only sure way to paradise is to die in jihad, killing "infidels"—who are actually God's chosen and redeemed people. Each time they commit some atrocity against the people of God, they are proving themselves to be children of Satan.

Does God not love these people? Did Jesus not die for them? Yes! And it is out of this great love even for Satan's children that Jesus Christ was crucified. But there is only one way for these deceived slaves of Satan to escape from this bondage to death, that is, by turning to faith in the Lord Jesus. This is not my word or my opinion, but God's Word.

John 1: 12-13

12 But to all who have received him—those who believe in his name—he has given the right to become God's children 13— children not born by human parents or by human desire or a husband's decision, but by God.

Acts 4:12

...there is salvation in no one else, for there is no other name under heaven given among people by which we must be saved.

Satan as Master Deceiver;
Islam His Masterpiece of Deception

Satan, through his servant Muhammad, has planted in the Quran direct contradictions to the biblical revelations of the way of salvation given by God the Father through faith in Jesus Christ, which is the basis of our Christian faith. Islam as the religion of Muhammad is Satan's masterpiece of deception to deny the name of Jesus Christ as the way of salvation.

Let me draw from Abraham Nhial's wonderful book, *Lost Boy No More: A True Story of Survival and Salvation.* The Christian and animist population of South Sudan have suffered the direct and terrible application of the lies of Satan by those in bondage to Islam. Read these purported words of Allah from the Quran rejecting foundational biblical doctrine. Does it not seem to have a little too much intentionality to suggest that they are anything but the deceptions of Satan? It was not until I read this sentence by sentence with the words from the Quran that I could see clearly the deception that is intended as a point by point replacement of the foundational truths of Christianity.

Bishop Abraham writes the following brilliant summary:

To the Muslim, Allah is the one and only absolute one. Christians believe in the Trinity: Father, Son and Holy Spirit. The Greatest sin a Muslim can commit is *shirk*, to give God more than one property or position, which is blasphemy to Allah. "They do blaspheme who say Allah is one of three in a Trinity: for there is no god except One Allah. If they desist not from their word (of blasphemy), verily a grievous penalty will befall the blasphemers among them." (Surah 5:73)

The Muslim believes Jesus was a mere man, a prophet from Allah. Allah would not lower himself to take a son. "And it [the Qur'an] warns those who say: 'Allah has taken a son.' Surely, of this they have no knowledge, neither they nor their fathers; it is a monstrous word that comes from their mouths, they say nothing but a lie." (Surah 18:4-5)

"O People of the Book! Commit no excesses in your religion: Nor say of God aught but the truth. Christ Jesus the son of Mary was (no more than) an apostle of God, and His Word, which He bestowed on Mary, and a spirit proceeding from Him: so believe in God and His apostles. Say not 'Trinity': desist: it will be better for you: for God is one God: Glory be to Him: (far exalted is He) above having a son. To Him belong all things in the heavens and on earth. And enough is God as a Disposer of affairs." (Surah 4:171)

The Muslim does not believe in Christ's death and resurrection. "That they said (in boast), 'We killed Christ Jesus the son of Mary, the Apostle of God'—but they killed him not, nor crucified him, but so it was made to appear to them, and those who differ therein are full of doubts, with no (certain) knowledge, but only conjecture to follow, for of a surety they killed him not." (Surah 4:157)

The Muslim believes his entrance into heaven is based on his good deeds outweighing the bad. "He forgiveth whom He pleaseth, and punisheth whom He pleaseth, for Allah hath power over all things." (Surah 2:284) "For those things that are good remove those that are evil." (Surah 11:114)

The Muslim has an assurance of paradise only through the jihad. This can be a spiritual struggle or a holy war against the unbeliever. "And if ye are slain, or die, in the way of Allah, forgiveness and mercy from Allah are far better than all they could amass." (Surah 3:157) If a Muslim dies in the midst of fighting the infidel, the unbeliever of Islam, he believes he is immediately escorted to paradise. "Let those fight in the cause of Allah who sell the life of this world for the hereafter. To him who fighteth in the cause of Allah—wither he is slain or gets victory— Soon shall we give him a reward of great (value)." (Surah 4:74)[2]

All this is presented as the infallible word of Allah that cannot be questioned or even critically reflected upon without the threat of death. However, Allah is supposedly ordering Christians to desist from the belief in a concept of the Trinity that is not found in orthodox Christianity.

> As the readers may already know, a cursory reading of the Islamic scripture shows that the author of the Quran distorted or was grossly mistaken about the beliefs of Jews and Christians. For example, the author accuses Christians of holding certain theological and Christological beliefs that do not correspond to the facts. The Quran erroneously assumes and condemns Christians for believing in three gods consisting of the Father, Mary his wife, and Jesus their offspring. Thus, the Quran erroneously assumes that the implication of Christian beliefs is that God acquired a son through procreation, that God and Mary had sexual relations in order to have Jesus their Son. (God forbid such horrendous blasphemy!)[3]

The dogmas the Quran condemns are in fact heresies that orthodox Judaism and Christianity also reject.

> In some cases, the "material" which forms the substance of Quranic narrative, details of the creeds of Christianity and Judaism for example, does not correspond to those religion's own understanding of their beliefs. This could be said, for example, of the notion of the Trinity found in the Quran, the story of Satan's refusal to bow down to Adam, the Docetist view of the crucifixion, all of which can be traced to the dogmas of Gnostic sects, which are heretical in relationship to orthodox Christianity and Judaism. The Trinity "seen" in the Quran is not the Trinity of the Apostles Creed, or of the Nicene Creed.[4]

When it comes to Islamic apocalyptic visions of the end of the world, the role of Jesus Christ is completely contrary to the revelation of the Bible. In fact, Islam turns "Isa" (Jesus) into the antichrist.

'Isa (Jesus) in the Hadith – 'Isa the destroyer of Christianity. The prophet 'Isa will have an important role in the end times, establishing Islam and making war until he destroys all religions save Islam. He shall kill the Evil One (Dajjal), an apocalyptic anti-Christ figure.

In one tradition of Muhammad we read that no further prophets will come to earth until 'Isa returns as "a man of medium height, or reddish complexion, wearing two light garments, looking as if drops were falling down from his head although it will not be wet. He will fight for the cause of Islam. He will break the cross, kill pigs, and abolish the poll-tax. Allah will destroy all religions except Islam. He ('Isa) will destroy the Evil One and will live on the earth for forty years and then he will die." (Sunan Abu Dawud, 37:4310) The Sahih Muslim has a variant of this tradition: "The son of Mary ... will soon descend among you as a just judge. He will ... abolish the poll-tax, and the wealth will pour forth to such an extent that no one will accept charitable gifts." (Sahih Muslim 287)

What do these sayings mean? The cross is a symbol of Christianity. Breaking crosses means abolishing Christianity. Pigs are associated with Christians. Killing them is another way of speaking of the destruction of Christianity. Under Islamic law the poll-tax buys the protection of the lives and property of conquered "people of the Book" [Jews and Christians]. (At-Taubah 9:29) The abolition of the poll-tax means jihad is restarted against Christians (and Jews) living under Islam, who should convert to Islam, or else be killed or enslaved. The abundance of wealth refers to booty flowing to the Muslims from this conquest. This is what the Muslim 'Isa will do when he returns in the last days.[5]

Satan masterfully orchestrated the deception of Muhammad. There is a well-spun web of deception beginning first within the Jewish and Christian communities themselves. These are related to the deep unbiblical hatred that had grown up between Jews and Christians. Then mixed in are the heresies that had taken root in the Christians of that area with whom Muhammad would have had direct contact. Satan built on all this to create the perfect conditions for a systematic set of lies that point by point reject and replace the basic doctrines of the Christian faith with its Jewish roots.

This is in contrast to the world's other great religions like Buddhism and Hinduism. These other religions have creeds and beliefs that are contrary to Christian doctrines, such as karma and reincarnation. However, in the sacred ancient texts of these religions there is nothing like the false god of Islam, Allah, giving direct commands against the core Christian doctrines of the Trinity, the divinity of Jesus Christ, and his death on the cross and resurrection. These other religions formed centuries before the coming of Christ. The prophet Muhammad comes nearly 600 years after Christ, which strengthens the argument that Islam is Satan's deception intended to replace Christianity.

Satan as Murderer and Radical Islam His Agent for Murder

Jesus goes on to say that Satan is not just a liar, but he will kill anyone who speaks the truth. Jesus said this to the unbelieving Jews to whom Jesus was speaking the truth, and who were trying to kill him. "You people are from your father the devil, and you want to do what your father desires. He was a murderer from the beginning, and does not uphold the truth..." (John 8:44).

Jesus says that lies and murder are bound as one. The lies of Satan first bring spiritual death because they take human beings away from God's established way of salvation. The second way they are connected is that in order to prevent the speaking of the truth the Devil will, if he has the earthly means to do so, kill those through whom God's truth comes. This is what Satan tried to do with Jesus Christ from the beginning: kill him. Through time, Satan has built strongholds that provide earthly power and permission to kill people. When deception fails, murder is always his effective means.

Historically this has been especially true when it comes to Satan's attempts to replace the way of salvation revealed in the Bible, as we saw with Hitler's attempts to kill not only Jews, but Christians who resisted the Nazi vision.[6] Islam, like the Nazis, from its beginnings has chosen death and subjugation as the means to enforce their creed on others. Therefore, Satan is using elements of Islam to build strongholds of death and subjugation today.

Second Confirmation:
The Parallels of Biblical Eschatology with Apocalyptic Islamic Hope of the Mahdi

There are many aspects of Radical Islam's own eschatology that seem to fit with Biblical end time prophecy. George Otis Jr., author of *The Last of the Giants: Lifting the Veil on Islam and the End Times,* fully explores this relationship. He sees the following direct parallels between Islam and the predicted Mahdi and the end times working of Satan:

> Although many sincere Muslims would no doubt resent the comparison, Islamic traditions of the Mahdi's emergence and actions are eerily akin to those associated with the false prophet in John's Revelation. Could it be that the Mahdi will be that miracle-working leader who will manage to heal the wounded head (the global Islamic empire) of the beast by resuscitating the faith of Muslims in the moment of their darkest defeat (by Israel in Ezekiel 38-39)?

That Islam is the ultimate systemic incarnation of the beast is suggested by: 1) the fact that the false prophet exercises the authority of the beast—thereby implying the system is essentially religious in nature; 2) the fact that no other religion exists with traditions matching the descriptions of Revelation 13 and 17; and 3) the fact that the nations following the beast hate and make war on the scarlet woman (the spirit of materialism and wantonness)—a graphic description of the sentiments and desires of today's Islamic fundamentalists vis-a-vis the "Great Satan" [who is the United States]. [7]

George Otis wrote in 1991, against the tide of thinking going back to the Reformation that the Antichrist would be the Pope. While the spirit of the antichrist has found expression in many different leaders including popes and dictators, the end times antichrist as revealed in Scripture seems to fit much better with George Otis's conclusion that he will be the Mahdi bringing the hegemony of Islam. Recently there are many teachers who are making a strong case for an Islamic Antichrist and Beast.

I would add a fourth point to this list of reasons to see Islam as part of the means of Satan fulfilling his aims in the last days. As demonstrated above, there is no other religious system on earth that has built into it such a calculated point by point replacement of Christian doctrine. There is no other religion on earth that calls for killing Jews and Christians who embody the covenants God has made with humanity—even down to beheading them![8]

Are the Present Islamic Leaders the Antichrist? Or the Beast?

Do these end times parallels to Biblical prophecy imply that the present day demonic strongholds based on Islam, such as ISIS or Hamas, or the mullahs of Iran are indeed the embodiment of the "Beast"? Are they the end times "Antichrist"? Is the "man of

Lawlessness" among them? I think it is dangerous to make such assumptions. Many people thought Adolph Hitler was the end time's Antichrist. One danger in trying to link up end-time theology with our role as intercessors is that a fatalistic passivity can overtake us and destroy our resolve as intercessors. Here is a personal example:

On September 3, 2015 the Holy Spirit called me into restless all night prayer concerning the nuclear deal with Iran. I kept hearing again and again the words, "This is appeasement;" it will, like the Munich conference of 1938, lead to Radical Islam gaining power to fulfill Satan's plans for genocide. This led me into prayer. I received guidance to pray that the Holy Spirit would expose Satan's true aims of the stronghold of Radical Islam in Iran for the entire world to see. I prayed especially that if their aims were "death to America and death to Israel," that this would be shown to the senators who are supporting the Iran deal. I prayed, "Lord if this agreement truly is appeasement and a furthering of Satan's genocidal goals, let that be exposed in the next two weeks." I further prayed, "Lord, if those are not Satan's goals through the Islamic Republic of Iran, then please reveal that also." And Lord, "Please reveal for all to see if this agreement is indeed a form of compromise. Lord, show us! In the name of Jesus Christ, expose what is really going on so that we will know how to cooperate with you to prevent evil and instead to advance your Kingdom."

I shared this with a friend who is very focused on the End Times. He said, "Oh I think we should keep our eyes on Jesus and let Satan work and gather the armies of Gog and Magog to attack Israel. Then we will see Jesus destroy the armies of Satan with the sword that comes out of his mouth." Then he told me, "You just need to relax; God is in charge and he is working everything out." That took me aback! My passion in prayer is to prevent the evil from taking place. This is why the Lord called me to gather the army of intercessors—to stop these terrible things from happening. But my friend had an entirely different attitude; it was one of passivity and disengagement from the battle because he was assuming that this is the last battle when Jesus Christ will supernaturally intervene without needing any involvement from human beings at all.

We must keep our balance when we are seeing evil. And what could be more evil than burning people alive in iron cages or beheading Christians including children—all acts of the Islamic State? We must seal upon our hearts John's words of warning that, as it is in the last days, "so now many antichrists have appeared," and Paul's affirmation in 2 Thessalonians 2:7 that the "hidden power of lawlessness is already at work." This means that although we will experience now all sorts of manifestations of evil, these are not necessarily the end of the age. We are in the battle that extends through all of history, the battle between the great Deceiver, and him who is the Way, the Truth and the Life.

Third Confirmation
Warnings by Leaders with God's Gift of Prescience

Just as in the period of the first gathering storm before the outbreak of World War II, political and military leaders of today are now warning us of the next gathering storm. Prime Minister of Israel Benjamin Netanyahu's speeches before the UN General Assembly and the Congress of the United States issue clear warnings of the dangers that we face in Radical Islam.

"America at Risk, the War with No Name," hosted by Newt and Callista Gingrich, vividly demonstrates the dangers facing America one decade after the attacks on 9/11.[9] Or review the text of a speech made on October 26, 2006 by republican Senator Rick Santorum. The Senator in 2006 used the very terms that I have used—of a "gathering storm" about the growing evil of Radical Islam. He called this movement "Islamic Fascism."[10]

Another insightful article is from (Retired) Lieutenant General

William G "Jerry" Boykin entitled "Shariah, the Threat to America: An Exercise in Competitive Analysis: Report of Team B II."[11]

Read Geert Wilders' powerful book, *Marked for Death: Islam's War Against the West and Me*, Regnery Publishing, 2012. Geert Wilders is a member of the Dutch Parliament and the founder and leader of the Freedom Party. He dared expose the true aims and purposes of Islam—to subjugate the world to Islamic tyranny.

Fourth Confirmation
The Leaders of Radical/Militant Islam Publicly Stating their Goals and Intentions.

I recommend two excellent behind-the-scenes documentaries to expose us to Islamic leaders themselves who state their aims and intentions. "*Obsession: Radical Islam's War Against the West* (2007)"[12], and "Islam: What the West Needs to Know."[13]

Geert Wilders' short video *Fitna* is also a devastating revelation of the words of the Quran and the Hadith, with contemporary Islamic jihadists quoting them, and then footage of their actions of death, violence and terror. Wilders just reports what the Islamic leaders themselves are saying and doing.[14] He shows clearly that their stated intentions are rooted in the Quran.

Why would Islamic leaders reveal their plans? Do you think it is probable that if your plans were as horrible as the extermination of a whole race or as outrageous as subjugating the whole world that you would speak them out over the airwaves or the internet for all to hear? Would you publish your atrocities committed in the name of Allah over the internet for all to see? Is that not the height of folly, especially when those who can thwart your plans may hear your words and take them seriously?

Satan's strategy, is to cloak his intentions so that his enemies will minimize the dangers until it is too late. He does this through cloaking philosophies like progressive liberalism and political correctness. But those whom Satan has called as his leaders, the ones through whom he will build his strongholds, must speak out their objectives plainly so that demonized or receptive people may hear those words and be attracted in increasing numbers. In chapter seventeen we shall explore this dynamic in greater detail. For now, this means that leaders speak out Satan's plans as part of the way that others will be brought into them. It also means that we must take what these leaders say with great seriousness. While it is true that Satan is an inveterate liar, in this case he must expose his plans so they can grow to fruition.

The same principle holds true on God's side of this conflict. God has revealed his plans to his friends (Jews and Christians) so that they will be able to act in accordance with his plans. But sometimes Christians do not appreciate the risks God takes in revealing his plans to his enemies by publishing them to his friends. Nor do we appreciate why Jesus spoke to his disciples in parables, so that some people would not be able to hear the Gospel of the Kingdom. Satan can read the Bible too, and the evidence shows that he is very skilled to know exactly what the Bible says down to the last detail. If God had decided to hide his Kingdom entirely, who could respond to the Gospel?

This necessity of speaking words out to recruit people for Satan's vision opens the door for all who can discern the times to discover Satan's plans, if we take this conflict seriously. To do so we must ignore Satan's cloaking devices, then listen carefully to the enemies of the Kingdom of God as they tell us in their own words what their goals and intentions are.

Let us review briefly a few of these openly expressed schemes of Satan. Here is a list of apocalyptic objectives, summarized by Joel Rosenberg:

> "We will conquer your Rome, break your crosses, and enslave your women, by the permission of Allah, the Exalted. This is his promise to us; he is glorified and he does not fail in his promise.

If we do not reach that time, then our children and grandchildren will reach it, and they will sell your sons as slaves at the slave market."—Excerpt from an article titled, "Indeed, Your Lord Is Ever Watchful," by the official ISIS spokesman, in Dabiq, Issue #4, September, 2014.

"Rush, O Muslims, to your state. It is your state. Syria is not for Syrians and Iraq is not for Iraqis. The land is for the Muslims, all Muslims. ... This is my advice to you. If you hold to it you will conquer Rome and own the world, if Allah wills."—ISIS leader Abu Bakr al-Baghdadi, audio recording, July 2014.

"The slogans of the Iranian nation on Al-Quds Day show what its position is. The slogans 'Death to Israel' and 'Death to America' have resounded throughout the country, and are not limited to Tehran and the other large cities. The entire country is under the umbrella of this great movement [of 'Death to Israel' and 'Death to America']."—Supreme Leader Ayatollah Ali Khomeini, July 18, 2015.

"It is the mission of the Islamic Republic of Iran to erase Israel from the map of the region."—Iranian Supreme Leader Ayatollah Ali Khomeini, January 2001.

"Israel must be wiped off the map."—Iranian president Mahmoud Ahmadinejad, October 26, 2005. [15]

We must take these words seriously. They confirm that these are indeed Satan's plans. Further they show that they have taken root in the hearts and minds of the deceived Islamic leaders through whom Satan is trying to fulfill them.

Fifth Confirmation
Revelatory Actions and Events

All human events to some degree express the intentions of those involved in them. There are, however, some events that stand out from the stream of human actions that especially reveal the intentions of human beings as well as God or Satan. An event becomes revelatory when it allows those with the gift of discernment to see a correlation between the stated intentions of the human leaders and the actions they are taking. With both God and Satan, working out either good or evil respectively, their visions and intentions must be clothed with actions. These actions are consistent with the vision and represent the first steps toward the fulfillment of the vision. When one's vision is clothed with actions, it builds faith in others that enables the author of the vision to continue working. When the al-Qaeda terrorists under the direction of Osama bin Laden flew the hijacked jet liners into the World Trade Towers and the Pentagon, several important dynamics were taking place.

First of all, Osama bin Laden's Islamic jihadist vision was clothed with actions. This built faith in those who shared this vision, and was then used by Satan to draw others into the vision and prepare for additional actions. No doubt this would have set off a chain of other terrorist events had not President George W. Bush launched a massive counterattack in the War on Terror.

Second, from the perspective of those who were attacked on September 11th, this was a revelatory event exposing the true purposes and aims of Osama bin Laden's al-Qaeda. These purposes and aims had previously been spoken as curses by bin Laden when he made formal fatwas calling for Muslims to kill Jews and Americans.[16] Our leaders rightly saw this event as an act of war which required the massive response that followed. For intercessors, it revealed how Satan had built the demonic stronghold of al Qaeda as the means of carrying out Satan's evil plans. We were called into the gap to pray. Events that are revelatory provide those with the gift of discernment the windows into the true intentions of human beings and the Devil.

As an example of seeing the revelatory significance of an event, see the article by Joseph I. Lieberman in the January 12, 2015 *Wall Street Journal* entitled, "*A Global War on Radical Islam: Atrocities like those in Paris won't stop until the civilized world mobilizes to wipe out the forces of violent jihad*" (Jan. 12, 2015 6:51 p.m. ET).

> In rapid order, the three attacks in France last week showed more clearly than ever that the international movement of violent Islamist extremism has declared war on Western civilization's foundational values, which are embraced by so many people throughout the world.
>
> The murders of police officers, cartoonists and Jews were attacks against the West's most central values and aspirations— the rule of law, freedom of expression and freedom of religion. Radical Islam will continue to threaten what we hold dear unless it is fought and eventually defeated.[17]

On the basis of this assessment of what the attacks in Paris actually meant, Joseph Lieberman, in the rest of the article, presents a set of action steps to defeat Radical Islam. This attack against freedom of expression, the rule of law and religious freedom is consistent with what the Islamists have been saying themselves about their plans and purposes. I take this discernment further than the human intentions and affirm that these actions reveal Satan's plans and purposes.

Sixth Confirmation
Analysis of Past and Present Facts
Reveal Persistent Patterns

Perhaps the most obvious way to confirm Satan's plans is by analyzing the facts of history. All the facts in the past and present, especially as they form persistent patterns, are revelatory of Satan's purposes.

For instance, Raymond Ibrahim, in his book *Crucified Again,* reveals the pattern of Islam's persecution of Christians down through history and across many cultures. This confirms that genocide is indeed Satan's intent, and that Satan is using certain texts from the Quran and the Hadith to deceive Muslims into cooperating with his plans. We will not understand or grasp the reality and validity of the threats that we face until we look at the track record of history right up to the present.[18]

Just as I am revising this chapter, a *Wall Street Journal* article appeared entitled "Exterminating Christians in the Middle East: Islamic State marks the houses of Christians with the Arabic letter 'N' for Nazarene."

> Recently I saw a riveting new play, "My Report to the World: The Story of Jan Karski." In 1943, Karski, a member of the Polish Catholic underground, was the first eyewitness to the Warsaw ghetto and a Nazi concentration camp to reach the U.S. He sought to convince President Franklin D. Roosevelt and Supreme Court Justice Felix Frankfurter that Judaism was being systematically wiped out by the Nazis. Frankfurter told Karski he couldn't believe it because the horror was unfathomable.
>
> A similar story is playing out again, as Christians are being wiped out in the Middle East. On his recent trip to Latin America, Pope Francis said, "Today we are dismayed to see how in the Middle East and elsewhere in the world many of our brothers and sisters are persecuted, tortured and killed for their faith in Jesus." He continued: "In this third world war, waged piecemeal, which we are now experiencing, a form of genocide is taking place." The author then calls for the action of allowing these persecuted Christians into America just as there were pleas to allow Jews to come to America and then he says this: "Furthermore, the world is no longer forced to rely on a single pair of eyes as in Karski's day. The forced conversions, the beheadings, the slaughter of Copts on a Mediterranean beach—these horrors are all available on YouTube."[19]

During the genocide of Armenian, Assyrian, and Greek Christians by the Ottoman Caliphate and the extermination of the Jews by the Nazis, there were voices of warning and calls to action. So now, with the extermination of Christians by Radical Islam, the Holy Spirit is raising up witnesses to expose this evil boldly. Yet Satan's cloaking devices, working within the sinful human heart as well as in a sophisticated fabric of deceptions, prevents most from seeing it. In the past, the leaders of Western nations have not acted until the evidence was overwhelming, and by then it was too late to prevent worldwide tragedies. Now again, Satan has already accomplished much; millions have died, and the stronghold has gained the tools and power to bring even more death and tyranny.

My motive for publishing this book to expose Satan's plans is to call intercessors worldwide into this prayer work to prevent the terrible mistakes of the past from being repeated, and to stop this unfolding horror before, this time, billions die.

These are Satan's Hideous Plans through Radical Islam

To arrive at the conclusion that these odious aims of Satan are being accomplished in the strongholds built from Islam, all of these discernment guidelines must line up with a positive affirmation. I believe they do.

If we are joining this battle to defeat Satan's terrible plans of genocide, subjugation and replacement through the means of Radical Islam, we must be very sure that these really are in fact Satan's plans. We are being called to a cause that may well cost us our lives. So I urge you to do your own research; come to your own conclusions.

For myself, I am absolutely convinced by the evidence that these objectives of Satan are real, and that Satan is actively and aggressively carrying them out through the virulent expressions of

Radical Islam. Further, the evidence shows that the Islamic State (ISIS), as well as the theocratic government of Iran, are indeed growing in power and in obtaining the spiritual, organizational, cultural, political, military, and financial means needed to continue to implement these plans

History has proven that the demonic strongholds Satan erects to impose his plans of death and tyranny are both spiritual as well as earthly power structures. Thus they will continue to be used by Satan to accomplish his genocidal purposes until stopped by a combination of opposing spiritual and earthly powers.

As of 2015-16 while we were preparing this prayer strategy, our focus is on victory over the Islamic State. But as we engage that particular stronghold, we must not forget that the Shiite expression in Iran and its proxies may in the long run be the greater danger unless stopped. It may be the most successful at carrying out Satan's plans. As Prime Minister of Israel Benjamin Netanyahu warned the joint session of the US Congress, "To defeat ISIS would win a battle, but to allow Iran to get the bomb would be to lose the war."[20] We must also recognize that ISIS is but one expression of the hydra-headed monster Satan is creating named "Radical Islam."

The Gathering of the Archons

As intercessors and spiritual warriors, where do we start in this battle to prevent Satan from bringing to fulfillment his fourteen-hundred-year old strategy to replace God's way of life and freedom with the death and tyranny of Islam?

For the sake of clarity of understanding and strategic impact, we must discern where Jesus Christ is calling us as intercessors to join the conflict. We must be led by St. Paul's words from Ephesians 6:12, *For our struggle is not against flesh and blood, but against the rulers, against the powers, against the world rulers of this darkness, against the spiritual forces of evil in the heavens.* So following His lead, we start discerning our spiritual enemies behind our human foes.

Into Satan's War Room
Levels of Demonic Beings behind Radical Islam

During one of our prayer engagements, we prayed that the Holy Spirit would show us the supernatural enemies we are up against in this war with the various expressions of Radical Islam. The Lord gave us a glimpse into Satan's war room. Through spiritual vision, we became akin to spies sent from Jesus to see the demonic entities that St. Paul lists in Ephesians 6:12. The details of the symbols the Holy Spirit used to show us this spiritual reality need not distract us. In the war room of the command and control center in the spiritual realms including Earth, Satan is always represented and sometimes actually present. Unlike our God he can only be in one place at a time. And not being God who is creator, he can only distort and corrupt what is already created, and in that he is immensely creative. He also must work through a hierarchy of evil entities starting with high level fallen angels who have jurisdiction over entire people groups and nations. He has an untold number of low level demons which, like an infantry, are swarming over the earth. Their assignments are given them by those higher up the chain of command. In a bewilderingly complex operational plan, each demon plays a role needed for fulfilling the master battle plan of overcoming the Kingdom of God and tormenting and subjugating the people of the earth.

Given the strategic importance of the strongholds of Radical Islam in this phase of the war, Satan may well be overseeing this operation in person. But we have no clear revelation about that, we just know that Satan is the prime motivator, and his character and nature drive the whole culture of his kingdom with an absolute dictatorship and fear. We are also certain that in this war we are dealing with much more than just one evil entity. Rather we must take seriously what John Calvin says in his summary of what the Bible teaches about the Devil.

> Scripture makes known that there are not one, not two, nor a few foes, but great armies, which wage war against us. But frequent mention of Satan or the Devil in the singular denotes the empire of wickedness opposed to the Kingdom of Righteousness.[1]

LEVELS OF SPIRITUAL WARFARE

Satan
Archon/High
Level Demonic
Beings

Corporate Level
Exousia Authorities

Human/Demonic
organzations

Personal Level - Demons
afflicting individulas

In the vision into Satan's war room we saw all these levels in great detail. I have written extensively elsewhere giving the biblical definition of each level of these demonic entities.[2] Others have done so as well. Go to them for the full description. In this book we must focus on the implications for exposing the strongholds Satan is building based on Islam.

Strongholds are interwoven human and demonic structures. We must gain a grasp of Satan's kingdom as it provides the structure and character of the human organizations that they are forming.

Also, when we move past gathering intelligence and step onto the battlefield, our engagement with demonic spirits will take place on different levels and will require different prayer and spiritual warfare tactics. Depicted in the chart are different levels of demonic beings in Satan's empire of darkness. The highest level of spiritual warfare is with Satan. This is called the cosmic level because it has to do with the victory of Jesus Christ over Satan. This level does not involve us. The second level, labeled *high level*, is well defined by Tom Wilcox:

> High-level Spiritual Warfare is primarily, at least from our perspective, a battle between the believing Church on earth and the invisible, spiritual forces of darkness. It often has to do with powerful demon rulers and authorities.

> These high level demons exert their evil power over people in communities or people in specific geographic regions. They are sometimes called "territorial spirits." These are the kinds of powers, principalities, and high things ("pretensions") Paul speaks of in Ephesians 6:12 and in 2 Corinthians 10:5. The Church seeks to stand firm against the enemy for itself. It also seeks to invade Satan's kingdom, to bind and loose in the spiritual realm, to wield divinely given power and authority, all in order to set the captives free.[3]

Our calling as intercessors will involve us with the demonic powers at this high level. These are the powers assigned to work in constructing strongholds beginning with the visionary leaders. These strongholds provide the means for Satan to accomplish his plans on earth.

Our prayer and warfare will also from time to time take us to what is called ground level spiritual warfare. This type of spiritual warfare involves binding spirits working in individuals who compose the human organization of the stronghold. At this level our prayer battles may be to prevent those individuals from carrying out Satan's plans. For example, we may be led to labor for a particular leader to be delivered from the deception of Islam and come to know the truth in Jesus Christ. This ground level warfare is connected with evangelism, and the Holy Spirit drawing Muslims to faith in Jesus Christ.

Our focus in this book, *Discerning the Times*, is on how high level demons or archons are at work in forming the strongholds. The second book will deal with the tactics for actually defeating these archons.

The Gathering of the Archons
in the Second Gathering Storm

We have discerned that at this season in history there is a gathering of high-level demonic spirits. In Ephesians 6:12, St. Paul calls these "rulers," or "principalities," from the Greek word *archon*.[4] They seem to be the highest level of demonic beings, above another level of beings called the "world rulers," or in Greek, the *kosmokrator*.[5] It is clear that these are demonic beings and not human rulers because Paul tells us that "our struggle is not against flesh and blood." Paul also makes it clear that while these are not human beings, their rule does interface with the human and earthly sphere.

These spiritual entities, which I have discerned to be gathering for Satan's present campaign through Radical Islam, may be in the highest category of archons. Or they may be under them as "world rulers." We may never know for certain. However, from all the intelligence that I have gathered, I am certain that Satan is using these high level demons and their accompanying hosts of evil spirits to influence directly and in some cases actually to possess the key leaders around whom he is building the demonic fortress of Radical Islam.

While we can never know for sure the names of the high level demons in Satan's empire, we can deduce their nature from the behavior and actions of Satan's agents. A further way of confirming that these are the actual demonic entities in Radical Islam is that they bring the talents needed to accomplish Satan's plans of replacement of Christianity, genocide and world subjugation. I list them here by their biblical names.

Gog
Ezekiel 38; Revelation 20:7-10

Gog, a high-level archon of tyrannical oppression and totalitarian government, destroys liberal, pluralistic, and democratic societies where human freedom flourishes.

Some commentators have identified Gog and Magog with Russia. But George Otis, Jr. gives a more plausible interpretation of the biblical text. His interpretation is that Gog and Magog represent a high level demonic power of "totalitarianism–which has incarnated various human vessels in the region over the course of many centuries."[6]

Gog is working through the Wahhabi interpretation of the Islamic texts to create the stronghold of radical, political Islam set on imposing Sharia law on all people. This includes the coercion to accept the Islamic creed[7] through the sword and subjugation. Once people are enslaved in this system of both spiritual and political oppression, they are held there by all the forms of coercion instituted by the Islamic totalitarian state.[8]

Moloch
Jeremiah 32:35; Acts 7:43

Moloch, the archon of death who murders children, thrives on the death of the innocent and consumes life, especially through fire. Wherever the choice is made to champion death and not life, Moloch is able and ready. When ISIS shows videos of burning people alive, Christian children being shot or beheaded, or the mass murder of apostate Muslims, all the while chanting "*Allah Akbar! God is greater!*" they reveal that they are listening to Moloch and to

Satan himself, who is a "murderer from the beginning."

Those who invoke the power of death, such as Muslims who chant "Death to Israel and death to America," unleash terrible power for themselves for a season. But Moloch's thirst for blood is unquenchable. After he has consumed the innocent, he usually turns and devours those who welcome him into their midst. God's law is: We reap what we sow.

The Spirit of Lawlessness
2 Thessalonians 2:1-12

This archon invites lawlessness and anarchy that opens the door for the imposition of tyranny—a paved road of welcome to the demonic to construct strongholds to grow and gain the power to accomplish their purposes. This demon is very much at work generating murder and chaos through ISIS, which intends to usher in the Mahdi. In the Shia Iranian version, this is the hoped for 12th Imam.

The Spirit of the Many Antichrists
1 John 2:18

Both Sunni and Shia apocalyptic versions see Islamic jihad-induced anarchy leading to the coming of a messianic figure who bears a striking resemblance to the Beast and the Antichrist of the book of Revelation. One version even includes the return of an Islamic Jesus Christ who is the complete opposite of the true Jesus Christ of the Bible.[9] "He will fight the people for Islam, breaking the cross, killing the swine, and abolishing the poll tax. In this time, [Allah][10] will destroy every religious community except Islam. He will destroy the Deceiving Messiah."[11] The final outcome of this twisted vision is global Islamic hegemony and the tyranny of Sharia law over all humankind.[12] This clearly fits the role of the Antichrist as an archon who specifically opposes the spread of the Gospel of the Kingdom of Yeshua.

<h2 style="text-align:center">The Demonic Spirit of the Amalekites
Exodus 17:16</h2>

Exodus 17:16: "...for he (Moses) said, 'For a hand was lifted up to the throne of the LORD—that the LORD will have war with Amalek from generation to generation.'" Here our God declared war against Amalek forever because this archon is committed to blocking God's Kingdom on earth and either to compromise or to destroy Yahweh's chosen and redeemed people, both Jews and Christians. We see it at work especially in Islam's abiding hatred of Jews and Radical Islam's stated intentions to destroy Israel and exterminate the Jewish people.

In Chapter 14, we shall demonstrate how this archon first found an open door in the heart of Muhammad and then has been passed down through generations of Muslims. The most recent pathway is through the Ottoman Caliphate/Occult German genocide of Armenian, Assyrian and Greek Christians. We will show that this spirit has now been transferred to modern Radical Islam through the Nazi/Islamist stronghold to exterminate the Jewish people and replace Christianity through genocide and subjugation.

Leviathan Holding these Archons Together

These five demonic powers are, however, only part of a hierarchy of evil. In 2011 a team of Canadian intercessors discerned that an archon named Leviathan was holding these five together, and coordinating their activities in the world. The Bible reveals the character of this high level demon and how this is possible.

Leviathan is described as a sea monster in Job 41 and Ezekiel 32. This is more than a description. It is depiction of a principality.

In Psalm 74:13-14 we read: *You split the sea by your strength and smashed the sea monsters. You crushed the heads of Leviathan and let the desert animals eat him.* Leviathan has many "heads" which suggests that he is more than an evil spirit. Leviathan is a principality that controls cultures against God and His people.

In the mid-1970s Bill Bright, Loren Cunningham, and Francis Schaffer spoke about seven mountains (or spheres) of culture.[13] Leviathan, with its many heads, seeks to control these spheres. The ancient Egyptian empire is a perfect example of a culture dominated by Leviathan. "Leviathan" is often associated with a "monster" (or monsters) of the Nile River. The Egyptian culture attributed their prosperity and victory to this leviathan. The "Leviathan" was worshipped and revered and controlled all of Egyptian culture. While described as monster, snake, dragon or crocodile, these are only depictions of a principality that seeks to control a culture at the expense of the people of God. Recall that Egypt was very happy to keep the Israelites in bondage, and tried to destroy them when they were set free by Yahweh through Moses.

The root word for Leviathan is "twisted" or "coiled." Leviathan is a sea monster or dragon that coils itself around the victim in order to twist the life out of him. This is the tactic and strategy of this archon—to coil itself around the people of God and twist them until there is no life. Note the leviathan strategy employed in the Garden of Eden. He twisted God's words so that Eve doubted God's goodness and His intentions toward Adam. Because of this twisting (deception), Eve and Adam entered into rebellion and were cut off from the source of life. Godly life and influence were choked out of them. Leviathan's strategy is to coil itself around a culture and twist the truth until people are in rebellion before God and are cut off from the source of life.

This is exactly what Satan is doing in pulling together these archons to create and then work through the demonic stronghold of Radical Islam. Leviathan's work includes not just building the fortress of Radical Islam through the five archons, but interweaving with it the demonic stronghold of Liberal Progressivism. [14] Leviathan is the coordinator of Satan's assault against the Church and Western culture from within. It may well be that Leviathan is in fact Satan himself. All the evidence suggests that could be the case.

Why the Intercessor Needs to Know these High Level Demons at Work Behind Radical Islam

The intercessor needs to know the identity of these high level demons for two important reasons.

First, knowing the names of the high level demons helps us understand the motives and behaviors of the human beings through whom they are at work. As Christians we all know that our enemy is Satan. But this knowledge is so general that it does not help much to describe with the specific way Satan is at work. If, however we view Satan as a skillful commander-in-chief who is gathering a team of generals with specific talents and characteristics needed for his master war strategy, then we may have a deeper knowledge of both the war plans themselves and the means by which they are to be implemented.

In World War II, the Supreme Commander of the Allied Forces in Europe, Dwight D. Eisenhower, was a master at putting together a team of generals with conflicting personalities, talents, and war experiences. But all were needed to defeat the armies of Nazi Germany. When we study these personalities, we see Eisenhower's genius. For instance, it was the combination of the rashness of General Patton with the methodical implementation of General Omar Bradley that advanced allied armies toward victory.

Similarly, in gathering these five archons, Satan has put together a formidable team. They are uniquely suited to fulfill his aims of the genocide of billions and the imposition of global Islamic tyranny. They have each proven themselves from Old Testament times up to the recent history of Nazism. In the present Islamic State Caliphate, they are demonstrating their aptitude by the extermination of Christians and Muslim infidels and the brutal imposition of the Wahhabi interpretation of Sharia law. By naming them and studying their roles in the past, we may understand a great deal about the behavior and tactics of their human agents. We may also learn from history the tactics that other great intercessors from Moses to Rees Howells used to defeat them.

Second, when we name these five high level demons and acknowledge their existence, we finally have a way to understand how it is possible for Radical Islamic propaganda to boast worldwide appeal. How can this apocalyptic vision of death and destruction have such appeal that middle class educated Muslims are being recruited by the thousands to this death cult? Certainly alienation from Western culture, injustices against Muslims, the Palestinian /Israeli conflict, and other sociological justifications have their merit. However, these human explanations do not sufficiently support the primal power of ISIS ideology and vision.

To comprehend the complete picture, we must add to these human factors the role of these demonic powers. Each of these archons has a global network of demons able to work anywhere they are given permission. This permission has been provided by the lies in Islam that reject the truth that Jesus Christ is the way, the truth, the life, and the only way to the Father (John 14:6). When we add this supernatural dimension to sinful human nature, we now gain an understanding how and why the Islamic State is recruiting more and more Muslims to its ranks.

This is not a hypothetical suggestion of the coordination between our sin-tainted hearts and the presence of demonic spirits ready to seize upon the opportunity to inflame universal human sinful tendencies. If we look deeply into our own hearts, we know the truth of Romans 3:22-23, *there is no distinction, for all have sinned and fall short of the glory of God.* If it were not for the grace of God and the strong restraints of the law, and a culture with Judeo-Christian values, we too would fall to Satan's recruitment efforts for accomplishing evil on earth.

These archons—Gog, Moloch, the demonic spirit of the Amalekites, the Spirit of Lawlessness and the Anti-Christ —under the coordinated leadership of Leviathan, when given the means of deceived human beings, are deadly, formidable adversaries. Defeating Satan's juggernaut of Radical Islam is going to require the convergence of all the human means of power with the spiritual means of the authority of Jesus Christ and the power of the Holy Spirit, guided by the revelation of God's eternal Word.

Having gathered this intelligence about Satan's purposes in Islam and the demonic powers that are gathering, we must turn our attention to understanding precisely how demonic powers work on earth.

Part Two

Satan Constructing the Demonic Stronghoulds of Radical Islam

How Satan Works On Earth

If we engage in a war with Satan, we must understand how he works on earth. We focus on this topic in these next two chapters. First, we deal with the general theme of how Satan, a spirit, must work through individuals and human organizations. We name these human demonic structures strongholds. In the following chapter, we will review the building blocks Satan uses to establish all strongholds. This leads to the specific development of the stronghold of Radical Islam based on the sacred texts of Islam as well as through the defeated, but reconstituted elements of Nazism. This "intelligence" will provide us with the basis of understanding how the Holy Spirit may lead us in defeating these strongholds.

The Taliban Massacre of Students
Demonstrates the Way Satan Works on Earth

While I was writing this chapter, I opened the December 17, 2014 issue of the *Wall Street Journal*. On the front page was a picture of mothers with Islamic head coverings in convulsions of grief over their dead children. The headlines read, "Taliban Massacre

Students. At least 141 Killed in Rampage."[1]

> Taliban gunmen stormed a military-run school in northwestern Pakistan and killed at least 141 people, methodically shooting schoolchildren in the head and setting fire to some victims in a horrifying 9-hour rampage.[2]

As I continued to read and checked other reports, the graphic horror of the massacre of innocent, school age children settled upon me.

> The attackers shouted "Allahu akbar" or "God is greater"[3] over and over as they shot each student, Mr. Ameen said.[4]

> A source told NBC, "They burnt a teacher in front of the students in a classroom. They literally set the teacher on fire with gasoline and made the kids watch." Harrowing eyewitness accounts revealed how students were forced to watch as bodies were burned beyond recognition. Other survivors told how they played dead while insurgents scoured[5] the school looking[6]for children to shoot, before opening fire indiscriminately— sometimes with smiles on their faces.[7]

This massacre reveals how Satan works on earth and how he uses both individuals as well as human organizations.

These are the Works of Moloch

When we see something this horrible, we must ponder whose nature these works reflect. Obviously, there were human beings involved. Their motivation is clear—they provide it themselves. The attackers shouted, "Allahu akbar" or "God is greater" over and over as they shot each student as Mr. Ameen said.[8] This is not collateral damage of war, but rather the intentional murder of innocents.

We must discern who this Allah is. If Allah reveals his greatness in the massacre of innocent children, in the beheadings of Christians, mass shootings and the burning to death of fellow Muslims, then, let us know unequivocally this is not the same spiritual entity revealed in the Torah and the Christian Bible. This is wholly another being. Remember that the word for god in Arabic is Allah. But it is possible for an alternate principality to adopt that word as his own name.

We do not speak here of the God who spoke to Moses out of the burning bush and gave His name as Yahweh. Further, the God who sent His Son Jesus to die for the world is full of grace and truth, love and life, and an entirely other being who behaves in a different—an opposite—way. If these atrocities show that Allah is "greater," then just who is this Allah?

As I was seeking discernment of this question, another article from the *Wall Street Journal* by Elie Wiesel came to mind, entitled: "I call upon President Obama and the leaders of the world to condemn Hamas's use of children as human shields." In early August, 2014, Hamas was sending hundreds of rockets into Israel. The IDF, in self-defense, was trying to take out the rocket launchers and the tunnels Hamas had built into Israel. Hamas intentionally placed these military installations amid the most vulnerable portions of the population to create the inevitable collateral casualties. The evidence pointed to the fact that Hamas intended the killing of innocent children, albeit through the response of the Israelis defending their own children.

> More than three thousand years ago, Abraham had two children. One son had been sent into the wilderness and was in danger of dying. God saved him with water from a spring
>
> . The other son was bound, his throat about to be cut by his own father. But God stayed the knife. Both sons—Ishmael and Isaac—received promises that they would father great nations.

With these narratives, monotheism and western civilization begin. And the Canaanite practices of child sacrifice to Moloch are forever left behind by the descendants of Abraham. Except they are not.

In my own lifetime, I have seen Jewish children thrown into the fire. And now I have seen Muslim children used as human shields, in both cases by worshippers of death cults indistinguishable from that of the Molochites. What we are suffering through today is not a battle of Jew versus Arab or Israeli versus Palestinian. Rather, it is a battle between those who celebrate life and those who champion death. It is a battle of civilization versus barbarism.[9]

For me, when Elie Wiesel called both Nazis and the Radical Islamic stronghold of Hamas "worshippers of death cults indistinguishable from that of the Molochites," the lights went on. This intentional killing of innocents, whether in the name of Nazism or Allah, is the work of a high-level demon, the Archon Moloch!

The Bible reveals that child sacrifice through fire and the death of innocent people, especially of the most innocent who are children, is the work of a high level demon. [10] Moloch is under the control of the chief fallen angel Satan, the Devil. Of him Jesus says, *"(He) was a murderer from the beginning, and does not uphold the truth, because there is no truth in him. Whenever he lies, he speaks according to his own nature, because he is a liar and the father of lies"* (John 8:44).

Thus, whenever we see the fruit of the power of death and lies shaping reality, we are seeing the works of the Devil. *"By their fruit you shall know them"* (Matthew 7:18) applies not just to human beings, but to spiritual beings as well.

Satan and the Archon
Express Themselves on Earth through People

In discerning that there is a high-level demon motivating the murder of innocent children, we return to the question of how a spiritual entity carries out its work on earth. Moloch did not manifest directly as a supernatural fire in that school in Pakistan in order to kill those children and burn the teacher to death. Human beings shouted "Allahu Akbar" with mocking smiles on their faces as they shot students and doused the teacher with gas to burn her to death. It is through human beings that the archon was at work.

In working through human beings, Satan perverts the means the Father has established for working in the material and human sphere. All of us were created in God's image with the capacity to interface between the spiritual and material realms. By applying our gifts of vision, reason, will and faith given to us by the Lord to exercise dominion, we may creatively shape reality in accord with God's intentions for the good of humanity. When we are born again into the Kingdom of God through faith in Jesus Christ and are filled with the Holy Spirit, we become His friends and coworkers. Then, as we cooperate with the Holy Spirit, we may work for the common good of humanity by building systems of government and economics that enable freedom and prosperity. Ultimately, we are also to advance the Gospel of Jesus Christ to fulfill the Great Commission.

Satan has hijacked this process by deceiving human beings away from the one true God to follow their own sinful propensities and evil intentions. The result is we yield our capacities for dominion to Satan's service and our thoughts and actions are in accord with his purposes. Under certain conditions such as unforgiveness, hatred and occult rituals, demonic spirits take control of individual human beings providing an avenue for them to express their vile nature on earth. This explains what happened at the school in Pakistan where Islamic radicals killed innocent human beings in the name of their god Allah. Satan was working through them to express his murderous nature and to implement his plans for death and tyranny on earth.

The Demonic Stronghold Behind the Seven Terrorists

Much evil in the world results from Satan working through individuals who are either deceived or demonized and have become his willing tools. However, there is another dimension to this atrocity. These seven men on their rampage of death were part of a larger organization, the Pakistani Taliban, which in turn is associated with the international Islamic jihadist group, al Qaeda.[11] The Pakistani Taliban as of October 2014, has pledged its support to ISIS as the Islamic Caliphate.[12] This organization indoctrinated these men, trained them, gave them the weapons and coordinated the attack. After the attack was successful, ISIS took credit for the murders as if they themselves had done the actual killing. They too demonstrate that they are instruments of the archon Moloch that is operating under Satan. This atrocity shows how Satan works not only through individuals, but also through corporate structures.

Corresponding to and actually intermingled with human organizations are demonic organizations. Our war, as St. Paul warns in Ephesians 6:12, is *against the rulers, against the powers, against the world rulers of this darkness, against the spiritual forces of evil in the heavens.* These intermingled human and demonic structures with power in the spiritual, human and material realms provide Satan his entrée and means to implement his malevolent purposes on earth.

To be well equipped to work with Jesus in fighting this war, we must understand the way Satan has worked not just through individuals, but also through the social organizations that include both the human and the demonic. These structures give Satan the agency to wage war against the Kingdom of God and to enforce his dominion across the earth. To accomplish his purposes requires the talents, the gifts, the economic, political, cultural, and military resources provided by human beings collectively. We are calling the social organizations Satan develops "demonic strongholds."

Satan Usurps God's Redemptive Structures to Implement his Purposes on Earth

Strongholds are actually Satan's distortions of God's structures designed for social order, justice and governance through human beings created in his image. These structures are God's means of provision for human material needs through earthly institutions. The Gospel of the Kingdom Jesus taught includes a complete restructuring of all these institutions in accordance with God's original intentions. At that time, Satan will be put away so that he can no longer deceive the nations. Ideally, when human beings are born again through faith in Jesus Christ, these social structures are formed into the Church. The Father has chosen us as his friends and coworkers, the "living stones" who form the Church as the primary way of working in the world (1 Peter 2:5). The Church becomes the way God chooses to express and carry out his redemptive plans for humanity.

These structures for spiritual entities expressing their presence within time/space reality are what St. Paul calls the "*exousia*"—powers or authorities. God forms these structures through human beings, but they interface with the spiritual realm through the Holy Spirit as well as through angels. St. Paul repeatedly points to this interface between the human and the spiritual world. For instance, he speaks of the treasure of the Gospel being in earthen vessels. (2 Corinthians 4:7)

In Romans 12:6-8 he lists the spiritual gifts as a mixture of both human talents and supernatural gifts. I quote here 1 Corinthians 12:28. *And God has placed in the church first apostles, second prophets, third teachers, then miracles, gifts of healing, helps, gifts of leadership, and different kinds of tongues.* This one verse describes the Church as a human community with a supernatural spiritual dimension. The human talents of helps, or administration and leadership needed for any human community are present. So, too, are the gifts of miracles and healing that stem not from human nature, but from the Holy Spirit. This reflects the divine and human interwoven nature of the Church as an *"exousia,"* the means of expressing authority and power.

In addition, in the book of Revelation, St. John addresses his letters not to the human leaders but to the angels of the seven churches. This also points to the spiritual *exousia* that interfaces with the human *exousia*, the people gathered who form the church in those locations. These are *exousia* because they represent how human beings and the Holy Spirit work together both on earth as well as in the spiritual realm. Social structures such as the Church of Jesus Christ, governments, kingdoms, and armies are the means of expressing power and authority in the human and spiritual spheres.

Satan usurps these *exousia* to be used for his evil rather than for God's good Kingdom purposes or for the benefit of humanity. Satan must work this way because, being spirit, it is through human beings that he can wreak his havoc within the human and material sphere. Without human beings through whom to work, he lacks the organization to express both his evil nature and to put into effect his plans in the human time-space world. This is why Satan had to deceive Adam and Eve; he needed them to disobey God and thus open a gateway into the time-space realm.

In summary, Satan, while not a creator, is nonetheless

extraordinarily clever at taking what God has intended for good in order to twist it for evil.

Now let us take the concept of Satan corrupting God's good creations one step further. Satan does not only corrupt these common grace social structures toward his ends, but he actively contrives his own social structures to express his evil plans on earth. These are demonic strongholds.

Demonic Strongholds

We return to the atrocity of shooting and beheading innocent schoolchildren in Pakistan by seven men shouting, "Allahu akbar!" We cannot discern with certainty to what extent demons were controlling their actions. That they were smiling as they were carrying out these heinous deeds suggests that they may well have been possessed. What we can affirm is that they were woven into a demonic stronghold under the human name, the Pakistani al Qaeda, which is both a spiritual and human organization. This stronghold is both a thought structure composed of an ideology that is rooted in the human mind, and a cultural system that expresses that ideology. This human organization and culture became the invitation to the demonic being, the archon Moloch, to express his evil on earth—in this case, the brutal murder of innocent children.

It is important to recognize, while the individuals may not themselves be demonized or possessed, they are nevertheless part of a social system that is governed by demons and in the service of the head of demons, Satan. We shall later show that the leaders who form the core of this stronghold are themselves the open door for Satan to control the entire organization. This terrible event in Pakistan was but one skirmish in a war Satan is waging against humanity and the Kingdom of God.

Satan has Built a Vast Array of Strongholds
for Accomplishing his Purposes on Earth

Down through history Satan has constructed from the building blocks of human beings, human knowledge, religious texts, and philosophical speculations a vast number of strongholds through which he is able to accomplish his purposes on earth. At this time in the history of Satan's war against the Kingdom of God, there are many strongholds under construction with some already operational. Some strongholds persist over decades. Others have been useful for centuries. They go by different names: anti-Semitism, Nazism, totalitarianism in Russia, fascism in Italy, and the Ku Klux Klan in America. Add to the list Liberal Progressivism, atheistic humanism, and the New Age Movement. The catalogue of strongholds is long.

At this particular phase in the war against the Kingdom of God, Satan is using the religion, culture, and particular sets of verses from the sacred texts of Islam to build the strongholds of Radical/Militant Islam. There are the present virulent and growing forms of the Sunni Islamic State and the Shia Revolutionary Regime of Iran. I am focusing in this prayer strategy on the stronghold of Radical Islam because Jesus has specifically called me to join him in defeating it. We must be aware, however, that in our warfare there are other potent and deadly strongholds with which we must also contend. Liberal Progressivism, anti-Semitism, totalitarianism, and anarchy seem to be at work in collusion with Radical Islam. This is truly a dangerous and complex battlefield, making our task of understanding how Satan builds these potent weapons essential as we devise strategies and tactics for defeating them.

Jesus calls us as intercessors to engage with Him in defeating these powerful structures of evil. These structures are not simply spiritual, but "flesh and blood." Therefore, the spiritual forces of

Part 2 Satan Constructing the Demonic Strongholds

Holy Spirit-empowered and directed prayer by Christian and Jewish religious organizations, spiritual warfare and evangelism, and a coalition of human structures including governments, armed forces, and western cultural institutions such as the free press are all needed to defeat these demonic strongholds based on Islam.

Forming the Core of the Stronghold
Satan's Deception of the Visionary Leader

The Apostle Paul gives us the following definition of the strongholds formed within the human heart:

2 Corinthians 10:3-5

3 For though we live as human beings, we do not wage war according to human standards, 4 for the weapons of our warfare are not human weapons, but are made powerful by God for tearing down strongholds. 5 We tear down arguments and every arrogant obstacle that is raised up against the knowledge of God, and we take every thought captive to make it obey Christ.

The term *strongholds*[1] is used only once in the New Testament, but many times in the Septuagint (the Greek Old Testament) to mean a fortress or a well-defended position against assaults from an enemy. Paul's meaning in 2 Corinthians 10:3-5 is that these are arguments or thought structures in a person's mind that oppose the true knowledge of God. The true knowledge of God is revealed in natural law confirmed by our conscience, and in the truth revealed in the Bible sealed upon our hearts by the Holy Spirit. Paul confirms this in Romans 2:14-16:

> 14 For whenever the Gentiles, who do not have the law, do by nature the things required by the law, these who do not have the law are a law to themselves. 15 They show that the work of the law is written in their hearts, as their conscience bears witness and their conflicting thoughts accuse or else defend them, 16 on the day when God will judge the secrets of human hearts, according to my gospel through Christ Jesus.

In order to prepare a person to become the seed of a stronghold of evil, Satan distorts three aspects of our *Imago Dei* (the image of God in us.) The first is the ability to form a worldview, which enables us to give meaning to our experience. The second is the process of receiving vision that provides the way for us to shape reality creatively. The third is the gift of leadership, which imparts worldview and vision to others who join in its propagation and implementation.

Thought Strongholds Are Formed from Worldviews

The thought strongholds of which Paul speaks have a basis in the human mind; but to understand them, we must move from the pejorative term strongholds to worldviews. When God created us in His image, He gave us certain capacities for sharing in his creativity as artists to shape reality. This includes the ability to understand and give meaning to our experience. The human mind is not a blank slate or a passive recorder of data. It actively brings order and meaning to our experience by filtering and interpreting data. This requires complex psychological processes as well as structures of thought that compose our worldview.

As Doug McMurry and I wrote in our book *The Collapse of the Brass Heaven,* worldview is a set of interpretive filters that bring meaning and order to our experience. These filters are shaped by the totality of our culture, our family, education, language, peers and lived experience. They also come from our interactions with the spiritual world and include truths from God and deceptions from Satan. When our culture, education and experience are rooted in God's truth in the Bible and through Jesus Christ, then our worldview helps us take part in the Father's redemptive building projects. But if our worldview has been shaped by lies and deceptions that Satan has sown into our culture, education and experience, it may be exploited by Satan to accomplish his evil plans on earth.

This sounds like a stark choice between God and Satan as the source of our worldview, but the true situation is more nuanced. Our worldview may also be shaped by the insights and values gained through natural revelation which is consistent with the Father's redemptive plans. This revelation of God's nature is revealed in creation, Romans 1: 20, *For since the creation of the world his invisible attributes—his eternal power and divine nature—have been clearly seen, because they are understood through what has been made.* The Creator, having made us in his own image, has also planted within all our hearts the foundational laws for human behavior (see Romans 2:13-16).

The witness of creation to the nature of God and his requirements written in all human hearts accounts for the glimmers of God's truth within the sacred texts of all the great religions and humanistic philosophical systems such as Confucianism. These truths provide the basis of systems of values and morality that form a worldview that can bring order and good to a society. For instance, in forming the Constitution of the United States, our founding fathers were grounded in the Old and New Testaments and well versed in the great Greek and Roman philosophers and statesman.[2]

Such systems, however, do not lead to salvation, as there is no other name given under heaven by which we must be saved except the name of Jesus, to paraphrase Acts 4:12—but they do provide the means of God's providential care of human kind. They also provide ways for releasing human creativity, industry and goodness and for constraining our innate tendencies toward evil. At the same time, embedded in such sacred texts and systems of philosophy, however consistent with natural revelation, there are lies and deceptions of Satan mingled in. These are like viruses or bacteria within an otherwise healthy body that Satan may activate for constructing strongholds of evil

Is God's Truth in the Quran and the Hadith?

This is the case with the Quran and the Hadith that are the foundation for the religion, culture, moral and political system of Islam. Within this system are foundational truths such as the belief that there is but one God and that all humanity is under God's sovereignty. On the basis of such truths built into the Islamic worldview, societies may be created for the good of humanity. Within the rich and varied history of Islam are the components for building a worldview that has enabled human beings seeking the common good of humanity to shape Islam as a religion of peace and justice for all. President Bush appealed to this worldview that Islam is a religion of peace after the terrorist attacks of 9/11. "The face of terror is not the true faith of Islam. That's not what Islam is all about. Islam is peace. These terrorists don't represent peace. They represent evil and war."[3] When I first heard this word by President Bush, I was appalled! That cannot be right! I thought he was playing politics, with a desire to appease the vast majority of Muslims world-wide not committed to jihad.

Then I did the research and found that he was not far from the truth of some aspects of Islam. Especially as I read the book, *Seeking Allah, Finding Jesus: A Devout Muslim Encounters Christianity,*[4] Nabeel Qureshi, describes his loving family—all devout Muslims—

and their view of the world. His father served as an officer in the United States Air Force. What I learned from his testimony has deepened my own sympathetic understanding of Islam and my appreciation for all those who come from that tradition who truly seek God.

Nabeel Qureshi's family comes from the Ahmadiyya sect of Islam founded in British India near the end of the 19th century. It originated with the life and teachings of Mirza Ghulam Ahmad (1835–1908) whose view of Muhammad and interpretations of the Quran and the Hadith all form a vision of Islam as a religion of peace. Indeed, I was astonished to find the following description of what they believe:

> Ahmadiyya adherents believe that Ahmad appeared in the likeness of Jesus, to end religious wars, condemn bloodshed and reinstitute morality, justice and peace. They believe that upon divine guidance he divested Islam of fanatical and innovative beliefs and practices by championing what is in their view, Islam's true and essential teachings as practiced by Muhammad and the early Islamic community. Thus, Ahmadis view themselves as leading the revival and peaceful propagation of Islam.[5]

All this sounds encouraging. But Islamic scholars from the Shia and Sunni schools of Islam have judged Mirza Ghulam Ahmad a heretic and called for his death.[6] Sunni and Shia Muslims are ruthlessly persecuting the Ahmadiyya sect of Islam.[7]

While these truths from which a worldview of Islam as a religion of peace are part of the Islamic traditions, at the very same time, intermingled with the truths are lies and deceptions planted by Satan. It is from these lies that, over the centuries, he has constructed a worldview that provides the basis for the demonic strongholds to carry out his plans for evil.

In saying this about what Satan has done with the sacred texts and traditions of Islam, those of us who are Christians must acknowledge that Satan has done the same thing using the Holy Bible and our orthodox Christian doctrine. We must face the fact that many times Satan has so subverted the Church of Jesus Christ that the church has become Satan's own war machine. Just think of the trail of blood and oppression against the Jewish people because Satan was able to craft from anti-Semitism and replacement theology a stronghold within the Church. The fact is that Satan may twist any organization, culture, movement, or tradition into strongholds for his evil purposes.

The Human Capacity to Receive Vision that Shapes Reality

A second component of our bearing *Imago Dei* is the capacity for envisioning a new reality different from the prevailing reality. When coupled with faith, will and reason, vision is the primary means human beings have to shape and create the reality of human life. Arnold Toynbee in his book *A Study of History*, explores the dynamic of those who shape human culture to become active growing civilizations. He concludes, following the French philosopher Henri Bergson, that it is the great mystics who have consistently provided the creative impulses that have taken whole societies in new directions.

For Bergson[8], it is the mystics who are the superhuman creators par excellence, and he finds the essence of the creative act in the supreme moment of the mystical experience. To pursue his analysis in his own words:

> The soul of the great mystic does not come to a halt at the [mystical] ecstasy as though that were the goal of a journey. The ecstasy may indeed be called a state of repose, but it is the repose of a locomotive standing in a station under steam

pressure, with its movement continuing as a stationary throbbing while it waits for the moment to make a new leap forward...The great mystic has felt the truth flow into him from its source like a force in action...His desire is with God's help to complete the creation of the human species...The mystic's direction is the very direction of the élan of life. It is that élan itself, communicated in its entirety to privileged human beings whose desire it is thereafter to set the imprint of it upon the whole of mankind...[9]

To grasp the full implications of this analysis, let us first expand the sphere of who would be included in Bergson's term "mystic." This term may include the prophet, the visionary, the leader, the artist, or the great entrepreneur, anyone who has received vision or a seminal idea, and then becomes a shaper of human reality. This expanded understanding of the meaning of the mystic is reinforced by Toynbee's analysis that all such individuals who have shaped human life have undergone a process of "withdrawal and return." This means the person has first withdrawn from society into the place where he or she is able to receive the vision, the great seminal idea, as well as a compelling drive or calling to implement what he or she has received. Then the second motion is returning to human society in order to implement the blueprint received during the phase of withdrawal.

We see this dynamic of withdrawal and return in the lives of many of the world's greatest leaders. Take, for instance, Jesus. This dynamic takes place repeatedly during his time on earth. The first great withdrawal took place after he was baptized in the Jordon River by John. At that point, the Holy Spirit fell upon him and empowered him to fulfill the mission of redeeming humanity. However, before launching out on this mission, the Holy Spirit drove him to withdraw into the wilderness for forty days. There Jesus went through a period of refinement by being tempted by the Devil. This is where, in the face of the temptations, not only was the mission refined, but he submitted to the Father's means of fulfilling his mission. Then, after time in the wilderness, he returned to human society where in the power of the Holy Spirit and in the authority of the Father, he worked to implement his mission on earth.

Throughout his life, Jesus maintained the dynamic of withdrawal and return. Often Jesus would withdraw to be alone with the Father and then return to implement the Father's plans. The last great withdrawal was after his death on the cross, resurrection, and ascent into heaven. The "return" will happen with the Second Coming when he will consummate his redemptive mission by vanquishing evil and inaugurating the New Heaven and the New Earth.

This describes perfectly the role of the man or woman of God who, through the Holy Spirit, receives from God a vision of the reality he wants to create. It is visionaries, then, who, by following Jesus, enable humanity to exercise creativity and dominion in the world, shaping reality to conform to the Kingdom of God. Examples of these great shapers of history are Moses and Jesus. Also a host of others: Martin Luther, John Calvin, Martin Luther King Jr., St. Theresa of Avila, and Mother Theresa of Calcutta received vision from God during times of withdrawal, and then returned in the power of the Holy Spirit to walk out the vision to advance the Kingdom of God.

Satan Subverts the Process and Projects Visions from Hell

Satan, however, may subvert this process of giving and receiving vision. His opportunity arises from two factors: First, not all visions come from God; and second, during the time of withdrawal, the visionary is extremely vulnerable to deception because he or she is completely alone.

The vision or revelation the mystic may receive while in the state of withdrawal can come from a variety of sources:

1) It may be God as revealed in the Bible.
2) It may be from the human mind, prone to pride, ambition, and selfishness.
3) Or, vision may come from the Devil and demonic spirits who communicate deceptions to suit his purposes.

These different sources of inspiration imply that all revelation must be submitted to a rigorous process of discernment. Otherwise, one may be deceived as to the actual source of their vision. This leads to disastrous mistakes of the mystic and their followers attributing to God what is in fact from their own imagination or the Devil.

The second factor that gives Satan the opportunity to implant his lies and deceptions is the extreme vulnerability of the person during the time of withdrawal. Jesus demonstrates this vulnerability during his time in the wilderness after his baptism. He has fasted for forty days and is hungry. In that time of great physical weakness and spiritual trial, Satan comes and tempts him. Note that it is the Holy Spirit who drives Jesus into the time of withdrawal in the first place. In Greek, this is the same word for driving out demons, implying a great forcefulness. Often it is by forcefulness that visionaries are driven into the time of withdrawal, even to the point of reaching the limits of human endurance. It may come from their own deep yearning and hunger for God, or from desperate circumstances, or from spiritual guidance from the Holy Spirit or evil spirits. However, their withdrawal comes about, they become extremely vulnerable to receiving solutions from beyond themselves to alleviate their spiritual hunger or powerlessness. Satan seizes the opportunity whenever he can.

I Have Experienced Satan Subverting this Process

I know from firsthand experience this vulnerability during the time of withdrawal.[10] I can recall states of extreme openness to the transcendent when the Holy Spirit was conceiving vision within me and Satan was seeking to corrupt the vision.

I am certain Satan would have deceived me and used me as a seed for building strongholds of deception if it were not for the following facts. First, I have been born again through faith in Jesus Christ, so I have the Holy Spirit dwelling within me. Second, I am rooted in the Bible as the word of God as my authority and my means of knowing what is true and false. Third, I am part of, and accountable to, a Christ-centered and Holy Spirit led fellowship that provides discernment in situations like this.

Satan is so clever at deception that, even though I am grounded in the Word Written and Incarnate in Jesus Christ, without the third protection of belonging to and actively participating in the body of Christ, I know I would have been deceived. For me, this fellowship of Christians consists of the PRMI Board of Directors, my staff, my personal accountability partners, and my wife. They all have helped in the discernment and the refinement of the vision as well as in fulfilling the vision. Without these three foundations, I know that I would be a person through whom Satan could work to deceive many. This hazard of being deceived is present for anyone who undergoes the dynamic of withdrawal and return. Yet it is because this process of withdrawing and returning is so potent that the enemy tries so hard to subvert it.

Muhammad During His Times of Withdrawal

An overview of Muhammad's life reveals this dynamic of withdrawal and return.[11] The first cycles took place when he began to receive, allegedly from the angel Gabriel, the revelations that he believed to be the verbatim words of Allah that form the Quran. His withdrawal involved times of solitude by going to the cave of Hira during Ramadan.[12] The second cycle takes place when Muhammad is forced out of Mecca and flees to Medina. He later returns to Mecca. We shall return to this cycle in a later section when we address the formation of the "creative minority" around the visionary leader. A reading of the original reports strongly suggests that Satan did indeed plant lies into Muhammad during these times of withdrawal.[13]

The following excerpts from an article entitled *The Dark Nature of Muhammad's Revelations* provide the evidence from Islamic sources supporting the conclusion of how the deception may actually have taken place. This article is from the web site *Answering Islam.* (www.answeringislam.org) For obvious reasons the author is not named, or at least, I have not been able to find his name. I have added the sources cited as footnotes.

First, the author addresses the Islamic understanding of divine revelation that is in stark contrast to the Jewish and Christian understanding.

Muslims believe that when Muhammad received the revelations that have been compiled to make up the Quran, he received them word for word, directly from Allah. As such, Allah is thought to be the actual author of the Quran. The Quran is thus intended to be read as if it is Allah speaking directly in the first person. Muhammad is merely viewed as the human messenger, or the apostle of Allah (rasul-allah). As one Muslim theologian has said, "The prophet was purely passive—indeed unconscious: the Book was in no sense his, neither its thought, nor language, nor style: all was of God, and the Prophet was merely a recording pen."[14]

This doctrine of the Quran's authorship discourages any discernment concerning the source of the inspiration and quenches any critical analysis of the text or content. This non-biblical understanding of revelation that has removed all human agency sets the stage for deception by evil spirits who have always operated by taking over personalities, which become passive.

Muslims believe Muhammad's initial encounter was with the angel Gabriel (*Jibril*) in the cave of *Hira*, which is located on a mountain above Mecca. The actual experience is described in the *Life of Mohammad.*

> When it was the night on which God honoured him with his mission and showed mercy on His servants thereby, Gabriel brought him the command of God. "He came to me," said the apostle of God, "while I was asleep, with a coverlet of brocade whereon was some writing, and said, 'Read!' I said, 'What shall I read?' He pressed me with it so tightly that I thought it was death; then he let me go and said, 'Read!' I said, 'What shall I read?' He pressed me with it again so that I thought it was death; then he let me go and said 'Read!' I said, 'What shall I read?' He pressed me with it the third time so that I thought it was death and said 'Read!' I said, 'What then shall I read?'—and this I said only to deliver myself from him, lest he should do the same to me again. He said:
>
> "Read in the name of thy Lord who created,
>
> Who created man of blood coagulated?
>
> Read! Thy Lord is the most beneficent,
>
> Who taught by the pen,
>
> Taught that which they knew not unto men.'

So I read it, and he departed from me."[15]

This encounter stands in stark contrast to the general nature of angelic and divine encounters found throughout the Bible, where the angels (or the Lord Himself) usually begin their conversation with the comforting phrase, "Do not be afraid." (See Genesis 15:1, 26:24, 46:3; Daniel 10:12, 19; Matthew 28: 5, 10; Luke 1:13,1:26-31,2:10; and Revelation1:17) While there are times when the Lord has overpowered human beings with his glory, driving people to their faces, this experience of being compelled to recite the words dictated by putting so much pressure on his chest that he could not breathe sounds very much like the work of a demon, not the Holy Spirit.

In fact, it sounds like a night terror attack when a demon actually falls upon a person while he or she is asleep. Note that Muhammad was asleep when the presence put such pressure on his chest. This experience was so terrifying and violent that Muhammad contemplated suicide. As reported by Guillaume:

> So I [Muhammad] read it, and he [Gabriel] departed from me. And I awoke from my sleep, and it was as though these words were written on my heart...Now none of God's creatures was more hateful to me than an [ecstatic] poet or a man possessed: I could not even look at them. I thought, "Woe is me poet or possessed. Never shall Quraysh [Muhammad's tribe and kinsman] say this of me! I will go to the top of the mountain and throw myself down that I may kill myself and gain rest." So I went forth to do so and then when I was midway on the mountain, I heard a voice from heaven saying, "O Muhammad! thou are the apostle of God and I am Gabriel."[16]

After this terrible experience, Muhammad returned home to his wife Khadija. Muhammad was still terribly disturbed by the encounter:

Then Allah's Apostle returned with the Inspiration, his neck muscles twitching with terror till he entered upon Khadija and said, "Cover me! Cover me!" They covered him till his fear was over and then he said, "O Khadija, what is wrong with me?" Then he told her everything that had happened and said, "I fear that something may happen to me."[17]

Muhammad thought he was demon possessed and apparently, a number of his contemporaries thought he was too.[18] He also apparently had other strange spiritual experiences, one of which is reported by our unnamed author:

> On another occasion, Muhammad was "bewitched," whereby he literally believed himself to be having sexual relations with his wives when he was actually doing no such thing. Guillaume notes that one Muslim scholar says that the spell lasted for an entire year. This episode of Muhammad's life is well documented in Islam's sacred traditions.[19]

Our unknown and certainly courageous author, by exposing the demonic origins of the revelations that were given to Muhammad, points to the need to discern not just the manner in which the revelations were given, but also the content of the revelations and above all their fruit.

> In the final assessment, we see that the revelations of Muhammad, the seeds out of which Islam sprouted, began amidst a violent and dark encounter with some form of spiritual being in the cave of Hira. We have also seen that Muhammad's life contained periods of either significant delusion or blatant spiritual oppression. It is this dimension of Muhammad's life that should indeed be noted as we develop the greater theme of this book. Also, when attempting to discern the primary spiritual source of Islam, it is essential not only to see the dark nature of the initial seed from which Islam sprouted, but even more so its ultimate vision of the future—its fully mature "fruit." The demonic and anti-biblical revelations that began in the Cave

of Hira find their culmination with the killing of every Jew, Christian, and non-Muslim in the world.[20]

In the last analysis, it is this terrible fruit of the prophecies, expressed through radical jihadists today who receive them as the word of Allah, that convinces me of their satanic origin.

Further Confirming Evidence that Satan Planted Lies through Islam's Prophet

This unnamed author certainly portrays a negative view of Muhammad. However, he has used the original Islamic sources that all may read. He seems to have had extensive experience with demonic manifestations in deliverance and exorcism, which I have also had. This assessment is not intended to offend anyone. As intercessors, we must press forward with what is true and how we know truth. I personally believe that Muhammad was a man truly seeking God.

Muhammad was obviously seeking help to discern the strange encounters with the supernatural that he was having during the period of withdrawal. It is noteworthy that the first person who affirmed Muhammad as the messenger of God was his wife Khadija. She also sought advice from her relative who had become a Christian and learned from those that followed the Torah and the Gospel.[21]

It is very interesting how Khadija, Muhammad's wife, discerned for Muhammad that this was actually the angel Gabriel and not a demon.

> Isma'il b. Abu Hakim, a freedman of the family of al-Zubayr, told me on Khadija's authority that she said to the apostle of God, "0 son of my uncle, are you able to tell me about your visitant, when he comes to you?" He replied that he could, and she asked him to tell her when he came. So when Gabriel came to him, as he

was wont, the apostle said to Khadija, "This is Gabriel who has just come to me." "Get up, 0 son of my uncle," she said, "and sit by my left thigh." The apostle did so, and she said, "Can you see him?" "Yes," he said. She said, "Then turn round and sit on my right thigh." He did so, and she said, "Can you see him?" When he said that he could, she asked him to move and sit in her lap. When he had done this she again asked if he could see him, and when he said yes, she disclosed her form and cast aside her veil while the apostle was sitting in her lap. Then she said, "Can you see him?" And he replied, "No." She said, "0 son of my uncle, rejoice and be of good heart, by God he is an angel and not a satan."[22]

In other words, the basis for the discernment was not on the content of the message as to whether they were consistent with the Torah and the Gospel, but that the angel left when his wife disrobed. But God made Adam and Eve naked, and it was good. So why would an angel reject the beauty and the goodness of the female form? This is so opposite the Judeo-Christian view where God created us male and female and it was all good. This is the view depicted by Milton in *Paradise Lost* in the beautiful passages of Adam and Eve making love. It is not God nor the angels who turn aside, but the Devil.

That shed May flowers; and pressed her matron lip

With kisses pure: aside the Devil turned

For envy, yet with jealous leer malign

Eyed them askance, and to himself thus plained.

"Sight hateful, sight tormenting! Thus these two

Imparadised in one another's arms

The happier Eden, shall enjoy their fill

Of bliss on bliss, while I to hell am thrust..."

(Book IV Lines 501-511)

When the presence turned away from Muhammad and his wife in similar embrace, it revealed itself not actually angelic, but demonic. I think Satan was just using this as a means to deceive both Muhammad and his wife and all future generations of Muslims. It also served Satan's purposes well of robbing the female sex of their having been created in the image of God and of shared dominion and equality with the male sex.

Notice too from this account, that while the experience started with the presence falling upon him while Muhammad was asleep, apparently after this the presence, invisible to others, would invade him while fully awake. This phenomenon is known the world over as a spirit speaking through a medium.

In another attempt to discern the revelation, a Christian relative apparently confirmed that Muhammad was the messenger of God.

> And when the apostle of God had finished his period of seclusion and returned (to Mecca), in the first place he performed the circumambulation of the Ka'ba, as was his wont. While he was doing it, Waraqa met him and said, "O son of my brother, tell me what thou hast seen and heard": The apostle told him and Waraqa said, "Surely, by Him in whose hand is Waraqa's soul, thou art the prophet of this people. There hath come unto thee the greatest Namus, (meaning Gabriel) who came unto Moses. Thou wilt be called a liar, and they will use thee despitefully and cast thee out and fight against thee. Verily, if I live to see that day, I will help God in such wise as He knoweth." Then he brought his head near to him and kissed his forehead; and the apostle went to his own house.[23]

Here again is a doubtful basis for discernment. We do not know to what extent this Christian relative actually knew the contents of the Torah and the Gospels. The teachings that

Muhammad was later to give concerning the "trinity" as God the Father having had sex with Mary and conceiving Jesus Christ, and that Jesus did not actually die on the cross, all prove that this Christian's understanding was just as confused as Muhammad's was. On the other hand, it may suggest that only the initial experience with the angel Gabriel was submitted for discernment, and not the content of the revelations. To me it appears to be an attempt to have a Christian appear to validate Muhammad as a true prophet. Also highly significant was the fact that the Jews who knew and lived the Torah could not embrace Muhammad as a true prophet because the revelations he was receiving were inconsistent with their own scriptures.

Muhammad was Seeking the One True God, but Satan Sowed the Seeds of Deception

This seeking for discernment and validation and being profoundly disturbed by the visitations to the point of wanting to commit suicide all confirm the true character of Muhammad. He was indeed seeking after God and the truth that was available in the Torah and in the Gospels. I would contend that the Holy Spirit was leading Muhammad to turn away from the worship of the Ka'ba with its 360 idols and pagan rituals. Apparently, the Holy Spirit was working in the hearts of some of Muhammad's own relatives to turn them to the monotheistic faith of Jews and Christians. Viewing the work of the Holy Spirit to draw Muhammad to faith allows us an attitude of charity and understanding. Let me quote from my book, *Prayer that Shapes the Future,* written with Doug McMurry.

> Christians, however, must not too quickly assume that all non-Christian prayer is a doorway into the demonic. Sometimes the prayers of non-Christian people are neither good nor bad. Sometimes they are ways of feeling for God, ways that God

honors because they are offering to him the best they know. The Bible calls such people "God-fearers"—a technical term in the Bible for pagans who have converted to monotheism without becoming Jewish converts (cf. Acts 17:17).[24]

We need to honor Muhammad as a "God-fearer." I would go so far as to affirm that the Holy Spirit was actively drawing him to faith in Jesus Christ as the only way to salvation (cf. John 6:44). However, Satan, the master deceiver, seems to have taken advantage of this hunger for the one true God and sown seeds of deception by adding lies to the truth to counter the truth revealed in Jesus Christ.

This is not only possible but probable because of the following verifiable facts: First, the Mecca of Muhammad's day was an occult center which presented open doors for demonic activities. Second, Muhammad took part in the many pagan rituals associated with Mecca and the Ka'ba, which by their nature opened the doors to demons. Third, Muhammad seems to have had a personality that was open to the spiritual realm and was actively seeking God. Fourth, he lacked accurate knowledge of the revealed word of God in the Jewish and Christian Scriptures so his doctrine was confused. Fifth, he was not born again through faith in Jesus Christ and thus not part of a community of faith and discernment.

Muhammad Kept the Pagan Rituals of Mecca, thus Opening the Door for Continued Demonization

A major source of continued deception for Muhammad and all future Muslims is that Muhammad kept the Ka'ba as well as the other rituals that went along with the worship of the idols at Mecca. Mecca was clearly an occult center.[25] Even Muhammad, after he started having his revelations from the being who claimed to be Gabriel, went back and walked around the Ka'ba. "And when the apostle of God had finished his period of seclusion and returned (to

Mecca), in the first place he performed the circumambulation of the Ka'ba, as was his wont." [26] Indeed, he made these rituals a requirement for every Muslim to bow five times a day toward Mecca, and at least once in their lifetime to make the Hajj or pilgrimage back to Mecca. These rituals give the original demons that were in Mecca legal access to the hearts of all Muslims who practice them.[27]

I believe Satan deployed an age-old tactic of "adaptive deceptions" to keep his foothold at Mecca and in Muslims' hearts and minds. George Otis, Jr. describes how demonic powers keep their power and influence in changing circumstances by this method:

> These deceptions, which can be defined either as necessary course corrections or as upgrades to the devil's product line, are introduced into situations in which traditional structures are in danger of losing their deceptive potency.[28]

It was certainly true that with Muhammad's monotheistic zeal smashing the 360 idols in the Ka'ba, Satan was about to lose the means of continuing his hold over the people of Arabia. Muhammad cleansed the Kaaba of its idols and permitted the worship of only one deity named Allah. In this choice, some have argued that this was not accepting the Creator God revealed in the Jewish Torah and the Christian Bible, but was actually the elevation of one idol, the moon god, above all the rest. He also kept the sacred black stone as an occult object. [29]

There is much debate about whether or not this Allah worshiped by Muslims is the same God as revealed in the Old and New Testaments. A comparison of the nature of Yahweh revealed in the Old and New Testaments and Allah revealed in the Quran and the Ahadith cannot possibly be the same deity. [30]

I do not want to engage this debate here. However, what is most probable is that Satan effectively used the "adaptive deceptions" to mislead Muhammad to keep the door to the demonic open through the Ka'ba. George Otis, Jr. provides profound discernment into Satan's methods.

> To appreciate how this could happen, it is important to remember that Islam, like the other great monotheistic religions, emerged in a profoundly pagan context. In early years the city of Mecca not only sanctioned worship of multiple gods and goddesses, but incorporated this idolatry into ceremonies associated with a great city feast. Muhammad, rather than dispense with these potent symbols, incorporated them into his new religion, giving birth to (among other things) the hajj.[31]

This is completely contrary to biblical revelation and practice. When the people of Israel came into the Promised Land, God gave them very explicit instructions to destroy completely all the places where Baal had been worshipped and to reject all the practices of Baal worship.

Deuteronomy 12:2-5

2 You must by all means destroy all the places where the nations you are about to dispossess worship their gods—on the high mountains and hills and under every leafy tree. 3 You must tear down their altars, shatter their sacred pillars, burn up their sacred Asherah poles, and cut down the images of their gods; you must eliminate their very memory from that place. 4 You must not worship the LORD your God the way they worship. 5 But you must seek only the place he chooses from all your tribes to establish his name as his place of residence, and you must go there.

"You must not worship the LORD your God the way they worship." The reason for such stern measures is that demons tend to inhabit such places, and rituals provide opportunities for demons to re-enter people. As a missionary in Taiwan, I saw people accept

Jesus Christ, but then remain vulnerable to re-demonization when they returned to a Buddhist temple. This can happen even when participating in Christian rituals that are similar to those of their pagan past, burning incense, for example.

Down through the centuries Christians have taken over non-Christian holidays and even the sacred places of pagans. Christians have certainly honored certain cities such as Jerusalem, Constantinople, Geneva or Rome, but the center of our faith is none of those places. Jesus Christ is not worshiped by praying in any particular direction or location, but everywhere "in spirit and in truth." (John 4:21-23)

But what was going on in the heavenlies with regard to Muhammad? Everything that I have read about the early life of Muhammad convinces me that he sought the one true God whom the Jews and Christians worshiped. This supports further my belief that Muhammad was indeed a God-fearer, someone led to seek God from the innate longing for the transcendent that is built into every human being.

Given all these conditions, it is not only possible but highly probable that demons were speaking to Muhammad in his time of withdrawal. This conclusion is supported by the actual content of the revelations that Muhammad received. They are completely contrary to the revelations about the nature of God and the way of salvation outlined in the Word of God written, and lived by Jesus, the Word of God Incarnate.[32] These facts provide us the basis for assuming that indeed Satan planted the seeds of deception in the prophet as the basis for building strongholds.

The Importance of the Dynamic of
Receiving Vision through "Withdrawal and Return"

Is it important to know the source of a visionary leader's visions? Why is it important to understand his or her worldview? Why review a founder's history and angelic encounters? It is important for two reasons. First, understanding the formation of worldview and the dynamic of receiving vision provides us with a tool for discerning those whom Satan may be cultivating to become his seeds for forming future strongholds.

To reiterate, the pattern of withdrawal and return shows up everywhere in the lives of those who have shaped reality. Osama Bin Laden is one prominent example, around whom the stronghold of Al Qaeda coalesced. Lawrence Wright in his brilliant book, *The Looming Tower: Al-Qaeda and the Road to 9-11*, documents this process of worldview formation and the dynamics of withdrawal and return that took place with Osama Bin Laden.

We find the pattern of withdrawal and return also at work in the formation of the Islamic State. William McCants documents this process in his book *The ISIS Apocalypse: The History, Strategy, and Doomsday Vision of the Islamic State.* Actually, a group of us intercessors praying for the defeat of al-Qaeda were warned that unless there were strong military and spiritual measures taken, the withdrawal forced upon the Sunni expression of Radical Islam through the success of the surge in Iraq and the killing of Osama Bin Laden would result in a deadly return. When Osama Bin Laden was killed, an intercessor saw a host of demons like black cyclones lifting off of the stronghold of al-Qaeda and landing on a new host.

We now know that that was ISIS. We can also see the folly of President Obama's retreat from the region by removing all American forces from Iraq. This removed the restraints on the government in Baghdad dominated by the Shia, and created the vacuum for the Sunni return in ISIS. This present violent return of Radical Islam in the form of ISIS would never have happened, or could have been destroyed at its fragile beginnings, if only the Obama administration had taken into account this dynamic of withdrawal and return. If only they had paid attention to those who understand history and the nature of evil and gave clear warnings concerning the reemergence of evil after having been defeated. [33]

The second reason why it is critical for the prayer warrior to understand the source of the vision is that when the prophet or the leader returns to shape a new reality, his worldview with the vision or the seminal idea embedded in him will be empowered by its source. For example, Martin Luther King, Jr., rooted in a deep faith in Jesus Christ, received a biblical vision of racial justice. Through him, Jesus waged war against the stronghold of racism in America. Martin Luther King, Jr. accomplished this in the anointing of the Holy Spirit and by upholding biblical ideas of justice. He rejected racial hatred and violence as the means for accomplishing his God-given biblical vision of social justice and equality.

Adolph Hitler, on the other hand, had a vision from the Devil that created hell on earth and led to mass death and oppression. As I shall show in a later chapter, there is very good evidence that during Hitler's times of withdrawal, Satan directly planted deceptive ideas in his mind and heart that formed the basis for the stronghold of Nazism. Hitler and his cohorts chose hatred, racial superiority, subjugation and death, which connected to the basest aspects of human nature as the means to implement his vision. This led to high-level demonic spirits, if not Satan himself, empowering and directing Hitler and the Nazi Party.

When Muhammad returned from his time of withdrawal, he chose death and subjugation to fulfill his vision laced with the lies of Satan, which opened the door for future followers to become the human conduit through whom Satan could fulfill his plans for genocide and tyranny.

In the following chapter, I turn to the next step in forming a stronghold, that is, how people coalesce around the visionary to form a core community, a creative minority. This is the way Satan expands his work from the deceived individual to organizations which mobilize the collective talents of people to enable him to propagate his evil on earth.

Forming the Core of the Stronghold
The Creative Minority

It is not enough to receive vision for changing the world while in a state of withdrawal. Next comes the process of return in which the visionary seeks to implement the vision. If this return does not take place, then the vision remains a fantasy with no connection to reality. The conditions for a successful return include sharing the vision with others, writing and refining the vision, and drawing others into the vision which requires the attribute of leadership.[1]

The gift of leadership comes from being created *imago Dei* (in the image of God) and is necessary in order for human beings to become co-creators with God exercising dominion over the earth. This ability to lead others into the reality of the vision takes place because the visionary embodies the content of the vision within himself or herself and has the personality attributes and talents of a leader. This gift of leadership enables the leader to impart the vision to others, and then gather together a core group of those who share the vision. Satan, however, can exploit this third feature, leadership, in constructing his strongholds.

Spiritual DNA

To summarize, in building a demonic stronghold, Satan often starts with a single individual in whom the three aspects of worldview, vision, and leadership converge. Using this process of forming a worldview and receiving vision, Satan plants systems of thought that are opposed to God's truth.[2] These core ideas are comparable to the DNA in a cell that contains the information needed to generate similar cells. These deceptive ideas, when coupled with hatred, unforgiveness or occultism, may provide the initial ground of entry for demonic spirits to gain access into these individuals.

These evil spirits then build the psychological constructs of deception that create the stronghold within the heart and mind.[3] If this happens with a person of real leadership, the stronghold will be transferred to others, and the creative minority begins to form.

This happens when three conditions are met:
1) The person's worldview includes Satan's distortions.
2) He has received a vision of the reality Satan wants to create.
3) He has the gift of leadership so he can draw others into his sphere of influence.

With this combination, the individual becomes the seed around which the demonic stronghold may coalesce.

The Formation of the Creative Minority

The next critical step in the formation of a stronghold is the formation of a cadre of supporters who coalesce around the leader to whom he or she transfers the "DNA" of the vision. Within this small group through many bonds—friend to friend, teacher and student, master and disciple—the leader imparts his worldview and vision to others. This may occur if the students share the same mystical experience as that of the leader. This group of supporters or disciples are the "creative minority"[4] who now embody the vision and make it possible to form an organization to accomplish Satan's plans.[5] We may find in the formation of this creative minority the same dynamic of withdrawal and return in which the vision from the founding leader becomes refined and internalized by the core group.

For example, let us return to the positive example of Jesus in forming the divine-human organization, the Church. First, implanted in Jesus Christ is the worldview and vision of the Kingdom of God. After being tested in the wilderness, and then an all-night prayer session with the Father, he begins to gather around himself certain chosen disciples.

Through a direct personal relationship with Jesus, the DNA of the truths from the Father and the reality of the Kingdom are planted within the hearts and minds of the disciples. They provide the core around which others are drawn in, to become part of the new reality. This core provides the means for the new reality to grow, centered around Jesus. First, the 12 men and several women begin following Jesus as his disciples. (The women become the source of material provision.) Then this number grows to include the 72 who are sent out two by two as witnesses. By the time of Pentecost, this core group has grown to 120, all of whom share the DNA of the Kingdom of God.

At Pentecost a radically new element is introduced into this dynamic. The Holy Spirit makes it possible for these disciples to share the same experience of the Father and the Kingdom that their leader Jesus has enjoyed. By means of the Holy Spirit, Jesus becomes not merely someone whose words would be memorized and behavior imitated; now they can know a personal relationship with the Father, Son and Holy Spirit. Through the Holy Spirit, their fellowship goes beyond relating one to another alone; they are invited into the eternal dynamic relationship of the Triune God of grace. Now they too may experience the Holy Spirit coming upon them to empower the mission of spreading that Kingdom DNA to the ends of the earth.[6] The process of forming the group moves beyond the power of an inspiring vision and imitation of the leader, to the inclusion of divine power and presence which enables the formation of a social organization that is both human and divine, the Church.

The vast expansion of the Church, however, could not take place until the Holy Spirit drove the nascent Christian community into a period of withdrawal into the wilderness just like Jesus. After Pentecost they underwent a wave of deadly persecution in which Stephen and others were martyred. Some, like Philip, were dispersed away from Jerusalem. Each Christian, now in personal relationship with the living, resurrected Jesus, could become the seed around whom the Holy Spirit formed an expression of the Kingdom of God. This is the history of the growth of the Church—a little group of disciples expands to include millions worldwide in an immense variety of organized expressions, all with the same Kingdom DNA.

Satan Usurps the Process of Forming the Creative Minority

Satan has now taken this dynamic which the Lord established, and has corrupted it for his own purposes. He replaces or distorts the leader's vision from God or the truths consistent with conscience, with his lies and corruptions.   Evil spirits surreptitiously replace the power and guidance of the noble aspects of human nature and the Holy Spirit with their own power and deceptiveness, which then perverts relationships among the creative minority. I have named this group the "creative minority," a concept I adapted from Arnold Toynbee's, *A Study of History*.

Another descriptive term for this group may be "true believers."[7] Movements tend to select particular names for those who follow the leaders, which reveal much about the nature of the movements. In the stronghold of Communism, the true believers are called "comrades." The followers of Muhammad, "companions." They are the ones who embody the reality around which Satan coalesces the larger social, political and cultural reality that forms the fully mature stronghold. This process follows well-established principles of the social construction of reality.[8] Shared deception and lies, and the bonding of evil spirits merge this core group as one. By using powerful demonic cloaking, Satan protects the core group from exposure to outside spiritual and physical attacks that would seek to stop the formation of the stronghold. This cloaking extends from the core outward to include the larger social-spiritual structure. As we have pointed out, during subsequent times of withdrawal, the DNA of the leaders becomes their own. They too become seeds for advancing the movement and formation of Satan's strongholds.[9]

A short summary of Muhammad's life by Toynbee clearly evidences the second withdrawal and return, when the stronghold is transferred from the original visionary to the core group:

> This life-work, upon which Muhammad appears to have embarked in about his fortieth year (circa A.D. 609), was achieved in two stages. In the first of these stages Muhammad was concerned with his religious mission; [in]the second stage the religious mission was overlaid, and almost overwhelmed, by the political enterprise.[10]

> The second, or politico-religious, stage in Muhammad's career was inaugurated by the Prophet's withdrawal or Hegira (Hijrah) from his native oasis of Mecca to the rival oasis of Yathrib, thenceforth known par excellence as Medina: "the City" (of the Prophet). Muhammad left Mecca as a hunted fugitive. After a

seven years' absence (A.D. 622-9) he returned to Mecca, not as an amnestied exile, but as lord and master of half Arabia.[11]

The time of withdrawal to Medina provided the opportunity for a larger group of believers to unite around the core group of believers to form the creative minority. In Islamic parlance, these are the "Sahabah," the companions of the prophet. This group started in the hundreds and grew to be thousands, became Muhammad's army. This expansion of the creative minority corresponded with Muhammad growing in both political and military power.

The companions also provided the human means for Muhammad to implement his vision. The accounts of this period tell of the raiding of caravans and the consolidation of military and political power. The companions were also the means through which the DNA of Muhammad's vision was passed on to future generations through the Quran and the Hadith.[12] A summary of what Satan was able to accomplish during this period of withdrawal based on the reading of what the Muslim writers have themselves reported is as follows:

> Stinging from the rejection of his own town and tribe, Muhammad's message quickly become more intolerant and ruthless—particularly as he gained power. Islam's holiest book clearly reflects this contrast, with the later parts of the Quran adding violence and earthly defeats at the hands of Muslims to the woes of eternal damnation that the earlier parts of the book promises those who will not believe in Muhammad. It was at Medina that Islam evolved from a relatively peaceful religion borrowed from others and into a military force that was intended to govern all aspects of society. During these last ten years of Muhammad's life, infidels were evicted or enslaved, converted upon point of death and even rounded up and slaughtered depending on expediency.[13]

During this time of withdrawal to Medina and the return to Mecca, the original seeds of revelation received in Mecca were passed on to the companions, but the same supernatural source kept giving Muhammad more revelations. Many of these (reputed to be Allah's words) such as the "sword verses"[14] promoting the advancement of Islam by the sword and subjugation, have now provided Satan with the key building blocks of Radical Islam. There are many dissenting opinions about the exact meaning and implications of these verses.[15] My point is not to debate whether this represents true Islam or not. What I am saying is that Satan has used this history and these specific verses to build the stronghold of Radical Islam today to fulfill his evil intention of genocide of "infidels," especially Jews and Christians, and subjugation of the world under Sharia law.

Why the Intercessor Must Know about the Core of the Stronghold

Most of this chapter has dealt with the formation of the creative minority. The critical work of the intercessor is, first, to discern with whom Satan is working in the world to build strongholds to oppose the Kingdom of God. Once discerned, the task of the intercessor becomes that of working with Jesus to neutralize or destroy the stronghold being built by the visionary and creative minority. Terrible consequences have come to the world when this does not take place.

For instance, what if someone had discerned Satan's work in Hitler when he was a lost, struggling artist, fuming with hatreds and resentments, and brought him the Gospel of Jesus Christ? Or, what if the US intelligence community had taken seriously Satan's work in Osama Bin Laden and the visionary leaders around whom he was going to unite the stronghold of Al Qaeda? There was a number of occasions during the presidency of Bill Clinton when he could have been removed and the disaster of the terrorist attacks of 9/11 averted. If only President Obama had not dismissed as "the JV team" the creative minority that was becoming the virulent stronghold of the Islamic State. This lapse in vigilance is inexcusable, as the evidence of their growing power was already clearly present in their raising their black flag over the city of Fallujah in Iraq.[16]

If, in 2014, the United States and our allies had reacted swiftly and massively as some of our military leaders were calling us to, this creative minority of ISIS could have been neutralized.[17] Now with each victory, they gain more momentum and are able to recruit more and more fighters—especially after they announced in fulfillment of their apocalyptic vision [18] that they were the new Islamic Caliphate, which demands the allegiance of all the world's Muslims.[19] If this had been discerned and decisively acted upon, we would not have to be dealing with this darkness now, and thousands of people's lives would have been saved. These lapses show a failure of discernment both by intercessors and by our national leaders.

In Chapter 13 we will tackle the next major building block of the stronghold, the means chosen by the visionary to implement his vision of reality.

The Means Chosen to Implement the Vision

Once a leader has chosen his core leaders, he must then choose a means for implementing that vision. Any vision or seminal idea that challenges the prevailing culture will encounter resistance. Most people, by our very nature, are stuck in habitual ways of thinking and doing. Change of any sort is resisted.

Therefore, the implementation of the vision always requires some means to overcome resistance. These means cover the spectrum of inspiration, from leading by example and persuasive oratory to the many forms of social coercion and tyrannical force. These means will be as important as the vision itself. Often it is when the fulfillment of a movement's vision is opposed by others that the true nature of the means is exposed. The means chosen, in turn, reveal the true source of the vision. Let us now contrast Jesus with Muhammad, as we examine how they implemented their respective visions.

The Means Chosen by Jesus to Implement His Vision

Jesus was given an extraordinary mission by the Father. It is summarized in the Gospel of John 3:13-17.

> 13 "No one has ascended into heaven except the one who descended from heaven—the Son of Man. 14 Just as Moses lifted up the serpent in the wilderness, so must the Son of Man be lifted up, 15 so that everyone who believes in him may have eternal life. 16 For this is the way God loved the world: He gave his one and only Son, so that everyone who believes in him will not perish but have eternal life. 17 For God did not send his Son into the world to condemn the world, but that the world should be saved through him."

Paul summarizes the means chosen to accomplish the mission of redeeming the entire human race in the letter to the Philippians 2:5-8.

> 5 You should have the same attitude toward one another that Christ Jesus had, 6 who though he existed in the form of God did not regard equality with God as something to be grasped, 7 but emptied himself by taking on the form of a slave, 8 by looking like other men, and by sharing in human nature. He humbled himself, by becoming obedient to the point of death—even death on a cross!

Jesus Christ, who is fully God and fully human, accomplished this incredible act of obedience of going to the cross by the power of the Holy Spirit. The Holy Spirit worked within Jesus giving him an intimacy with the Father so that he could say, *"The Son can do nothing on his own initiative, but only what he sees the Father doing. For whatever the Father does, the Son does likewise."* (John 5:19) Jesus also experienced the Holy Spirit upon Him in the manner of an Old Testament prophet, priest and king, which granted Him the means to accomplish his vision.

Jesus passed on these same means of accomplishing the vision to His disciples and the creative minority. They were to accomplish His vision by the power of God's love. *The person who does not love does not know God, because God is love. By this the love of God is revealed in us: that God has sent his one and only Son into the world so that we may live through him* (1 John 4:8-9). Jesus tells us, *"If anyone wants to become my follower, he must deny himself, take up his cross, and follow me"* (Mark 8:34). They were to do all this in the very same power and authority that Jesus Christ their leader did— by the Holy Spirit dwelling within them, changing their hearts to produce the fruit of love, peace and joy. They were also to have the Holy Spirit upon them just as Jesus had, moving in supernatural powers with the gifts needed to accomplish their mission(see Acts 1:4-8). They were full participants in fulfilling the mission, and their prayers, faith, love and obedience were all needed. However, the source of the effectiveness of their work was not their own, but God in three persons working through them.

John 14:12-14

12 "I tell you the solemn truth, the person who believes in me will perform the miraculous deeds that I am doing, and will perform greater deeds than these, because I am going to the Father. 13 And I will do whatever you ask in my name, so that the Father may be glorified in the Son. 14 If you ask me anything in my name, I will do it."

In order to deal with the resistance of those who rejected their message and opposed the fulfillment of the mission, Jesus gave them the following guidelines that were consistent with his own life and consistent with the vision. When sending the disciples out as witnesses he said, *"If anyone will not welcome you or listen to your message, shake the dust off your feet as you leave that house or that town"* (Matthew 10:14). The disciples were not to force anyone to accept the Gospel. There were consequences for not accepting this good news, but that would come on the Day of Judgment and it was God's business, not theirs. *"But I say to you who are listening: Love your enemies, do good to those who hate you, bless those who curse you, pray for those who mistreat you."* (Luke 6:27)

These means are consistent with the message of the Gospel. They are contrary to all of our sinful tendencies. And they are only possible for human beings to achieve through a relationship with Jesus Christ and empowered by the Holy Spirit. Jesus intends for us to accomplish his work his way! He tells us, *"I am the vine; you are the branches. The one who remains in me—and me in him—bears much fruit, because apart from me you can accomplish nothing."* (John 15:5)

Satan Twists Jesus' Way

Satan has persistently tempted the Church to turn away from Jesus' way to accomplish the mission. Even while Jesus was still with his disciples, walking with them in the flesh, he had to correct them for replacing God's means with their own human means or Satan's means. For instance, when Peter rejects the means the Father has established for redemption, which entails Jesus' crucifixion.

Matthew 16:23-24

23 Jesus rebuked him and said, "Get behind me, Satan! You are a stumbling block to me, because you are not setting your mind on God's interests, but on man's." 24 Then Jesus said to his disciples, "If anyone wants to become my follower, he must deny himself, take up his cross, and follow me..."

Luke 9:52-56

On another occasion, [Jesus] 52 sent messengers on ahead of him. As they went along, they entered a Samaritan village to make things ready in advance for him, 53 but the villagers refused to welcome him, because he was determined to go to Jerusalem. 54 Now when his disciples James and John saw this, they said, "Lord, do you want us to call fire to come down from heaven and consume them?" 55 But Jesus turned and rebuked them, 56 and they went on to another village.

Even while dying on the cross and being mocked by those He came to save, Jesus did not depart from his way. But Jesus said, *"Father, forgive them, for they don't know what they are doing"* (Luke 23:34). Jesus was able to stick to fulfilling the mission by the means given him, namely, total dependence on the Father in the power of the Holy Spirit to impart life and not death. We who have followed him have not done so well. We have often not depended on the power of the Holy Spirit, but upon ourselves. We see this when a pastor or church leader becomes manipulative and controlling. In the history of mission, there have been cases when Jesus' way for advancing his Kingdom have been abandoned and human means adopted.

Tragically, this most often has happened when well-intended mission work went hand-in-hand with colonialism and racial prejudice. Some have tried to advance the Gospel not in the power of love and the Holy Spirit, but in hatred or coercion, all of which fit into Satan's plans to aid him in constructing strongholds of evil.

An example of this is the enforced Christianization of native peoples at Christian schools in Canada and the United States. Well intended but deceived Christians adopted non-Christian coercive means to strip children of their native culture and traditions to force them into the mold of Western Christian culture.[1] Sexual and physical abuse, prohibitions against using their native languages or practicing their tribal rituals and customs were methods of forced conversion. These methods are not in step with Jesus' first creative minority as recorded in the book of Acts. These are Satan's means and, while done in the name of Christ, only add to Satan's evil empire.

The Example of Martin Luther and the Jews

We must face the terrible reality that because of the original sin that resides in every human being, Satan has been able to subvert even the greatest Christian leaders and visionaries away from Jesus' way, to exercise Satan's means. Take, for instance, the great reformer Martin Luther. The Holy Spirit used Martin Luther to restore the Church to the foundations of the Old and New Testament. Martin Luther reestablished the biblical revelation that salvation is not based on our works, but by faith in Jesus Christ alone. The means chosen by Luther to implement the vision of the Gospel were almost completely true to God's Word and consistent with the model and method of Jesus Christ.

At the start, Martin Luther was perfectly consistent with Jesus' model for implementing the mission to take the Gospel to the nations, including to the Jewish people. In his approach, he opposed not just anti-Semitic elements in his own culture, but also the traditional teaching of the Roman Catholic Church.

> In 1519 Luther challenged the doctrine Servitus Judaeorum ('Servitude of the Jews'), established in Corpus Juris Civilis by Justinian I from 529–534. He wrote: "absurd theologians defend hatred for the Jews...What Jew would consent to enter our ranks when he sees the cruelty and enmity we wreak on them—that in our behavior towards them we less resemble Christians than beasts?"

In his 1523 essay, "That Jesus Christ Was Born a Jew," Luther condemned the inhumane treatment of the Jews and urged Christians to treat them kindly. Luther's fervent desire was that Jews would hear the Gospel proclaimed clearly and be moved to convert to Christianity.[2]

In this essay, he made statements that were consistent with Romans 11:

When we are inclined to boast of our position [as Christians] we should remember that we are but Gentiles, while the Jews are of the lineage of Christ. We are aliens and in-laws; they are blood relatives, cousins, and brothers of our Lord. Therefore, if one is to boast of flesh and blood the Jews are actually nearer to Christ than we are. If we really want to help them, we must be guided in our dealings with them not by papal law but by the law of Christian love. We must receive them cordially, and permit them to trade and work with us, that they may have occasion and opportunity to associate with us, hear our Christian teaching, and witness our Christian life. If some of them should prove stiff-necked, what of it? After all, we ourselves are not all good Christians either.[3]

But later in his life, a terrible shift took place: love was replaced by virulent hatred. Jesus' means of implementing the vision of the Gospel were replaced by the means of the Devil.

In 1543 Luther published "On the Jews and Their Lies" in which he makes some of the most hatful anti-Semite statements ever uttered. In summary:

The Jews are a "base, whoring people, that is, no people of God, and their boast of lineage, circumcision, and law must be accounted as filth." They are full of the "devil's feces...which they wallow in like swine." The synagogue was a "defiled bride, yes, an incorrigible whore and an evil slut ..."

He argues that their synagogues and schools be set on fire, their prayer books destroyed, rabbis forbidden to preach, homes razed, and property and money confiscated. They should be shown no mercy or kindness, afforded no legal protection, and these "poisonous envenomed worms" should be drafted into forced labor or expelled for all time. He also seems to advocate their murder, writing "[w]e are at fault in not slaying them." Luther calls prophet Jeremiah a heretic: "Jeremiah, you wretched heretic, you seducer and false prophet." He claims that Jewish history was "assailed by much heresy," and that Christ the logos swept away the Jewish heresy and goes on to do so, "as it still does daily before our eyes." He stigmatizes Jewish prayer as being "blasphemous" (sic) and a lie, and vilifies Jews in general as being spiritually "blind" and "surely possessed by all devils."[4]

Appalling! Is this coming from the same heart and pen that urged that we see the Jewish people as "blood relatives closer to Christ than we are, to be treated with Christian love?" Apparently, later in life, this love turned to hatred because the Jews did not respond to the Gospel, and there were rumors that the papists had bribed some Jews to murder him.[5] It is obvious that hatred had replaced Christian love. Had this hatred opened the door to evil spirits to deceive Luther?

As I ponder the question of why so great a man of faith as Martin Luther could depart so profoundly from the essence of the Gospel that he was preaching, I am led to one conclusion: his unforgiveness. He could not forgive the Jews for rejecting the message of the Gospel of Jesus Christ. There are hints that the Jews offended him in other ways. However, all that is speculation.[6] In any event, unforgiveness opens the door for anger that can so easily turn to hatred. Hatred is Satan's tool for entering into a person and sowing seeds of deception. I think this is what happened to Martin Luther. While this does not invalidate the truth of his original message of justification by faith alone, it does demonstrate that Satan can turn any one of us away from the way of Jesus to take up his means, which results in evil.

Satan Used Martin Luther's Words to Build the Stronghold of Nazism

Some four hundred years later when Satan went about building the stronghold of Nazism with the purposes of exterminating the Jewish people and replacing the Christian Church with Nazi paganism, the anti-Semitism of Luther would be an important building block. William Shirer, in exploring the passivity of the Protestant Church to the rise of Nazism, states this:

> It is difficult to understand the behavior of most German Protestants in the first Nazi years unless one is aware of two things: their history and the influence of Martin Luther. The great founder of Protestantism was both a passionate anti-Semite and a ferocious believer in absolute obedience to political authority. He wanted Germany rid of the Jews and when they were sent away he advised that they be deprived of "all their cash and jewels and silver and gold" and, furthermore, "that their synagogues or schools be set on fire, that their houses be broken up and destroyed...and they be put under a roof or stable, like gypsies...in misery and captivity as they incessantly lament and complain to God about us"—advice that was literally followed four centuries later by Hitler, Goering and Himmler.[7]

Nazi leaders themselves confirmed Martin Luther's critical part in developing their thinking.

> In *Mein Kampf*, Hitler listed Martin Luther as one of the greatest reformers. And similar to Luther in the 1500s, Hitler spoke against the Jews. The Nazi plan to create a German Reich church laid its basis on the "spirit of Dr. Martin Luther." The first

physical violence against the Jews came on November 9-10 on Kristallnacht (Crystal Night) where the Nazis killed Jews, shattered glass windows, and destroyed hundreds of synagogues, just as Luther had proposed.

In Daniel Jonah Goldhagen's book, *Hitler's Willing Executioners*, he writes: "One leading Protestant churchman, Bishop Martin Sasse, published a compendium of Martin Luther's anti-Semitic vitriol shortly after Kristallnacht's orgy of anti-Jewish violence. In the foreword to the volume, he applauded the burning of the synagogues and the coincidence of the day: 'On November 10, 1938, on Luther's birthday, the synagogues are burning in Germany.' The German people, he urged, ought to heed these words 'of the greatest anti-Semite of his time, the warner of his people against the Jews.'"[8]

As Christians we need to face this terrible history and be vigilant that in our zeal to advance the good news of Jesus Christ we do not depart from the Father's love and the power of the Holy Spirit, the means that Jesus himself gave us to accomplish his mission.

The Means of Violence and Subjugation Chosen by Muhammad at Medina

Having looked at Martin Luther, we must now turn to Muhammad, the prophet of Islam. What means did he choose to implement the words of Allah that he received during the times of withdrawal, first to the cave of *Hira,* and then later when he had to flee to Medina? Here we find some disturbing parallels in Satan's work in both these two shapers of reality—Muhammad and Luther. Both start with a conciliatory approach to those who opposed their message. However, when met with resistance and rejection, both were deceived by Satan to use means consistent with fallen human nature that played directly into Satan's hands.[9]

There is much debate about this topic partly because Muhammad recommends different means at different phases of his life, just as Martin Luther did. I do not want to engage in the debate about what is or is not true Islam. What I am saying is that the Devil has used specific verses from the Quran as well as the words and deeds of Muhammad recorded in the Hadith to construct the stronghold of Radical Islam, a stronghold in which the means chosen are coercion, subjugation, death and genocide of Jews and Christians.

One person calling for the reform of Islam is Ayaan Hirsi Ali, born a Muslim in Somalia. She has a discerning article in the *Wall Street Journal* entitled, "Why Islam Needs a Reformation: To defeat the extremists for good, Muslims must reject those aspects of their tradition that prompt some believers to resort to oppression and holy war."[10] She points to the difference in the choice of means made at different periods in Muhammad's life.

> In the early days of Islam, when Muhammad was going from door to door in Mecca trying to persuade the polytheists to abandon their idols of worship, he was inviting them to accept that there was no god but Allah and that he was Allah's messenger.

> After 10 years of trying this kind of persuasion, however, he and his small band of believers went to Medina, and from that moment, Muhammad's mission took on a political dimension. Unbelievers were still invited to submit to Allah, but after Medina, they were attacked if they refused. If defeated, they were given the option to convert or to die. (Jews and Christians could retain their faith if they submitted to paying a special tax.)[11]

> It is Medina Muslims who call Jews and Christians "pigs and monkeys." It is Medina Muslims who prescribe death for the

crime of apostasy, death by stoning for adultery and hanging for homosexuality. It is Medina Muslims who put women in burqas and beat them if they leave their homes alone or if they are improperly veiled.[12]

It is my contention exposed in the process of discernment that Satan is very effectively using those whom Ayaan Hirsi Ali has named the Medina Muslims, along with selected passages from the Quran and the Hadith that reflect this period, to build the stronghold of Radical Islam. This development received its biggest boost in the emergence of Wahhabism in the 18th century.

This Islamic sect appeared in Arabia through the leadership of Muhammad ibn Abd al-Wahhab (1703–1792). The means chosen to enforce their vision are described by Bernard Lewis.

> The ire of the Wahhabis was directed, not primarily against outsiders, but against those whom they saw as betraying and degrading Islam from within: on the one hand those who attempted any kind of modernizing reform; on the other hand, and this was the more immediate target—those whom the Wahhabis saw as corrupting and debasing the true Islamic heritage of the Prophet and his Companions. They were, of course, strongly opposed to any school or version of Islam, whether Sunni or Shi'ite, other than their own. They were particularly opposed to Sufism, condemning not only its mysticism and tolerance but also what they saw as the pagan cults associated with it.

> Whenever they could, they enforced their beliefs with the utmost severity and ferocity, demolishing tombs, desecrating what they called false and idolatrous holy places, and slaughtering large numbers of men, women, and children who failed to meet their standards of Islamic purity and authenticity. Another practice introduced by Ibn 'Abd al Wahhab was the condemnation and burning of books. These consisted mainly of Islamic works on theology and law deemed contrary to Wahhabi

doctrine. The burning of books was often accompanied by the summary execution of those who wrote, copied, or taught them.[13]

The virus of this fanatical cult would have remained buried in the desert sands of Arabia if there had not been the promotion of Wahhabism through the rise of oil rich Saudi Arabia.[14]

The root motive for the slaughter of innocent people in the name of Allah is the determination of radical Islamists to purify their religion. Satan is incorporating this willingness to kill in the name of Allah into the present day strongholds of Radical Islam.

This choice of means is well documented by Raymond Ibrahim in his book, *Crucified Again: Exposing Islam's New War on Christianity.* Here I offer his summary conclusions. For the full and exhaustive documentation from Islamic history as well as contemporary reports, please see his eye-opening book that reveals the deadly danger we all face from this stronghold today.

Many have contended that all the violence and oppression so thoroughly documented by Raymond Ibrahim is not true Islam, but extremist "hijacking" of the true Islam, which they view as a religion of peace. To put to rest those objections, we must lay out the means Muhammad demonstrably chose to implement his vision for humanity.

The Choice of War as the Means of Coercing Non-Muslims into Islamic Bondage

The Quran and Hadith, the foundational documents of Islam, show that Muhammad and the companions that formed around him chose waging war as the means to force others to convert to the Islamic creed.

The idea of fighting non-Muslims until they pay tribute is foundational to Islam—and hardly limited to the Koran. In a well-known canonical hadith, Muhammad commanded his jihadis to invade the realms of the infidels and order the latter to convert to Islam: "If they refuse to accept Islam, demand from them the Jizya. If they agree to pay, accept it from them and hold off your hands. If they refuse to pay the tax, seek Allah's help and fight them." In another canonical hadith Muhammad proclaims: "I have been commanded to wage war against mankind until they testify that there is no god but Allah and that Muhammad is the Messenger of Allah; and that they establish prostration-prayer, and pay the alms-tax [that is, until they become Muslims]. If they do so, their blood and property are protected." There are literally hundreds of similar Islamic texts enjoining Muslims to fight non-Muslims until the latter either convert or pay tribute and live in submission.[15]

It is clear from the history and the texts that this is not spiritual warfare that Muslims are commanded to wage against humankind, but physical and *military* warfare with physical weapons intended to kill people. By choosing the means of war and death to extend the creed of Islam, Muhammad and Muslims have opened the door to Satan who is a murderer from the beginning. Today when Muslims chant "Death to America and Death to Israel," they are announcing this decision that is consistent with 1400 years of Islamic history.

Islam's History of Forced Conversions Exposes the Means Chosen by Muhammad

How are people brought into the Islamic faith? This question reveals the heart of the type of Islam that has come from the Medina period. As demonstrated above, the means of advancing the Islamic faith is by warfare in which people are given the choice of being murdered, converting, or if they are Jews or Christians, being humiliated. The purpose of the humiliation is to force them to convert to Islam. Raymond Ibrahim exposes this means of force to drive people to conversion.

> Forced conversions permeate the whole of Islamic history. While the Koran states that "there is no coercion in religion"— and even Koran 9:29, which abrogates such verses, allows at least Christians and Jews the option to exist as dhimmis—the fact is, from the dawn of Islamic history up to the present, forced conversions have been a normal aspect of Islam. Not all were forced at the point of the sword; most forced conversions have been subtle and gradual, and yet forced nonetheless. As should be clear by now, the non-Muslim dhimmi's life is made so miserable by oppressive Sharia stipulations—punctuated by sporadic persecutions—that converting to Islam is the only way to end the suffering, not to mention joining the winning team. It is disingenuous not to count such conversions as "forced" or at least "coerced," as Islam's apologists habitually do.[16]

> It is not an exaggeration to say that "the Islamic world" would be a fraction of its size, or might not even exist at all, were it not for the fact that non-Muslims were compelled to convert to Islam simply to evade oppression—beginning, as we have seen, with the earliest Arabs attacked by Muhammad. Once all these Christians converted to Islam, all their progeny became Muslim in perpetuity, thanks to Islam's apostasy law.[17]

> As for the classic forced conversion—at the point of the sword—this too, has been a regular feature of the Islamic world, past and present.[18]

The choice of force to make people convert plays directly into Satan's hands. Satan's evil empire is characterized by coercion and the obliteration of human freedom.

Islam Destroys Freedom
of Speech, Religion, and Thought

How does Satan hold a person in bondage to the Islamic faith? How are the core lies from Satan shielded from exposure and challenge? Once again, I turn to Raymond Ibrahim for help in understanding this. In the chapter "Islam's war on Christian Freedom" in *Crucified Again*, he observes that there are three laws that come from the Quran and the Hadith that are imposed in nearly every Islamic majority nation in the world today. These laws not only destroy the freedom of Christians, but of Muslims as well. Here is Raymond Ibrahim's summary:

> The precarious status of churches and other forms of Christian expression under Sharia law is emblematic of Islam's innate hostility to Christianity. But Islamic law goes further, denying freedom of speech to all Christians and even freedom of conscience and conviction to Christian converts. Sharia curtails these freedoms by means of three laws that, though separate, often overlap: the laws against apostasy, blasphemy, and proselytism. For example, the Muslim who converts to Christianity is guilty of apostasy. But he can also be seen as a blasphemer, whose very existence is an affront to Islam. And when he speaks about Christianity—as enthusiastic new converts are wont to do—around Muslims, he exposes himself to charges of proselytism. These three Islamic laws effectively ban freedom of speech, freedom of religion, and even freedom of thought.[19]

It is worth pausing a moment to consider the laws concerning apostasy from Islam.

> Irtidad, or apostasy from Islam, is one of the most reprehensible crimes—if not the most reprehensible crime—in Islamic law, deserving of great punishment, including execution. So great a

crime is it that if several people apostatize at once, the Muslim state is obliged to proclaim an official jihad against them. Moreover, because he has actively left or "betrayed" Islam, the apostate is seen as worse than the born infidel. The absolute condemnation of apostasy in Islam is so well known that it is almost redundant quoting sources. Nevertheless, some striking passages from Islamic authorities follow. [20]

This is so contrary to the Western worldview built on the Judeo-Christian revelation of God, that many simply cannot believe that Islam today could continue to purvey a culture we regard as "barbaric." We want to believe that such narrow-mindedness must surely come from a few fringe elements or "ultra-fundamentalists" among the greater body of Muslims who are really just like us at heart. But this is true Islam, as described by the late Majid Khadduri, internationally recognized as one of the world's leading authorities on Islamic law and jurisprudence. He states the following as a summary of the whole force of Islamic law and tradition concerning apostasy from Islam.

Khadduri quotes the various Koranic verses—2: 2:214, 5:59, 16:108—that condemns apostates and then focuses on 4:90-91, which calls for the killing of the apostate from Islam, and concludes...

Although only [verse 4:90-90] specifically states that death sentence should be imposed on those who apostatize or turn back from religion [of Islam], all commentators agree that a believer who turns back from his religion (irtadda) openly or secretly, must be killed if he persists in disbelief. The traditions are more explicit in providing the death penalty for everyone who apostatizes from Islam. The Prophet Muhammad is reported to have said: "He who changes his religion [Islam] must be killed." Cases of those who apostatized and escaped punishment are few, but the rule was certainly more strictly enforced after Muhammad's death as a result of the victories won during the wars of the ridda (secession). The law of apostasy endorsed by the practice of the early caliphs has been sanctioned by ijma [that is, consensus among Islam's scholars]. And there is no disagreement as to its validity.[21]

Not only is this the law of Islam, it is being enforced!

What is amazing is that not only are apostates still being attacked and killed around the Islamic world, but the smallest details of their persecution are consistent across the whole history of Islam, from its beginnings to today.[22]

By contrast to Jesus, "who came that they may have life," Islam has chosen death, and the threat of death, as its means of propagation. The threat of death, in turn, extinguishes freedom of speech, conscience, religion, and thought.

Satan has used those who have chosen these means now to craft a demonic stronghold of Radical Islam which is itself a totalitarian slave state. Ominously, the whole structure has the purpose of imposing this same slavery upon the rest of the world. Further, to these already evil means of war, subjugation and quenching freedom, there has now been added the intent to commit genocide against Jews and Christians. We now turn to examine the historical and spiritual basis for this terrible choice.

Preparing to Commit Genocide
First Stream
Islam Growing a Culture of Hate

A remarkable confirmation that the genocide of billions of people is the method chosen by Radical Islam was revealed in a speech made by the President of Egypt, Abdel Fattah al-Sisi. He was speaking before Al-Azhar[1] and the Awqaf Ministry[2] on New Year's Day, 2015 in connection with Prophet Muhammad's birthday to an assembly of scholars and ulema.[3]

> I am referring here to the religious clerics. We have to think hard about what we are facing—and I have, in fact, addressed this topic a couple of times before. It's inconceivable that the thinking that we hold most sacred should cause the entire umma [Islamic world] to be a source of anxiety, danger, killing and destruction for the rest of the world. Impossible!
>
> That thinking—I am not saying "religion" but "thinking"—that corpus of texts and ideas that we have sacralized over the centuries, to the point that departing from them has become almost impossible, is antagonizing the entire world. It's

antagonizing the entire world!

Is it possible that 1.6 billion people [Muslims] should want to kill the rest of the world's inhabitants—that is 7 billion—so that they themselves may live? Impossible!

I am saying these words here at Al Azhar, before this assembly of scholars and ulema—Allah Almighty be witness to your truth on Judgment Day concerning that which I'm talking about now.

I say and repeat again that we are in need of a religious revolution. You, imams, are responsible before Allah. The entire world, I say it again, the entire world is waiting for your next move...because this umma[4] is being torn, it is being destroyed, it is being lost—and it is being lost by our own hands.[5]

When you realize that President Sisi is lecturing at the preeminent Islamic University in the world to those who are responsible for interpreting the Islamic faith, it is incredible that he would have to tell them such things. Sisi expresses his own astonishment of the facts by the word, *"Impossible!"*

This reveals beyond all doubt that genocide of Christians, Jews, and everyone else who is not Muslim is very much a part of what President Sisi is naming, "...not their religion but 'thinking'— that corpus of texts and ideas that have been sacralized over the centuries to the point that departing from them has become almost impossible." That is what is "antagonizing the entire world." This is confirming evidence to me that Satan is using a system based on the Quran and the Hadith to build strongholds with the intention of seeking to kill up to seven billion people, unless, of course, they convert to Islam.

As we have already seen, war is the means chosen by Muhammad and the "companions" who gathered around him to form the creative minority to grow Islam as a political and religious culture. War implies killing people, but the purpose of Islam's war is to force conversion to their creed. The traditional approach of subjugating Christians and Jews for the purpose of robbing them of their wealth, their women and children, and forcing their conversion to Islam, is now replaced in Radical Islam by genocide.

Satan has used the confluence of three streams to construct the demonic stronghold of Radical Islam as the means of carrying out this intended genocide. These three sources are:

(1) The original hatred of Muhammad embodied in the Quran and the Ahadith that Satan has used to create a climate of hatred.

(2) The Ottoman-German genocide of Armenian, Assyrian and Greek Christians during the waning years of the Ottoman Caliphate during World War I.

(3) The Nazi-Islamic shared ideology of world domination with their common goal of exterminating the Jewish people.

These three streams are woven together by the documented personal associations between the key leaders as they decided on the goal of genocide. Harder to document, but much evidenced nonetheless, is the transfer of the same high level demonic spirits or archons.

First Stream
Muhammad's Hatred Grows a Climate of Hate

The "sword verses" in the Quran and the Hadith and other words of Muhammad from the period of Medina are what Sisi has identified as "that corpus of texts and ideas that have been sacralized over the centuries."

Satan has used these verses to create a climate of hatred of Jews and Christians, which has prepared the way for countless atrocities committed by Muslims down through the centuries. As I have read these verses in the Quran and the Hadith, I cannot help but think that they flow from Muhammad's inability to forgive the Jews and Christians who did not accept his identity as the messenger of God. In this, they are comparable to the passages of Luther that embody his hatred of the Jews. This hatred, regardless of the original cause, gives ground to Satan. This is an open door for demonic spirits of hate and murder which attach themselves not only to human beings, but also to the social structures built upon these verses.

Through the sacred text of Islam, hate is passed down from generation to generation. This has happened not just through memorizing the sacred texts, but also by the attachment of evil spirits passed down from generation to generation because of the hatred. Often apologists for Islamic violence and hatred are deceived by attributing this hatred and violence solely to the atrocities of the Crusades against Muslims, and more recently to colonialism and to the resettlement over land Israel won back in 1967.

The pattern, however, is deeper and older than that. These "modern reasons" are merely a part of Satan's smoke screen to obscure the true root of this hatred: the heart of Muhammad, who is the heart of Islam.

On the 70th anniversary of the liberation of Auschwitz, the *Wall Street Journal* featured an article in which I found the following quote that gets past Satan's deceptions to the root source of Islamic hatred of Jews and Christians:

> According to the Middle East Media Research Institute, an Egyptian cleric, Muhammad Hussein Yaqub, speaking in January 2009 on Al Rahma, a popular religious TV station in Egypt, made the contours of the new hate impeccably clear: "If the Jews left Palestine to us, would we start loving them? Of course not. We

will never love them...They are enemies not because they occupied Palestine. They would have been enemies even if they did not occupy a thing...You must believe that we will fight, defeat and annihilate them until not a single Jew remains on the face of the Earth...You will not survive as long as a single one of us remains."[6]

This hatred by Muslims exists because it is planted in their hearts by the Quran and the Hadith, by the preaching of hatred in the mosques and the relentless indoctrination of their children. This has created a culture of hatred. I base this statement on listening to what Radical Muslims are saying themselves. We must listen to them! As I am writing this chapter, there is a renewed outbreak of violence in Israel by Palestinians. Both men and women with butcher knives are attacking defenseless Israelis—families with young children, teenagers, the elderly. Noted by Bret Stephens in the *Wall Street Journal,* Palestinian Authority President Abbas just added to the hatred and encouraged the violence with the following words, usually left out of the liberal press's narrative of the causes of the violence:

"Al Aqsa Mosque is ours. They [Jews] have no right to defile it with their filthy feet." And, "We bless every drop of blood spilled for Jerusalem, which is clean and pure blood, blood spilled for Allah."[7]

These statements that Jews are "filthy," that they are unclean, that killing Jews is somehow a service to their god Allah, are hate-filled, death-inspiring words. If Allah welcomes these hateful words and actions, then who else could this be but Satan himself?

This conclusion that Muhammed's hatred has been used by Satan to create a culture of hatred is also based on the careful research and documentation provided by Raymond Ibrahim:

Islamic doctrines unequivocally create hostility toward Christians. As we have seen, Muslims around the world are quite deliberately enforcing the provisions of Sharia law against Christian worship, Christian evangelism, freedom of speech, and even freedom of conscience. But Christians also suffer violence at the hands of Muslims for reasons that go beyond conscious applications of Islamic doctrines. The hostility Sharia engenders toward Christians has permeated the culture, mentality, and worldview of the average Muslim. The extent to which violent hatred toward Christians animates an individual Muslim depends on many factors, of course. But clearly one of those factors—in many cases, the deciding factor—is how much or how little that particular Muslim is immersed in and influenced by Islamic civilization.[8]

Ibrahim thoroughly documents this culture of hate in the education systems, Muslim mob mentality, and jihadi terrorism. The result of this hatred permeating Muslim minds, hearts, institutions, and culture is an open door to incalculable numbers of evil spirits. These demonic spirits thrive on the hatred and use it to prepare Muslim cultural institutions to become instruments of murder.

Satan accomplished the same thing through hatred of Christians in the Ottoman Empire and the hatred of Jews among the German and Austrian people. This hatred prepared the cultural climate for building the demonic strongholds for carrying out genocide of Christians and Jews.

Preparing to Commit Genocide
Second Stream
Uniting Islamism with German Occultism

It is not until the twentieth century, so full of evolutionary hope and intellectual promise, that we begin to see Islam's culture of hate evolve into true genocide. In this chapter, we explore the spiritual roots of the intentional rape, murder, and plundering of the property of over two million Armenian, Assyrian, and Greek Christians. These atrocities were committed by Muslims under the orders of the Ottoman Caliphate during the first decades of the 20th century. When we explore the roots of this genocide, we find what appears at first to be a tangled web of political, military, cultural, and economic causes and explanations. When, however, we seek discernment from the Holy Spirit about how Satan was working out his master plans through these human causes, then the structure and sinister purposes of Satan's stronghold of Radical Islam become frighteningly clear.

The Dangers of Gazing into the Abyss of Satanic Evil

I need to add a personal note here. When I asked the Holy Spirit to reveal these spiritual links leading to Islamic genocide, he gave me a glimpse into radical evil and the unfathomable abyss of human suffering. This would have seared my soul had I not been hidden in Jesus Christ and upheld by the love and prayers of family, friends and coworkers. To explore these topics is to look into the face of Satan and grasp the reality of hell. I have many times recoiled in horror at what I have seen in the realm of the spirit and in the documentation I have read. At the same time, I have had to resist the power of evil wanting to invade my own soul and spirit. Repeatedly as I have looked at pictures or read descriptions of ordinary human beings committing monstrous deeds of rape, pillage, and mass murder, I have had to admit that because of my own sinful tendencies, "there go I except for the grace of God." The Lord has called me and others into this process of discernment, as dangerous as it has been, in order that we may have the intelligence necessary to develop this prayer strategy to cooperate with Jesus in defeating Satan's plans in Radical Islam.

Germany's Part in the Ottoman Empire's Genocide of Christians

When I started research into the spiritual roots of the genocide of Armenian, Assyrian and Greek Christians by the Ottoman Turks, I assumed it had grown entirely from Islam or was simply based on Turkish nationalism. But I was in for a shock. One thread, of course, was Islam; but Satan had woven in a new strand of both ideology and spiritual evil that came from Germany. These were welded as one to produce genocide. The astonishing fact is that Germany was responsible for mobilizing the jihad against Christians using the texts of Islam. It was part of the Imperial German strategy at the end of the 19th and the beginning of the 20th centuries to use Muslims and the religion of Islam as a weapon against the rival powers of Russia, Great Britain and France. To see the hidden workings of Satan we must first review some German history.

This history is complex, but the gist of it is that the German Imperial government under Kaiser Wilhelm II developed a plan for working within the Ottoman Empire to extend their cultural, political and military influence. This project culminated in 1908 with the revolution by the Young Turks who were mostly German-trained young military officers.[1] We need to understand that, "The Young Turks were not Islamists but modernizing ethnic nationalists who wanted their country to be like Germany."[2] They gladly received from the Germans all the assistance they were offered in order to become a modern European nation. The many cultural affinities between the Ottoman and Prussian military cultures facilitated this cooperation.

Kaiser Wilhelm II - Deutches Reich - German Emperor - Peter Crawford

On the German side, there was the need for natural resources, new markets and spheres of influence to enable its continued growth as a nation. In addition, Kaiser Wilhelm II held a romantic fascination with the Middle East and with Islam. "Fascinated by the Middle East, Wilhelm dreamed of being an oriental potentate or reincarnation of Alexander the Great. Two trips to the Ottoman Empire, in 1889 and 1898, convinced him that this was his destiny."[3]

As Europe moved into hostilities in 1914, Kaiser Wilhelm II accepted a plan proposed by Max von Oppenheim, who was well versed in the language and culture of the Islamic Middle East, for mobilizing a Muslim jihad against the French and the British.[4] Implementing this strategy involved them with the secular Young Turks whom they had trained. The astute Germans, able to determine who provided the entry way into Muslim hearts and minds, turned to individual religious leaders or brotherhoods, and also to the Ottoman Empire's Mehmed V, the Ottoman sultan who as caliph, nominally led all Muslims.[5] As such, he could declare jihad for every Muslim in the world, setting off what the Kaiser called a "furor Islamiticus," an Islamic fury against British (but not German) infidels. Seeing the Ottoman Turks as a kindred people, Germans dubbed them "the Germans of the Middle East.[6]

In the chapter, "A Jihad Made in Germany," the authors carefully document how a master plan for launching this jihad was prepared. Propaganda for the home front prepared the German public for, "an unprecedented...and frightening undertaking: A European Christian-manufactured jihad against other European Christians."[7]

Within the Ottoman Empire, the Muslim religious establishment obliged their German benefactors with fatwas—some written in Berlin—to back up their calls for jihad. The Germans went beyond giving the justification for jihad from Islam; they provided "how-to" manuals for jihad.

These are the American ambassador to the Ottoman Empire Henry Morgenthau's own words describing the content and the intentions of these secret German inspired booklets:

> The Sultan's proclamation was an official public document, and dealt with the proposed Holy War only in a general way, but about this same time a secret pamphlet appeared which gave instructions to the faithful in more specific terms. This paper was not read in the mosques; it was distributed stealthily in all Mohammedan countries—India, Egypt, Morocco, Syria, and many others; and it was significantly printed in Arabic, the

language of the Koran. It was a lengthy document—the English translation contains 10,000 words—full of quotations from the Koran, and its style was frenzied in its appeal to racial and religious hatred. It described a detailed plan of operations for the assassination and extermination of all Christians—except those of German nationality.

Specific instructions for carrying out this holy purpose follow. There shall be a "heart war"—every follower of the Prophet, that is, shall constantly nourish in his spirit a hatred of the infidel; a "speech war" with tongue and pen every Moslem shall spread this same hatred wherever Mohammedans live; and a war of deed-fighting and killing the infidel wherever he shows his head. This latter conflict, says the pamphlet, is the "true war." There is to be a "little holy war" and a "great holy war"; the first describes the battle which every Mohammedan is to wage in his community against his Christian neighbors, and the second is the great world struggle which united Islam, in India, Arabia, Turkey, Africa, and other countries are to wage against the infidel oppressors.[8]

Rubin and Schwanitz summarize the results of this Holy War as follows:

Since the plan identified the enemy as not only the British, French, and Russians but also non-Muslim minorities, Christians and Jews who supported the Allies, this meant Germany's endorsement of a war against civilians and spreading religious hatred. Thus, German strategy would be intimately involved in the Ottomans' mass murder of Armenians.[9]

When Muslims, following the fatwas of the religious leaders, began killing Christians, reports of these atrocities started to leak out to the German public and to the world. German missionaries returned with reports of the massacres. One great champion for the plight of the Armenians was the American Ambassador to the

Ottoman Empire, Henry Morgenthau. He exposed the massacres to the world through newspaper articles and diplomatic reports. He worked tirelessly as a diplomat with the Turks and world leaders in an attempt to prevent the genocide. He formed a foundation to raise millions of dollars for the Armenians.

Finally, finding his efforts futile, he resigned as Ambassador:

> Exasperated with his relationship with the Ottoman government, he resigned from the ambassadorship in 1916. Looking back on that decision in his *The Murder of a Nation,* he wrote he had come to see Turkey as a place of horror. "I had reached the end of my resources. I found intolerable my further daily association with men, however gracious and accommodating...who were still reeking with the blood of nearly a million human beings." His conversations with Ottoman leaders and his account of the Armenian genocide were later published in 1918 under the title "Ambassador Morgenthau's Story."[10]

Later, Morgenthau exposed the lies of the Turks, maintained to this day, that their campaign to exterminate Armenian Christians was because of their alignment with Russia.

> In 1918, Ambassador Morgenthau gave public speeches in the United States warning that the Greeks and Assyrians were being subjected to the "same methods" of deportation and "wholesale massacre" as the Armenians, and that two million Armenians, Greeks, and Assyrians had already perished.[11]

Muslims exterminated these Armenian, Greek and Assyrian Christians because they were Christians. This was an Islamic jihad of genocide against Christians carried out under the smoke screen of nationalism and war by the last Islamic Caliphate. All of this provides us with a warning of what is already happening and will continue to happen as the various expressions of the stronghold of Radical Islam battle out among themselves as to who will become be the true Islamic Caliphate.

At the heart of the past and present working of Satan through Islam is the historic reality of the complicity of the German Government.

> By early 1916 German officials in the Ottoman Empire had no doubt about what was happening. Even the Kaiser heard the news. The head of his military cabinet, Moriz von Lyncker, wrote in his diary on August 8, 1916: "Most terrible how the Turks rage against Christian Armenians, their subjects. Thousands—men, women and children—are slaughtered, others are driven purposely to death by starvation. Our diplomats appear at this point powerless." But in fact the German government never made the slightest attempt to discourage the mass murders.[12]

Not mentioned in this report above, but witnessed as a regular part of the genocide was the treatment of Christian women.

> Rape was an integral part of the genocide; military commanders told their men, "to do to [the women] whatever you wish," resulting in widespread sexual abuse. Deportees were displayed naked in Damascus and sold as sex slaves in some areas, including Mosul according to the report of the German consul there, constituting an important source of income for accompanying soldiers. Rössler, the German consul in Aleppo during the genocide, heard from an "objective" Armenian that around a quarter of young women, whose appearance was "more or less pleasing" were regularly raped by the gendarmes, and that "even more beautiful ones" were violated by 10–15 men. This resulted in girls and women being left behind dying.[13]

But, does any of this truly connect to the first stream which is Islam? It seems from reading the history that these horrors are explained by Turkish nationalism and the atrocities that always take place when there is ethnic and cultural strife. There is certainly this dimension. However, the role of Islam and the words of the prophet Muhammad are demonstrated in one photograph from among hundreds that reveal the connection of Islam in the past to the present genocide of Christians. This juxtaposition of photographs from 100 years apart made by Raymond Ibrahim says it all with the title, "The Islamic Genocide of Christians: Past and Present."[14]

Muslims are doing what their prophet Muhammad told them to do. First in the "sword verse" in the Quran 9:29 (Sahih International version):

Fight those who do not believe in Allah or in the Last Day and who do not consider unlawful what Allah and His Messenger have made unlawful and who do not adopt the religion of truth from those who were given the Scripture - [fight] until they give the jizyah willingly while they are humbled.

A second verse from the Quran 5:33-34 (Sahih International):

Indeed, the penalty for those who wage war against Allah and His Messenger and strive upon earth [to cause] corruption is none but that they be killed or crucified or that their hands and feet be cut off from opposite sides or that they be exiled from the land. That is for them a disgrace in this world; and for them in the Hereafter is a great punishment, Except for those who return [repenting] before you apprehend them. And know that Allah is Forgiving and Merciful."

Adding to the horror of their present day crucifixions, ISIS has proudly posted videos displaying the beheading of Christians. Here is one report of Muslims beheading Christian children because they would not renounce their faith in Jesus Christ:

Four Christian children were beheaded by ISIS militants in Iraq for refusing to denounce Jesus and convert to Islam, according to the leader of the Anglican church in Baghdad. Canon Andrew White, known as the, "Vicar of Baghdad," fled Iraq in October 2014 for Israel and recounted in a video posted on the Christian Broadcasting Network website how brutal the country has become for Christians. "ISIS turned up and said to the children, 'You say the words that you will follow Mohammed.' The children, all under 15, four of them, they said, 'No, we love Yeshua [Jesus], we have always loved Yeshua.' They chopped all their heads off. How do you respond to that? You just cry."[15]

Now why are these Muslims beheading Christians, even Christian children? Here too, Satan is using the words of their own Quran to inspire and condone such evil:

When thy Lord was revealing to the angels, "I am with you; so confirm the believers. I shall cast into the unbelievers' hearts terror; so smite above the necks, and smite every finger of them!" Quran (Arberry Sura) 8:12

I know that many have argued that these verses have been taken out of context or have been misinterpreted. Just look at the Muslim web sites on Google interpreting these verses to see these efforts. They may well have! Nevertheless, the argument of this prayer strategy is that Satan has used these verses to build strongholds of death and to prepare Muslims to take part in his plans for genocide, which are unfolding before us now in the 21st century.

All this is in continuity with the genocide of Armenian, Greek, and Assyrian Christians during the Ottoman Caliphate a hundred years ago. These horrors into which we have glimpsed are consistent with what is going on today with the ISIS expression of the Islamic Caliphate. This consistency is because of the same spiritual root in the Quran and in the Hadith which convey the words, deeds, and hatreds of Muhammad.

The racial and religious hatred Germans encouraged and connected with in the hearts of Muslims opened the doors to demonic spirits within Muslim hearts. These demons further intensified the hatred and empowered the deadly violence. The contribution of the German effort was to move the Muslims away from their traditional treatment of Christians (keeping them as subjugated people from whom they received tribute) to exterminating them because they had not submitted to Islam. It is my contention that this addition of genocide, which robs Muslims of a source of wealth, is from Satan and is part of his master plan. These facts are documented, and not merely the work of people who are trying to slander Islam.[16]

Kaiser Wilhelm II Opens the Door for Demonic Spirits

As intercessors we must go behind the historical and political facts and expose the role of high-level demonic spirits who assisted in making this shift from subjugation to genocide. We must move from the original open doors to the demonic in Muhammad to the pre-World War I German leadership who departed from their traditional faith in Jesus Christ and sought power from the occult.

The two key figures are Kaiser Wilhelm II and Houston Stewart Chamberlain.

As I have studied this history, I have pondered several questions. How could Kaiser Wilhelm II and his fellow implementers foment Islamic jihad against fellow Christians for political gain? How could they launch a policy fomenting genocide of fellow Christians? Moreover, when they heard firsthand from their own representatives the actual extent of the atrocities, how could they do nothing to stop them? This is betrayal of Jesus Christ and high treason against the Kingdom of God.

This takes us to the occult connection. From all I have read and studied, the Kaiser was not a follower of Jesus Christ. Apparently, he abandoned orthodox Christian faith and was deceived by occult movements popular at the time. These movements, besides opening the doors to evil spirits, were the carriers of a virulent ideology of racial superiority that would prepare both Muslims and Germans to welcome and empower Satan's plans for genocide.

The key figure in these plans was a strange Englishman named Houston Stewart Chamberlain who adopted Germany as his home culture. Though he was no doubt a literary genius, he was also demonized, receiving inspiration as a spirit medium. Chamberlain became Kaiser Wilhelm II's occult advisor and steadfast friend until his death in 1927. William Shirer writes,

> The book which most profoundly influenced that [German] mind, which sent Wilhelm II into ecstasies and provided the Nazis with their racial aberrations, was *Foundations of the Nineteenth Century*, a work of some twelve hundred pages which Chamberlain, again possessed of one of his "demons," wrote in nineteen months between April 1, 1897, and October 31, 1898, in Vienna, and which was published in 1899.[17]

It is beyond our scope to explore all the ideas of this book and the movement that it ignited among Germans, but suffice it to say that it contained the racial theories that justify the extermination of the Jewish people, the destruction of the Church of Jesus Christ, and the enslavement of all non-Aryan people. What is important to know for our task as intercessors is that through Chamberlain's ideas and friendship, Satan himself implanted the DNA for building the strongholds that led to genocide against Jews and Christians.

Germany's plans to use this jihad to defeat England and France during World War I failed. [18] However, their sell-out to Satan and their connections to the Islamic world led to the next stream, which involves the link between the Ottoman genocide of Christians, the Nazis and the Grand Mufti of Jerusalem.

Preparing to Commit Genocide
Third Stream
Al-Husseini's Link with Adolph Hitler

Because of the continuing presence of evil spirits and human sin, streams of evil do not disappear. They morph into other streams of deception and false belief systems. The third stream has its spiritual and ideological roots in the Ottoman Islamic Caliphate/German jihad against Christians. It was refined in the turbulent period after World War I.

In the grand scheme of Satan's work, the defeat of Germany and their Ottoman/Islamic allies was a time of withdrawal, during which demonic powers were able to make more virulent the deceptions and hatreds that had launched the slaughter of World War I and the genocide of Christians. The following evidence shows that Satan used this period to prepare for his next attempt to exterminate Jews and Christians.

This involved many complex ideologies and movements, but for our purposes, we will focus on the following two individuals:[1] The first is Haj Muhammad Effendi Amin al-Husseini, who was the Grand Mufti of Jerusalem. Around him formed a stronghold of

Radical/Militant Islamism. The second is Adolph Hitler, around whom coalesced the stronghold of Nazism. Both these men independently, from different spiritual roots but in parallel movements, developed their ideologies of hate and death. They then connected to form a cooperative relationship to accomplish goals they held in common. The incubator of both men and their different movements was the dynamic of withdrawal enforced upon both Islamists and German nationalists in the defeat of World War I. It was to be al-Husseini who merged Islamic and Nazi ideologies to become the DNA of today's Radical Islam as a tool for genocide.

I will review these two leaders separately, and then look at their interface together.

The Grand Mufti of Jerusalem

Haj Muhammad Effendi Amin el-Husseini – 1929, by American Colony (Jerusalem), Photo Dept., photographer, Licensed under Public Domain via Commons

It seems that Satan was busy guiding the fate of Muhammad Effendi Amin al-Husseini. [2] Against all odds he was prepared and protected as the carrier of deceptions that provided the DNA for Radical Islam. We do not have the space to document his amazing rise to power. Others have done that careful historical work which forms the basis of my discernment.[3] But the hand of Satan is evident.

In summary, "He had been one of those Arabs who had at first remained loyal to the Ottoman Empire on imperial Islamist grounds, serving as an officer in its army and fighting alongside Germany. Then he changed sides to support the anti-Ottoman Arab revolutionaries and became a British agent."[4] In addition, and at the same time, he went to work with the French as an intelligence agent to subvert British rule in Palestine.[5]

Al-Husseini's door to power that allowed him to wield profound influence in the Islamic world was his appointment in 1921 as the Grand Mufti of Jerusalem. This appointment was made by the first British high commissioner in Palestine, Herbert Samuels, who was Jewish and pro-Zionist. It must have been Satan cleverly at work blinding Herbert Samuels to this man's true character. This betrays an astonishing lack of discernment that was to play directly into Satan's long-term plans.[6] The opportunity given al-Husseini by the British was used by Satan to build the predecessor strongholds that were to reject and destroy the forces for peace and moderation in the Middle East.[7]

There is much awful history that may seem distant and irrelevant for us today, but is nonetheless profoundly important for exposing Satan's strategies for genocide. The issue of Jewish immigration to Palestine provided Satan with his opportunity. In the early 1930s, while Hitler had already declared his intentions to exterminate the Jewish people, the Nazi government was reluctant to descend into the moral abomination of genocide. Along with Hitler, they were looking for another solution to the Jewish problem. They found it in allowing the Jews to ransom their emigration to Palestine.[8]

However, it was Satan's agent al-Husseini who blocked this escape rout of immigration both for the Jews and the Nazis. Barry Rubin and Wolfgang Schwanitz offer profound insights into this history of how the Islamist al-Husseini directly contributed to the Holocaust.

> Perhaps there might have been an entirely different kind of Final Solution for Germany, with emigration instead of firing squads and gas chambers. But al-Husaini did not want this outcome. He insisted on stopping all Jewish migration to

Palestine. And since any European Jews let out of Europe might later go to Palestine, al-Husaini made it clear that if Hitler wanted Muslims and Arabs as allies, he must close Europe's exits to Jews. At the same time, al-Husaini and Arab rulers also told Britain that if it wanted to keep Arabs and Muslims from being enemies, it must close entrance to Palestine to all Jews. By succeeding on both fronts, al-Husaini contributed to the Holocaust doubly, directly, and from the start.[9]

This is not to absolve Hitler and the Nazis for the Holocaust, but it does indeed point to al-Husseini and Islamic complicity. Their evil is compounded in that Islamists chose for themselves the option of genocide as they had during the Ottoman Caliphate.

Once again Barry Rubin and Wolfgang Schwanitz summarize their historical research with this profound indictment of al-Husseini and the Islamists who gathered around him and followed him. This ideology of genocide was also to provide the DNA for forming the demonic strongholds of Radical Islam today.

> As for what should be done to the Jews, al-Husaini was crystal clear, publicly advocating genocide even before the Nazi government did so. His 1937 *"Appeal to All Muslims of the World"* urged them to cleanse their lands of the Jews, and it was translated into German in 1938.[10] Urging the use of force against all Jews in the Middle East, al-Husaini both gave his parallel version of Hitler's doctrine and laid the foundation for the anti-Semitic arguments used by radical Arab nationalists and Islamists down to this day. A half-century later, every speech and sermon from Hamas, Hezbollah, Iran's regime, the Muslim Brotherhood, and al-Qaeda echo all the grand mufti's main points in his declaration.[11]

As for the points of this *"Appeal to All Muslims of the World,"* it "combined traditional Islamic hatred of Jews with arguments framed by modern political concepts."[12]

Al-Husseini was not just empty rhetoric; he implemented his

own killing of Jews in Palestine. Later he joined the Nazis in implementing the Final Solution. It is of profound importance that we recognize that this choice of genocide of the Jewish people came from the root of Islam itself. In other words, they drew on deceptions that go back to the beginnings of Islam itself. To wit, they did not simply borrow from Nazism.

All the historical evidence points to the conclusion that both Islamism and Nazism provided two separate but interconnected tracks for accomplishing Satan's purposes of the genocide of the Jewish people.[13]

Before turning to the other parallel track of Nazism, we must pause and ask the question whether or not Haj Muhammad Effendi Amin al-Husseini was demonized or possessed by evil spirits. Or, was he merely a tool of Satan? The historical evidence of his participation in the Ottoman genocide, his hatred of the Jewish people, his affinity to Hitler, and his ability to stir crowds to hatred of Jews, all suggest to me that he was demonized, to some degree or another.[14]

Hitler and the Creative Minority of Nazism Were Demon-Possessed

Now we turn to the German side of the equation. To begin to understand this track of Satan's work in Germany in building strongholds for genocide, we must start with the direct lines connecting Kaiser Wilhelm's occult involvement before and during World War I, with the heavy occult involvement of Adolph Hitler and the inner circle of Nazi leaders

The figure linking Kaiser Wilhelm with the Nazis is Houston Stewart Chamberlain. From a reading of even secular historians like William Shirer who wrote *The Rise and Fall of the Third Reich,* it is clear that Chamberlain was possessed by high level demonic spirits.

Houston Stewart Chamberlain - http://www.britannica.com/biography/Houston-Stewart-Chamberlain

I believe that Chamberlain provided the means for both Kaiser Wilhelm II and Adolph Hitler to be implanted with Satan's deceptions concerning race. Whether they were both demonized through association with Chamberlain may be impossible to determine. It is evident, however, from the historical record, that Adolph Hitler and the creative minority formed around him were themselves highly demonized and equipped as channels for the Devil's power.[15] As intercessors, a glimpse into this demonic dimension will help us later in discerning both the ground of entry as well as the nature of the demons that have been passed on to present day Radical Islam.

It is certain that Satan's deceptions concerning race were planted in Hitler's heart through Houston Chamberlain. He may also have contributed to the transferring of demonic spirits into the members of the nascent Nazi party. Except for Chamberlain's well-documented association with the occult beginnings of the party, I have found nothing clear about how these demons were actually transferred.

I have searched for years for a description of how and when evil spirits actually entered into and took possession of Hitler. I was sure this would help account for the nature of the demons and Hitler's commitment to destroy the Jewish people and the Church. I finally found what may have been the open door. I had seen this information before, but it was when I read how the pastor of Moody Church and author of *Hitler's Cross*, Erwin W. Lutzer, described it, that I felt the Holy Spirit say, "That is the open door!"

This is connected with what had become an occult object

known as the "Spear of Destiny." This was supposedly the spear that was used to pierce the side of the already dead Jesus hanging on the cross. For many through the centuries, the spear was an object of veneration of Jesus Christ who defeated the powers of Satan through his death on the cross. The spear provides the objective verification to the decisive victory as water and blood came from Jesus' side.[16] Satan has masterfully twisted this good news of our salvation and made the spear the symbol of the power to kill God and control humanity. Thus, whoever possesses it would gain great power from the Devil.

There are a number of such spears in existence, but for our story, we look to the one in the Hofburg Library in Vienna. This particular spearhead has undergone extensive research and has various overlays attached to it, one of which is an iron nail similar to those used in Roman crucifixions. What concerns us here, however, is not the actual history of this relic, but the nature of the faith brought to it that would open the door either to the Holy Spirit or to evil spirits. Hitler's worldview and "faith" (definitely not orthodox biblical faith) opened the door to the demonic and to his possession by demons. Lutzer reports the following account of Hitler being possessed by demons while he meditated on this spear.

> One day when Adolf Hitler was in his early twenties, he overheard a tour guide point the spear out to a group of visitors and say, "This spear is shrouded in mystery; whoever unlocks its secrets will rule the world." Later Hitler said those words changed his whole life. Hitler stared at this object for hours, inviting its hidden powers to invade his soul. He believed that this ancient weapon was a bridge between the world of sense and the world of spirit. He felt as if he had held it in his hands in an earlier century.[17]

The moment of demonic inhabitation seems to have been witnessed by Walter Stein, a doctor who had befriended Hitler during his desperate days as a homeless student in Vienna. This is from Ravenscroft's book *Spear of Destiny*:

> Walter Stein found that he was not the only one moved by the sight of this historic Spearhead. Adolf Hitler stood beside him like a man in a trance, a man over whom some dreadful magic spell had been cast. His face was flushed and his brooding eyes shone with an alien emanation. He was swaying on his feet as though caught up in some totally inexplicable euphoria. The very space around him seemed enlivened with some subtle irradiation, a kind of ghostly ectoplasmic light. His whole physiognomy and stance appeared transformed as if some mighty Spirit now inhabited his very soul, creating within and around him a kind of evil transfiguration of its own nature and power.[18]

After observing this event, Dr. Stein reported that he asked himself,

> Was I the witness of the incorporating of the Spirit of the Anti-Christ in this deluded human soul? Had this tramp from the dosshouse momentarily become the vessel of that Spirit which the Bible called "Lucifer...?"[19]

Apparently there are some questions about the veracity of these reports.[20] I believe, however, that these are a glimpse into the possession of Hitler through the ancient relic that he believed to have pierced the side of Jesus Christ. This process of demonization deepened during mentoring by those involved in the occult, most notably Dietrich Eckart who was one of the founders of the occult society that grew into the Nazi Party. There is no need to go too deeply into the process of Hitler's possession by demons. A short summary from Lutzer and a report by those who knew Hitler personally will be sufficient.

After Eckart's death, Karl Haushofer became Hitler's spiritual mentor, taking him through the deepest levels of occult transformation until he became a thoroughly demonized being. Hitler was even transformed sexually; he became a sadomasochist, practicing various forms of sexual perversion. He was stimulated sexually by violence, brutality, and blood. Hermann Rauschning, a friend of Hitler's, said this of him, "Hatred is like wine to him, it intoxicates him. One must have heard his tirades of denunciation to realize how he can revel in hate."[21]

Virulent hatred and involvement in the occult provided Satan with powerful means to coalesce around Adolph Hitler the core group for the stronghold of Nazism. Lutzer confirms this entanglement between human beings and demons:

Hitler's closest associates were occultists in their own right... Himmler was a dedicated occultist; so were Rosenberg and Goebbels. As the Nazi party grew, it attracted those who belonged to numerous satanic organizations. The inner Nazi circle drew power directly from these hidden forces.[22]

As history shows, this small group of deceived and demonized men formed the creative minority for a mass movement that deceived a nation and drove the world into a catastrophic war.

The Death Curse, the "Final Solution of the Jewish Problem" Shared by Hitler and al-Husseini

History shows two separate but parallel avenues used by Satan to provoke genocide of Christians and Jews: the Islamist stream embodied in al-Husseini, and the German occult embodied in Hitler. For Satan to accomplish his plans of genocide, these two men had to meet and be fused into one stronghold. This would provide the concentration of demonic power with the political, cultural and military force to carry out the extermination of millions. The decisive meeting took place between the Grand Mufti and Hitler on Friday November 28, 1941.

A significant and growing partnership between the Nazis and al-Husseini and the Arab Nationalist-Islamist movement existed prior to this particular meeting.[23]

November 28, 1941 al-Husseini met Hitler
Bundesarchiv_Bild_146-1987-004-09A,

This partnership was a continuation of the relationships formed before World War I. It persisted and was effective because of similar ideology and goals. Similar demonic entities were also at work—the "spirit of Amalek" characterized by a virulent hatred of the Jews and the intention to block the fulfillment of God's covenant promises through them. No doubt the Gog spirit of totalitarianism was also working in both men and the movements they embodied. But with this meeting of al-Husseini and Hitler, the cooperation and partnership between Islamism and Nazism reached a new level in both the human and the demonic realms.

At four P. M. on Friday, November 28, Hitler met with al-Husaini, beginning the occasion with a warm on–camera handshake. Their talk in the Nazi leader's office in the presence of von Ribbentrop, Grobba, and the French-language translator Paul Schmidt lasted an hour and thirty-five minutes, ending just after

5:30. Behind closed doors, Hitler promised al-Husaini that Arab aspirations would be fulfilled. Once "we win" the battle against world Jewry, Hitler said, Germany would eliminate the Jews in the Middle East too. The Fuhrer would announce that the Arab world's hour of liberation had arrived and the grand mufti, the Arab world's new leader, would implement the task, already secretly prepared, of eliminating all the Jews in his domain. Hitler asked al-Husaini to keep this confidential declaration secret—to lock it deeply in his heart—until the time was ripe.[24]

In this meeting between Hitler and the Mufti, much more was taking place than the passing on of some war plans or reveling in a similar hatred of the Jews. Satan was using both of these men to establish a bridge between the demonic and earthly realms.

Thus two key parts of his stronghold building plans were lodged in place. First, at that meeting the high level evil spirits from the roots of Islam and Ottoman genocide were united with the high level spirits possessing Hitler. This was in order to form the hybrid of Islamic and Nazis ideologies as the core of the strongholds through which these demonic spirits would express Satan's purposes. Satan needed the personal connection between these two human beings because they both gave him ground on earth through which to work. Each of these men had influence over the hearts and minds of millions of people, and provided Satan with carte blanche on earth for carrying out his purposes. Al Husseini and Hitler built extended human systems based on lies, hatred, and deadly force. They gave Satan an open door to inhabit the entire system and hold millions of Muslims and Germans in his thrall.

The second powerful event of that day hit when the death curse for the extermination of the Jewish people was set in motion. This curse had already formed in both al-Husseini and Hitler long before they met. In writing and in speeches even before the war started, Hitler had spoken of the "annihilation of the Jewish race throughout Europe" which would be the result of "the Jews having started a world war." He viewed this as a type of prophecy.[25] Hitler had a profound understanding of how a prophetic word such as this would function not in predicting the future, but in creating the future.

To understand how Hitler's word about annihilating the Jewish race could function as a prophecy, we must expand our understanding of prophecy from that of foretelling the future, to words spoken or written that are inspired either by the Holy Spirit or evil spirits, used by these spiritual entities to create the reality envisioned. When the source of these words and visions are satanic, they function as curses that enable demonic spirits to work in human minds and hearts.

The prophecy about the "annihilation of the Jewish race" was expressed as a curse, the "Final Solution of the Jewish Problem" that set in motion the human and demonic actions resulting in the extermination of over six million Jews. This curse was spoken by the demon-possessed Hitler to his inner circle.

> What became known in high Nazi circles as the "Fuehrer Order on the Final Solution" apparently was never committed to paper—at least no copy of it has yet been unearthed in the captured Nazi documents. All the evidence shows that it was most probably given verbally to Goering, Himmler and Heydrich, who passed it down during the summer and fall of 1941. A number of witnesses testified at Nuremberg that they had "heard" of it but none admitted ever seeing it.[26]

Such a curse is passed on verbally, either orally or in writing, often with a person in a direct personal relationship that allows the demonic spirits who empower the curse to be transferred. This can happen when a person possessed by demons holds another person in his power.

In the report of the meeting, Hitler revealed to al-Husseini the Nazi secret that they intended to exterminate all the Jewish people.

The exposure of this hideous secret to an outsider came as a surprise to the other Nazis who witnessed it.[27]

By revealing the secret of the final solution to the Grand Mufti who was the gateway into the Arab Muslim world, Satan planted seeds in Muslim hearts already well prepared to take the next step in his infernal purposes of genocide. Hitler and al-Husseini were both true believers in their calling to exterminate Jews. This agreement enabled the demonic spirits possessing them to empower the curse, "the final solution of the Jewish problem."[28] A curse functions as an entryway into the human heart for demonic spirits to enter in and start their work through individual actions and corporate expressions to carry out the curse.

How do we know that all this took place at the brief hour-and-a-half meeting? We must review what resulted from their meeting. First, Adolph Hitler:

> After the meeting, Hitler called in Foreign Ministry official Emil von Rintelen, to whom he dictated "four points following the reception of the grand mufti," including a press release on his "important talk" with al-Husaini "about the future of Arab people..."

> At this same moment, Hitler made a fifth decision that would end millions of lives. He ordered Heydrich to organize a conference within ten days to prepare the "final solution of the Jewish question." Thus, Hitler made his key decision to start the genocide with al-Husaini's anti-Jewish rhetoric and insistence on wiping out the Jews fresh in his ears.[29]

This must have been given to Heydrich orally. The order led to the infamous Wannsee conference in which the decision was made to deport all Jews under German control to concentration camps where they would be murdered.[30]

It would be incorrect historically to see this as the initiation of Hitler's plans to exterminate the Jews. This program had already begun with the "Einsatzgruppen—Special Action Groups, or what might better be termed Extermination Squads."[31] In 1939 these had become operational in Poland, and later followed Germany's conquering armies east into Russia.[32] It was, however, at Hitler's direct orders that the next phase of the Final Solution of industrialized mass murder was put into place. This was to take place within all areas of Nazi control and was planned to involve over eleven million Jews.[33] It is here that the means were developed and implemented to fulfill Hitler's prophetic vision of "the annihilation of the Jewish race throughout Europe."

As for the Grand Mufti, who had already been murdering Jews in Palestine, he was brought into the Nazi plans for the Final Solution and started to take part in implementing it. This came through al-Husseini's close relationship with Adolf Eichmann:

> Another significant link was that Adolf Eichmann, who had prepared the background briefing for the genocide discussion at Wannsee, was ordered to give al-Husaini a preview before any high-ranking Germans had heard the briefing. Probably on Thursday, December 4, Eichmann took al-Husaini into the map room at the Reich Main Security Office's Jewish Affairs division to explain how Germany would "solve the Jewish question." Al-Husaini was so impressed that he asked to have one of Himmler's aides, likely Dieter Wisliceny, sent to Jerusalem after Germany won the war in order to make a similar plan for wiping out the Middle East's Jews. Both men expected this to happen in 1942, or at the latest, in 1943.[34]

The Grand Mufti not only became a protégé of Hitler and Himmler, but actually took part in implementing the Final Solution by recruiting 20,000 Muslim volunteers for the SS. They participated in the killing of Jews in Croatia and Hungary.[35] He also became Satan's means of spreading Satan's curses of death and Muslim/Nazi poison into the Muslim world.[36]

History shows that the Grand Mufti was Satan's key person around whom the demonic stronghold of Radical Islam intending death upon Jews and Christians was to form.[37] When one looks back at this history, it becomes clear that Satan was planning ahead. If plan A, the extermination of the Jews through Nazism, was to fail, in al-Husseini he had plan B to continue his objectives of genocide of Jews and Christians through Radical Islam.

How the Demonized Leader and Creative Minority Impact an Entire Culture

We have focused on just two men, al-Husseini and Hitler. How was Satan able to work through them to deceive millions of people, and to continue even to this day to deceive the masses? This question is posed by Lutzer whose gifts of discernment help us intercessors pierce the veneer of human causes into the deep workings of Satan.

> But even if we grant, as I believe we must, that Hitler was indwelt by an evil spirit(s) or possibly by Satan himself, we are faced with questions: what about his millions of followers? What made them fanatically committed to the dictates of "The Fuhrer"?[38]

This question must be asked concerning any number of demonized leaders around whom Satan is forming the stronghold of Radical Islam today. How is it that their impact extends far beyond their creative minorities to millions of people with open hearts and minds ready to fulfill their evil vision?

The first reason noted by Lutzer is found in the way Satan works through the leader and by extension through the creative minority. *Let us remember that a demonic leader is able to unleash spiritual forces that influence others. As Houston Chamberlain said, 'Hitler is an awakener of souls, the vehicle of Messianic powers.'"*[39]

This demonic empowerment takes place when a person becomes a gateway for demonic spirits. Satan is able to use their words, actions and attitudes to awaken the latent evil that resides in the hearts of others. They are able to make the vilest evils seem the greatest good by giving sanction from beyond the individual— for instance, Islamists committing their atrocities in the name of Allah. Or Nazis exterminating supposed inferior races out of the delusion of Aryan supremacy that has become to them a god.

The demonized leader is able to awaken the souls of others to Satan's lies by embodying the lies in his own words and clothing them in actions. Satan then uses these words and actions to build "faith" in the leader and the movement. This faith, in turn, opens the door for Satan to bring people under the deception and enable Satan to work through them as well. This is the very same dynamic of a Christian leader who is anointed by the Holy Spirit, to be able to "awaken souls" to the truth and reality of Jesus Christ. This awakening then welcomes the Holy Spirit to work through the person to accomplish Christ's purposes in the world. Likewise, if the faith is in Satan's leader embodying his lies, then the door opens for evil spirits to work through the individuals.

The demonized leader, however, is only part of Satan's equation. The other is the cultural, spiritual, and political ethos that nurtures the fertile soil in which the lies planted in the leader may take root and flourish. For Hitler, this was the German culture of the opening decades of the 20th century, in which virulent anti-Semitism, the myths of Aryan superiority, and glorification of Germanic paganism by Wagner, flourished. Above all, the political leaders rejected biblical faith in Jesus Christ and became enmeshed in a national obsession with the occult.

This was especially the case in the desperate years after World War I when spiritualism swept not just defeated Germany, but also Great Britain and the United States. Satan had already prepared German hearts and minds with these ideologies in preparation for the advent of Hitler the Aryan Messiah.

Satan accomplished the same thing with the Islamic track through selected words of the Quran and Hadith, and through centuries of hatred of Jews, Christians and apostates. This prepared the way for al-Husseini in the 1930s and 40s, and it is preparing the way for the present generation of demonized Islamic leaders to form the strongholds of today.

There is a dynamic relationship between the culture and the demonized leader. First, the culture provides the soil in which the leader and the creative minority may grow. Then the leader and the creative minority, upon reaching a tipping point of power and influence, begin to shape the culture according to Satan's plans given the leaders. This is what is happening right now with Radical Islam in relationship to general Muslim culture. The more power ISIS and the Iranian theodicy wield, the more they are radicalizing Muslim culture. If this process is not soon stopped, the world faces the terrifying possibility of increasing numbers of Muslims becoming the Satan's pawns unto global genocide. These dynamics can help us understand how a small group of extremists can, under the right circumstances, become a dangerous world movement.

Intercessors Must Know the Methods and Plans of Satan

It has been a terrible struggle for me to write these last chapters, especially on genocide. Doing the research has had me looking into the abyss of human and demonic evil. Why not just skip over these terrible topics and avoid altogether the risks of having our souls and minds seared by such evil? There are several reasons why we must take the risk.

First, we will not understand the full depth of evil and the potential for evil that Satan is planning through the strongholds of Radical Islam unless we take seriously its demonic roots.

Second, history teaches us not to underestimate the horrors that will explode upon humanity if strongholds intended by Satan for genocide and subjugation are allowed to reach their full maturity.

Third, we can see that we are engaged with formidable foes in both the human and demonic realms who can only be defeated by the power of Jesus Christ in combination with all the human resources at our command.

In the next chapter we address how Satan hides all this intelligence that we have gained from the process of discernment. Satan is a master of deception and actively cloaks his plans from those with spiritual and earthly power and authority to prevent their fulfillment.

Demonic Cloaking

When it comes to the growth of great evil in the world, there seems to be an inexplicable phenomenon—both the intended victims as well as those most able to prevent the evil who do not see it until it is too late to be stopped. For instance, despite the repeated public announcements and the detailed revelations in *Mein Kampf*, most did not believe Hitler's plans for the extermination of Europe's Jews. Incredibly, it required them to see the pictures of mountains of emaciated corpses bulldozed into mass graves before many believed the Holocaust was real.[1] Even today, despite massive and indisputable evidence, some, especially in the deceived Muslim world, deny the historicity of the genocide.

Or to take a more contemporary example, why did the United States for years not see the danger and preemptively destroy the growing demonic stronghold of al-Qaeda forming around Osama Bin Laden? This despite the February 26, 1993 truck bomb attack below the North Tower of the World Trade Center, and then the August 1998 attacks against US embassies in Kenya and Tanzania? In addition to these, there were many other clear signs that al-Qaeda had both the intention and developing means to murder

Americans.[2] The intelligence was available just as it was for the growing danger of Nazism, but it was not seen or acted upon until the aims of these strongholds had been so obviously expressed that they could no longer be ignored. So how do we account for this blindness and inaction even when human intelligence is available to warn of the danger?

To answer this urgent question, I propose a paradigm that is not properly a building block of a demonic stronghold, but an essential component of Satan's work to shield his plans and intentions in the strongholds he is constructing. This is "demonic cloaking."

Our challenge in discerning the times is Satan's mastery of deceit. Our call to develop a successful prayer strategy and the military's responsibility to defeat Radical Islam in battle, must take into consideration how clever he is at hiding the strongholds and the evil he intends through them.

Satan accomplishes this by a complex web of lies that provides a cloaking over the stronghold and hides his true purposes. A first task in our warfare is to understand the nature of Satan's cloaking. This will prepare us to develop the spiritual and human tactics and strategies needed to defeat Radical Islam.

In this chapter we must develop a working knowledge of both the spiritual and human psychological process that make us so vulnerable to Satan's cloaking. In our present age with weapons of mass destruction and mass migrations of Muslims into the West, this blindness to Satan's plans in the religion of Islam and the demonic stronghold of Radical Islam could have cataclysmic consequences.

Cloaking on Three Levels of Reality

A Canadian intercessor anointed to discern Satan's work in national and international events provided the following paradigm to understand the different levels of reality where Satan's cloaking might take place. He sent me the following notes from his prayer journal:

> On April 25th as I was praying for guidance about countering the threats to Israel and the Jewish people, I received an insight which triggered deeper understanding into what is happening today. This word was "Layers to remain hidden" that led me to visualize three different levels with different agendas.
>
> **Level I:** What is on the surface, which is visible to us that may be reported in the news media.
>
> **Level II:** The agendas of human beings, which are partly visible.
>
> **Level III:** The agendas of the rulers (archons), the powers, the world rulers of this darkness, the spiritual forces of evil in the heavens. (Ephesians 6:12) These are invisible to us.
>
> An analogy to this tri-level structure is the composition of the Earth, namely its crust, mantle, and core. The core supports and energizes the mantle, which in turn supports the crust and determines what happens across its expanse. Level III would then be equivalent to the core, level II would be characterized by the mantle, and level I is the crust itself.[3]

I personally found this extremely helpful for understanding both the complex multidimensional battle and how Satan cloaks his work at each level. Let us review this, starting with Level III, which is the basis for what takes place in the other two levels.

Level III
The Agendas of the Demonic Powers

Satan's cloaking at this spiritual level may come over an individual, a movement, or a whole people as spiritual blindness or delusion that prevents people from knowing and seeing what is true. In 2 Thessalonians 2:7-12, this supernaturally imposed blindness is called a "strong delusion" that prevents people from being able to discern the deceptions from the "spirit of lawlessness." People believe the lies from Satan, cannot see the truth, and are held in bondage leading to death.

Within the strongholds of Radical Islam, there is a "strong delusion" blinding all in its grip from knowing the truth of Jesus Christ by using their reason, which would provide liberation from this captivity. Satan also uses select verses of the Quran and Hadith to weave a comprehensive web of lies that forms the thought fortress of Radical Islam. This fortress is guarded by the threat of death to all those who would dare seek freedom of thought or try to escape to life in Jesus Christ. Through this entire system, penetrating to the deepest levels of the human mind, heart and spirit, Satan has fashioned a slave army ready to do his bidding.

Satan also seeks to cast his deceptive web of lies over those who are not in bondage to Islam, blinding us to his true intentions. This cloaking work is often evidenced at Levels II and I, but also may be experienced in Level III, as the demonic powers impinge upon our hearts and minds.

For example, on the intercessory prayer "reconnaissance" trip to Israel that my wife and I took with Doug and Carla McMurry in February 2015, we were all praying constantly. Our ceaseless praying was not just because I was driving the rental car (which was certainly prayer inducing) but because we were being obedient to Jesus' guidance that we were to pray and discern the demonic strongholds at work in Jerusalem opposing God's plans. We were driving through a Jewish area following Google maps. Outwardly, (Level I) there was a sense of order and vibrant life. People looked cheerful and happy going about their business. On Level III, it felt good spiritually. There was a clear, open heaven. It felt peaceful and safe, like God's hand of protection was present.

Then I missed a turn. We had gone no more than several hundred feet when suddenly everything changed. Outwardly (Level I, the visible level) chaos replaced order. Men were shouting at each other, and the cars were jammed up with drivers relentlessly blowing their horns. Peace had been replaced with an undertone of anger, and we could feel hatred, not directed at us, merely in the atmosphere. We had turned into a Muslim section. What happened in the spiritual realm of Level III was even more shocking than the external physical change of cultures. We could feel the demonic oppression. We could feel the presence of demonic powers that had control over the people's hearts as well as over the culture. All of us in that car could feel viscerally and in our spirits these demons seeking to engulf us in their deception. It was like running into an invisible force field or an alternative reality. We all started praying in the Holy Spirit to Jesus for protection and guidance to get us out of there.

Was this just a form of culture shock? No doubt part of it was. It was a jolt to move from the Jewish section, which is essentially Western culture, to Muslim Arab culture. However, this was much more than culture shock. Confirming the deeper spiritual dimension was the recognition that the demons inhabiting that Islamic enclave in Jerusalem were familiar to me; I had encountered them before.

Then I remembered the time when I was in the United Kingdom being driven by a local pastor to conduct a seminar in Yorkshire for pastors. I was to start teaching the moment we arrived, so I was completely engrossed in my notes and was paying no attention to where we were on the journey. Suddenly I felt an abrupt change in the spiritual atmosphere. It was like a blanket of fear and oppression had fallen on me. I felt demonic spirits pressing against me and found it hard to breathe. I looked up and saw that we were in a Muslim area with angry looking men and women in black burkas. When I asked the pastor where we were, he said we were in the city of Bradford. Without seeing the external surroundings, I had experienced in my spirit the demons in that location which were intermingled among the people and their Islamic culture.

The cloaking at Level III is not only real, but is experienced through the other levels of reality. I would go further and affirm that these hidden demonic entities whose presence I felt and observed have contributed greatly to the creation of the culture and the externals of the Islamic quarters in both Jerusalem and Bradford.

Level II
The Agendas of Human Beings

The agendas of human beings are partly visible to us. They may be deduced from careful study of human events, a deep understanding of human nature, making connections, as well as listening to the stated intentions of those who are in leadership of movements and nations. In our present battle, this level includes the stated agendas of the Iranian leadership to, "wipe Israel off the face of the earth."[4] Or in ISIS's message to all Christians, "You Will Soon See an Ocean of Blood for All the Nations of The Cross."[5] Or "We will raise the flag of Allah in the White House,"[6] or bring "a new Holocaust to the Jewish people."[7]

These human agendas, which are inferred from observation, analysis, and listening to the leaders, are also vulnerable to Satan's sophisticated cloaking devices. Because we all have worldviews that filter information according to certain paradigms and assumptions, Satan has an opportunity to inject lies and false assumptions into these systems of thought to create effective cloaking.

For those outside the stronghold of Islam, Satan is presently developing this cloaking from the tenets of postmodernism incorporated in the prevailing ideologies of liberal progressivism and multiculturalism. This worldview denies the reality of God and the Devil, does not believe in sin, makes tolerance the chief virtue, and sees all cultures as equal. These paradigms have effectively blinded people from seeing the intentions and true evil nature of the stronghold of Radical Islam (This blindness also extends to other strongholds Satan is building in Russia and China that threaten liberal democratic free societies the world over.[8]).

Examples of this demonic cloaking working through our worldview are seen most clearly in retrospect. For instance, in the 1930s during the formation of the stronghold of Nazism, much of world was blind to Hitler's agendas, despite the fact that he stated his objectives clearly in speeches and in his book, *Mein Kampf.*

> For whatever other accusations can be made against Adolf Hitler, one cannot accuse him of not putting down in writing exactly the kind of Germany he intended to make if he ever came to power and the kind of world he meant to create by armed German conquest. The blueprint of the Third Reich and, what is more, the barbaric New Order which Hitler inflicted on conquered Europe in the triumphant years between 1939 and 1945 is set down in all its appalling crudity at great length and in detail between the covers of this revealing book.[9]

Yet, because of the demonic cloaking produced through a liberal worldview and the inability to imagine such evil, many could not see Hitler's agenda.

The same is taking place today. Its leaders have stated the aims and goals of Radical Islam in public. With the internet, these intentions of world domination and genocide are broadcast worldwide. The Islamists make the connection repeatedly that they are following Muhammad and are acting in accord with the edicts of the Quran and the Hadith.

This photo of Abelhamid Abaaoud, the mastermind of the terrorist attacks in Paris on the evening of 13 November 2015 that killed 130 people is an example of how Islamists clearly show us that their agenda is based upon Islam.

Abdelhamid Abaaoud. (Militant Photo via AP)

Pictured is the 27-year-old jihadi leader holding in one hand the Quran, and in the other the black flag of ISIS. The meaning of the Quran is obvious. The flag needs more explanation to those who do not speak Arabic and are not familiar with Islamic history. The color black goes back to the banner of Muhammad. Black is particularly significant for ISIS because it was used by the Abbasid Caliphate started in 747.[10] The mission of ISIS is to reestablish the Caliphate. The second meaning of the color black points to ISIS as an apocalyptic cult. "It is also a symbol in Islamic eschatology (heralding the advent of the Mahdi)."[11]

The Arabic at the top is the first part of the "shahada," the Islamic declaration of faith, "There is no God but Allah." The white circle with the Arabic in black contains the second part of the shahada, "Muhammad is the Messenger of Allah." This represents the official seal of the prophet Muhammad.

Now whether this is true Islam or not is not the issue. What is absolutely clear is that in this photo and in the actions of ISIS, they see themselves as the true followers of Muhammad, and their agenda is to spread the Islamic creed by the sword to the entire world.

Yet many in the West have great trouble seeing the connection between Radical Islam and its roots in the religion and the sacred text of Islam. I have noticed this problem ever since President Obama came into office. The following article "How to Beat Islamic State" by Majid Nawz, who is a Muslim and former jihadi [12], appeared in the *Wall Street Journal* December 11, 2015.

> President Barack Obama and many liberal-minded commentators have been hesitant to call this Islamist ideology by its proper name. They seem to fear that both Muslim communities and the religiously intolerant will hear the word "Islam" and simply assume that all Muslims are being held responsible for the excesses of the jihadist few.
>
> I call this the Voldemort effect, after the villain in J.K. Rowling's Harry Potter books. Many well-meaning people in Ms. Rowling's fictional world are so petrified of Voldemort's evil that they do two things: They refuse to call Voldemort by name, instead referring to "He Who Must Not Be Named," and they deny that he exists in the first place. Such dread only increases public hysteria, thus magnifying the appeal of Voldemort's power.
>
> The same hysteria about Islamism is unfolding before our eyes. But no strategy intended to defeat Islamism can succeed if Islamism itself and its violent expression in jihadism are not first named, isolated and understood. It is as disingenuous to argue that Islamic State is entirely divorced from Islam as it is to assert that it is synonymous with Islam. Islamic State does indeed have something to do with Islam—not nothing, not everything, but something. That something is the way in which all Islamists justify their arguments using Islamic scripture and seek to recruit from Muslims.[13]

Majid Nawz's observation of the "Voldemort effect" is brilliant and exposes one of the method's Satan uses to bring the strong delusion—our reluctance to identify an evil by its true name. The deeper reason why many liberals are unable to name the evil is that Satan is effectively using their worldview that does not accept the reality of either original sin or supernatural evil. These are dimensions of reality that for them do not exist and therefore cannot be named.

Level I
What is on the Surface

Satan effectively cloaks from view even what is on the surface and is plainly visible to all. The news media report this level as the facts. Or, so it seems. Upon closer study of "what is on the surface" and what is reported in the news media, we find that Satan has many means for obscuring and distorting facts and covering the true agendas of human beings.

This demonic cloaking is so pervasive and effective that we must explore more deeply the means that Satan uses to blind individuals and entire nations. Being aware of these means will aid us in the tactics of piercing the cloaking.

Satan's Cloaking Through Worldview

Worldview was introduced in Chapter 11. To further sharpen our gifts of discernment we must understand how Satan uses our natural capacity to form a worldview as an effective means of cloaking his actions and intentions in a stronghold.

Our worldview with its set of culturally determined filters helps us see with great clarity those aspects of reality that a culture has deemed to be important. For instance, in traditional Confucian

Chinese culture, family is the most important unit of society. This focus is reflected in the reality that family name is always spoken or written first and then the given names. So I introduce myself in Chinese as Long Zeb Bradford. In our Western worldview the individual is the most important unit of society, so we start with our given names that are unique to us as individuals so my name in the Western context is Zeb Bradford Long.

Language also reflects worldview. For instance, in English we have the one word "uncle," and then we must qualify whether this is a paternal or maternal uncle. In Mandarin Chinese, a large vocabulary precisely distinguishes the different family relationships. In this way our different worldviews enable us to see with great clarity different aspects of reality.

But the converse is also true; our worldview blinds us from certain aspects of reality. For instance, the traditional Taiwanese have a supernatural worldview in which evil spirits and the departed souls of the ancestors are real and present. They are acutely aware of these spiritual entities. Most Westerners, on the other hand, have a scientific, materialistic worldview. The result is that Westerners are often obtuse to the spiritual world, but very astute when it comes to seeing the human and material world. This capacity for worldview to blind us gives Satan an opportunity.

As already noted in Chapter 11, Satan may sow into our culture ideas that shape our worldview—lies or half-truths that form the filters that block out aspects of reality. In modern Western culture in Western Europe, the United Kingdom, Canada and the United States after World War II, a certain worldview developed, "Liberal Progressivism." This worldview contains a number of foundational concepts that are derived from our Judeo-Christian values. However, this worldview has replaced much of the rich spiritual and moral legacy of Judaism and Christianity. The result is varying degrees of blindness to the spiritual and moral dimensions of reality. Satan is effectively using this blindness to cloak both the reality of the supreme good in God, and his own evil intentions. When this happens to those in leadership, the results can be catastrophic.

This has happened before! In the 1930s the German Church was profoundly influenced by the liberal worldview that denied the supernatural aspects of the Christian faith. It reduced the Gospel of Jesus Christ with its dependence on the power of God, into a "social Gospel." Further, when Kaiser Wilhelm II and many others in leadership gave up orthodox Christian faith for the occult, the result was that Satan was able to blind the Church and the German people to the demonic power of Nazism. Many in the rest of the world were blinded as well. Moreover, we all know from our history how this blindness led to this demonic stronghold growing to its terrible maturity.

Satan is using the same methods of a liberal progressive worldview to blind the present leaders of the West to the true demonic roots of Radical Islam. Our powers of reason and analysis may help us in determining the human agendas in Level I and II as well as deducing the role of the demonic in Level III. However, our reason will produce distorted results and half-truths if our worldview prevents us from discerning certain aspects of reality. I am convinced that the Liberal Progressive worldview is preventing many from providing the discernment as well as leadership to combat the enemy effectively. This is true not just of political leaders, but of many Church leaders who have given up a traditional biblical worldview for a liberal progressive worldview. This is especially true of the mainline Protestant denominations in the United States, Canada and the United Kingdom. Like the Church in Germany, blind to the Devil in Nazism in the 1930s, they are blind to the work of the Devil in Radical Islam.

Satan's use of a worldview to blind people from certain aspects of reality has been well demonstrated in President Obama. He has denied that ISIS has anything to do with Islam. On September

10, 2014, he made the following remarks in his otherwise powerful speech launching the plans to "degrade and ultimately destroy ISIL."

> ISIL is not "Islamic." No religion condones the killing of innocents, and the vast majority of ISIL's victims have been Muslim. And ISIL is certainly not a state; it was formerly al Qaeda's affiliate in Iraq and has taken advantage of sectarian strife and Syria's civil war to gain territory on both sides of the Iraq-Syrian border. It is recognized by no government nor by the people it subjugates.
>
> ISIL is a terrorist organization, pure and simple, and it has no vision other than the slaughter of all who stand in its way.[14]

The speech displayed a good strategy for defeating this foe. It included increasing air attacks, forming a coalition, etc.[15] However, in my opinion, President Obama's fatal flaw is that he does not name the true enemy and the true aims and motivations of this enemy. The spiritual blindness demonstrated in this statement is deeply troubling. The categorical statement that "ISIL is not 'Islamic'" rules out rational analysis of the root causes of this evil, which are indeed in Islam. This precludes the development of effective strategies to defeat it.

Obama seems to prove his point that ISIL is not "Islamic" by saying, "No religion condones the killing of innocents." From my reading of the Quran and the Hadith and reviewing 1400 years of bloody history, I declare there is such a religion. It is Islam! How does the fact that most of their victims are Muslim make ISIL not Islamic? The statement that "they have no vision other than slaughter of all who stand in their way" is astonishing for its blindness to the real vision or agenda of ISIS which is to establish the Islamic Caliphate.

Does President Obama not know this is their agenda? Is he that blinded by his worldview? Or does he know that this is their agenda and chooses to join the cloaking agenda to hide from us all their true genocidal purposes? If he knows and is lying, then he is evil and a full participant in Satan's plans through Radical Islam. If he sincerely and naïvely believes these statements against all the evidence to the contrary, then as President of the United States he is Satan's (and the Islamist's) "useful idiot."[16] Either way he has been used by Satan to provide the cloaking of the stronghold of Radical Islam that intends our destruction as a free society.

Another example of this blindness and the resulting inability to understand our enemy is displayed in the following headlines.

"State Department Spokeswoman Floats Jobs as Answer to ISIS." February 17, 2015. She is quoted as saying, "We're killing a lot of them, and we're going to keep killing more of them...But we cannot win this war by killing them," department spokeswoman Marie Harf said on MSNBC's "Hardball." "We need...to go after the root causes that lead people to join these groups, whether it's lack of opportunity for jobs..."[17]

Marie Harf is of course right; we must get to the root causes of what it is that drives young people to join the Islamic jihad. She is also right in that no jobs, lack of opportunity, injustice, oppressive governments, and colonialism are all part of the equation and must be taken seriously as part of the strategy for defeating terrorism. However, there is much more that the liberal progressive worldview has excluded—the spiritual and religious dimension, which is at the heart of the violence.

In the *Atlantic* article "What ISIS Really Wants," Graeme Wood exposes the blindness of this interpretative framework and the consequences.

The reality is that the Islamic State is Islamic. Very Islamic. Yes, it has attracted psychopaths and adventure seekers, drawn largely from the disaffected populations of the Middle East and

Europe. But the religion preached by its most ardent followers derives from coherent and even learned interpretations of Islam.

Virtually every major decision and law promulgated by the Islamic State adheres to what it calls, in its press and pronouncements, and on its billboards, license plates, stationery, and coins, "the Prophetic methodology," which means following the prophecy and example of Muhammad, in punctilious detail. Muslims can reject the Islamic State; nearly all do. But pretending that it isn't actually a religious, millenarian group, with theology that must be understood to be combated, has already led the United States to underestimate it and back foolish schemes to counter it.[18]

This inability to see the complete picture of the root causes of Radical Islam and ISIS is clear evidence that Satan has effectively used the liberal progressive worldview to blind people to the religious and spiritual dimensions of this movement. That the religion of Islam as believed by those in ISIS could be the root cause and motivation for people joining a movement like ISIS or cutting people's heads off, is just not part of the liberal progressive worldview. As a result, Satan may achieve his purposes of hiding his full terrible purposes in Radical Islam as well as preventing those in political, military and even religious authority from being able to develop a comprehensive and effective strategy to defeat it. As intercessors, we must not let that happen to us!

Worldview Leads People to Focus on the Instruments Used to Express Evil Rather than the Source of the Evil

The method of cloaking by use of the Liberal Progressive worldview was also demonstrated in the Islamic terrorist attack that took place on December 3, 2015 in San Bernardino, California, in which a couple killed fourteen people at their holiday work party. The media was careful not to identify this as Islamic terrorism until the facts became clear. On December 4, 2015 however, "FBI Director James Comey confirmed that the probe into the massacre in San Bernardino is now 'a federal terrorism investigation' as a result of evidence that the killers were 'radicalized' and 'potentially inspired' by foreign terrorist organizations."[19]

What is revealing is that the immediate reaction to this attack by those whose worldview I would suspect is liberal progressive was to focus on gun control rather than on the source of the evil which is the ideology of Radical Islam. William McGurn, in his *Wall Street Journal* article of December 7, 2015, offered profound discernment into how Satan is using worldview to divert attention away from the true source of the threat. The following quote is from his article "The Liberal Theology of Gun Control: Guns are what you talk about to avoid having to talk about Islamist terrorism."

> It's what you talk about so you don't have to talk about the reality of Islamist terror. And focusing on the weaponry is part of a liberal argument that dates to the Cold War, when calls for arms control were likewise used to avoid addressing the ugly reality of communism.
>
> Understand this, and you understand why Senate democrats reacted to San Bernardino by putting forth antigun legislation. Why the *New York Times* ran a gun control editorial on its front page, and the *Daily News* used its own cover to feature the National Rifle Association's Wayne LaPierre underneath San Bernardino killer Syed Farook—labeling them both terrorists. And why President Obama used Sunday night's address to whine about those resisting his call for gun measures that would not have stopped any of the shooters.
>
> Put simply, today's liberalism cannot deal with the reality of evil. So liberals inveigh against the instruments the evil use

rather than the evil that motivates them. Not that there aren't measures society can embrace to keep the innocent from being shot and killed...

Meanwhile, we've just endured what may be the first successful ISIS-inspired attack on the homeland. And, like her former boss, Hillary Clinton is demanding the government "take action now" on guns.[18]

William McGurn offers brilliant discernment and an insightful example of how Satan is using the liberal progressive worldview to prevent the discussion of those topics that might lead to an active national response to his evil plans being implemented through Radical Islam. Now, am I saying that people like me with a biblical worldview can see with far greater clarity? Yes! There are whole areas of reality that a biblical worldview does allow us to see that gives us far deeper insights into the nature of good and evil. But at the same time, no one can see with perfect clarity. My point is that Satan is relentlessly seeking to exploit the blind spots in our worldviews to cloak his evil plans. The key is being aware of Satan's tactics, knowing our blind spots, and allowing the Holy Spirit to give us the gift of discernment.

Satan's Cloaking through the Destruction of Free Speech

On the surface, a strange collusion appears to be going on between Liberal Progressivism and Islamic jihad. What could appear more mutually contradictory than the draconian application of Sharia law that stones homosexuals, oppresses women, and silences any critical reflection on their belief system through threats of death; and, on the other hand, Liberal Progressivism that celebrates gay rights, liberates women from all biological or social constraints, and rejects faith in God as unreasonable? Yet both seek to silence free speech. The root of their cooperation is that Satan is using both of these ideologies to impose tyranny. The first step on the road to tyranny is always to extinguish free speech. Pamela Geller and Robert Spencer are two leaders on the front lines of exposing this war from these two contradictory directions. In the chapter "On Free Speech and Jihad," in their powerful book, *The Post-American Presidency: The Obama Administration's War on America,* they make the case for the centrality of free speech:

> The Bill of Rights reads: "Congress shall make no law abridging the freedom of speech or of the press." It is our foremost safeguard against tyranny. The most basic tenet of our great and noble nation is freedom of speech. It is the cement that holds together the bricks of life, liberty, and the pursuit of happiness. There is no possibility of a constitutional republic without freedom of speech. If one group is allowed to suppress the speech of another, the suppressing group has achieved total hegemony: and more to the point, in the words of Ayn Rand, the principle of free speech is "not concerned with the *content* of a man's speech and does not protect only the expression of *good* ideas, but of *all* ideas. If it were otherwise, who would determine which ideas are good and which to be forbidden? The government?[20]

Islam quenches free speech through death threats. The Western politically correct media caves in and removes from critical discourse reflections on how Islam is not only completely incompatible with but also destructive of our Western democratic culture based on the Judeo-Christian faith and worldview. At present, the epicenter of the battle is over Radical Islam's attempts to silence those who draw cartoons critical of their prophet.

While some doubt that there is an orchestrated campaign by Islamists to quench free speech, the evidence is there for all with eyes to see. There is not space here to prove their plan to silence free speech, but it is succeeding in many places in Europe and increasingly in America. Please read the afore-mentioned book by

Geller and Spencer. Also the older, but no less sobering book, *Lights Out: Islam, Free Speech and The Twilight of the West,* by Mark Steyn substantiates this evidence.

For our work as intercessors, we must understand the clever and effective way that Satan is cloaking his true aims in Radical Islam. We must recognize that the stakes in this battle to preserve free speech are very high. If the West loses this battle, we will be bound over to the totalitarian fascism of Islam, which has always protected itself from exposure by destroying human freedom.

Demonic Cloaking by Discrediting Those who Deliver Prophetic Warnings

As we seek out and listen to those whom God is calling to reveal the nature of this threat, we must be aware that Satan will work very hard to silence these prescient and prophetic voices, or at least, make sure that their warnings are not heard. A ploy Satan has often used is choosing a person who has been publicly very wrong on some other topic, which now prevents us from taking him seriously when he is right where Satan is plotting great evil.

A sobering example of this ploy is Winston Churchill. For years, Churchill stridently and persistently warned the British government and public of the growing dangers of Nazism–mostly in vain. The worldview of those in power seeking peace at any cost was partly to blame, but not entirely. The other reason was in the personality and actions of Churchill himself. I hate saying this about my hero, but his own brash personality as well as the military disaster of Gallipoli during World War I made it hard for many to take his warnings seriously. The decisive factor, however, was his position on granting dominion status to India. The British public and much of the government were all supportive of granting freedom of self-rule to India. But Churchill, in all his brilliance as a writer and speaker, railed against loosening the grip of colonial control over India. I am convinced that Satan, in a masterpiece of cloaking, cleverly used Churchill's mistakes as well as his personality flaws to prevent those in power at that time from heeding his warnings on the growing evil of Nazism.

We must be careful today that we do not let Satan do the same thing to us. Some who are seeing clearly into the threat of Radical Islam have, in the eyes of the press or public, been very wrong in other areas either in their personal lives, their tone, or past wrongheaded stands they may have taken. In any event, we must discern on a case-by-case basis whether what a flawed person may be saying is true or not, and not be fooled.

I fear this is happening today with people such as Glenn Beck, Robert Spencer of Jihad Watch, Newt Gingrich, Joel Rosenberg, Joseph Lieberman, Benjamin Netanyahu, and Geert Wilders of the Netherlands. I am convinced that on the issue of the threat to the world and the genocidal goals of Radical/apocalyptic Islam, they are telling us the truth. I have been warned that even mentioning them in this book is too polarizing. But I have ignored this advice because I am convinced that they are among the prophetic voices of today. I urge us all to listen to them; but do so, as always, with discernment.

In summary, when we put these three levels together and see how Satan may work within each level to hide his true intentions, the task of gathering accurate actionable intelligence is not only daunting, but all the more necessary if we are not to be deceived. Being aware of the ways Satan may apply the cloaking is a very good first step. However, it will not be enough; we will need to employ prayer tactics in cooperation with the Holy Spirit to pierce the demonic cloaking. This will be covered in Book II of *A Prayer Strategy for the Victory of Jesus Christ, Defeating the Demonic Strongholds of ISIS and Radical Islam.*

Having dealt with the reality of Satan's cloaking as part of his stronghold in Radical Islam, we must gather up the intelligence yielded through discerning the times and move toward a coherent map of our human/demonic adversary.

A Map of the Strongholds Created from Islam

In this chapter I will summarize the intelligence gathered so far into a map of the structure of the demonic stronghold of ISIS and Radical Islam. This will provide the starting point for developing the strategies and tactics for defeating these strongholds and thwarting Satan's plans.

A short description of each component of the stronghold follows the map. Most components have already been covered in depth, some have not been but are necessary to include in order to complete the structure of the stronghold.

I have also included some starting points for developing the strategy for defeating this stronghold. It may help to imagine this stronghold as a fortress that must be dismantled block by block. Different approaches and weapons are required to remove each block. The complete development of the strategy and specific prayer tactics again are published in the next volume of this series.

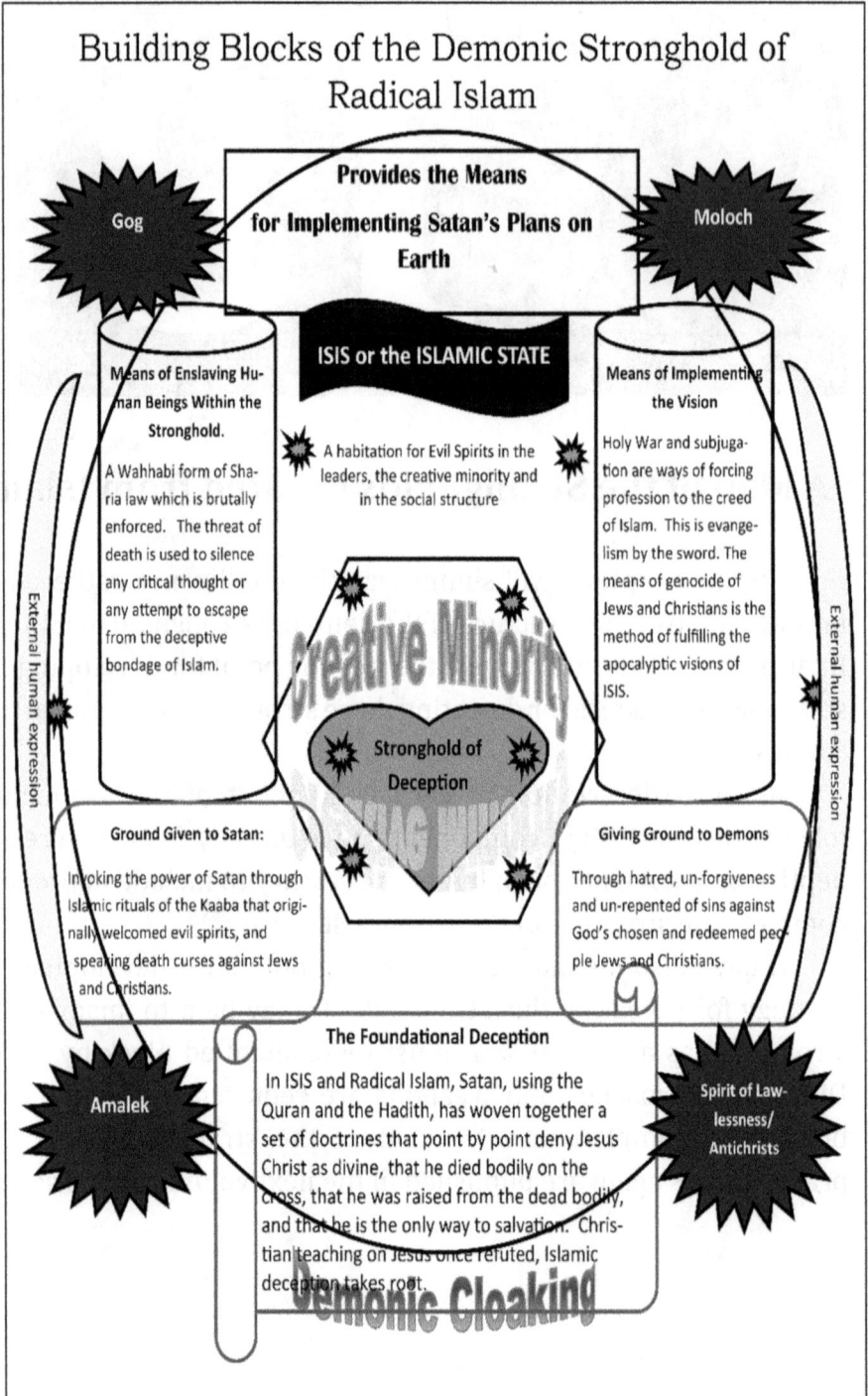

Building Blocks of the Demonic Stronghold of Radical Islam

Gog

Moloch

Provides the Means for Implementing Satan's Plans on Earth

ISIS or the ISLAMIC STATE

Means of Enslaving Human Beings Within the Stronghold.

A Wahhabi form of Sharia law which is brutally enforced. The threat of death is used to silence any critical thought or any attempt to escape from the deceptive bondage of Islam.

A habitation for Evil Spirits in the leaders, the creative minority and in the social structure

Means of Implementing the Vision

Holy War and subjugation are ways of forcing profession to the creed of Islam. This is evangelism by the sword. The means of genocide of Jews and Christians is the method of fulfilling the apocalyptic visions of ISIS.

Creative Minority

Stronghold of Deception

Ground Given to Satan:

Invoking the power of Satan through Islamic rituals of the Kaaba that originally welcomed evil spirits, and speaking death curses against Jews and Christians.

Giving Ground to Demons

Through hatred, un-forgiveness and un-repented of sins against God's chosen and redeemed people Jews and Christians.

External human expression

External human expression

The Foundational Deception

In ISIS and Radical Islam, Satan, using the Quran and the Hadith, has woven together a set of doctrines that point by point deny Jesus Christ as divine, that he died bodily on the cross, that he was raised from the dead bodily, and that he is the only way to salvation. Christian teaching on Jesus once refuted, Islamic deception takes root.

Demonic Cloaking

Amalek

Spirit of Lawlessness/ Antichrists

A Summary of the Building Blocks of the Stronghold of ISIS and the Strategies for Defeating it

Moving from the center outward:

1.The Stronghold of Deception within the Mind and Heart of the Leader

All strongholds start in the human heart and mind and consist of ideas and systems of thought planted by Satan that oppose God's truth as revealed through natural and biblical revelation. (See II Corinthians 10:14.)

Stronghold of Deception

In Radical Islam, the source of deception is the Wahhabi interpretative framework, which reforms Islam by returning to Satan's original deception of Muhammad through whom was given the revelations that formed the Quran. Next in authority is the compilation of the reports of what Muhammad said and did, along with commentary, which form the Hadith. From the vast and varied material of the Quran and the Hadith, Satan has chosen a particular set of texts to form a worldview consistent with his goals.

Specifically, these are the reports and stories from the time when Muhammad and his band of followers had to withdraw to Medina—these have become known as the "sword verses." This stronghold of deception is both conceptual and emotional. That is, ideas and feelings such as hatred of Jews and Christians are fused together. The stronghold of deception gives ground to demonic spirits who may take root in the leader's heart, intensifying the lies and the emotions. The ideas, emotions, and demons coalesce to form the stronghold, which is comparable to DNA that may be passed on to others.

2. A *Creative Minority* Forms Around the Leader

Around the leader coalesces a small core group with complementary personalities, talents, similar thoughts and attitudes. The stronghold of deception carried by the leader infects this core group. The core may also be demonized or possessed by demons, which gives them power and authority as well as guidance. This group may well be called *the creative minority*, those who embody the reality around which Satan coalesces the larger social, political and cultural reality that forms the fully mature stronghold. This process follows well-established principles of the social construction of reality.[1] Shared deceptions and evil spirits hold together this core group.

The basis for the present day stronghold of Radical Islam is the original creative minority, the companions who formed around Muhammad, enshrined in the Quran and Hadith. The present day stronghold of ISIS has formed around an imitation of this original creative minority. There a set of deceptions exists that Satan has constructed from many sources, but especially from the Quran and the Hadith refracted by the Wahhabi interpretive framework. In addition, in both the Sunni version and the Shia version, apocalyptic expectations have been added.

The ideology of the genocide of Christians (rather than subjugating them) is added from the Ottoman Caliphate/Occult German genocide of Armenian, Assyrian and Greek Christians. The racial ideology, hatred, goals of exterminating the Jewish people, and replacing the Church of Jesus Christ with Islamic/Nazi ideology—all these are grafted onto this Islamic root and carried into the present by the al-Husseini/ Adolph Hitler embodiment of the ideals.

These have all formed a coherent system of ideas, beliefs and attitudes, which form the grounding for the stronghold of Radical Islam. This coherent system is first held by the core leaders and the creative minority, then infused throughout the entire social organization that constitutes the stronghold known by its own particular name.

3. Demonic Spirits Exert Control over the Leaders and the Core Group

Demonic spirits are welcomed both into individuals as well as into the social fabric of the stronghold through Satan's deceptions, unconfessed sins such as murder, hatred, unforgiveness, and through intentional invocation by prayer, religious rituals, and worship of false gods. The attachment of these demonic spirits enables the stronghold to become a human-demonic, intermingled entity.

In Radical Islam, these demons have also been passed down through the generations beginning with Satan's original deception of Muhammad. More recent open doors to demons are the unconfessed sins of the Ottoman Caliphate/German Occult Nationalist genocide of Armenian, Assyrian and Greek Christians. A second pathway for demons into the present stronghold is Muslim unconfessed complicity in the extermination of the Jewish people under al-Husseini.

Implications for Battle Strategy and Tactics

Since the leader and the creative minority form the core around which the entire stronghold is formed, they must be removed in order to prevent the stronghold from reaching its full maturity. At many points in the development of the stronghold, the removal of the leader and the creative minority will result in the stronghold coming unraveled and ceasing to be a threat.

For intercessors, this will begin in the spiritual realm. It will include such tactics of bidding the Father that the Holy Spirit may penetrate their hearts with the truth of Jesus Christ to overcome Satan's lies which comprise the stronghold of deception. This work in the heavenlies will also involve binding the demons that may have gotten into them. In some cases, this may involve high-level engagements with the archons that are working through them to exert control over the entire stronghold. These engagements with the demons working through the core leaders will require many different tactics of binding evil spirits and breaking the curses spoken through them. Under the right circumstances, the tactic of dividing Satan's kingdom standing behind these human organizations can be employed. The battle tactics for removing these leaders depends upon identifying them, discerning their roles in Satan's work, and then seeking the guidance of the Holy Spirit as to how we are called to cooperated with Him in removing them.

If the human leaders of the core of the stronghold are not removed or neutralized by either being converted or cut off from the demons which empower them, then they may need to be removed from the core of the stronghold through other means.

The tactics here depend on the type of system the leaders and creative minority have created. Radical Islam, like Nazism and Stalinism, has chosen the means of death and a totalitarian oppression. So the tactics for removing them by necessity become more drastic. This may take place by praying for their friends to turn against them. Most often, this removal requires military intervention as it did with the removal of Osama bin Laden by Seal Team Six. In all these options, the intercessor is to cooperate with the Holy Spirit to become the means through whom Jesus works out his plans in the human sphere.

4. The Human Name Given to the Demonic Stronghold

This is the outward expression of the words, curses, and lies that Satan used to speak into "the hour of the power of darkness" that when received in "faith" by human beings, actually plants in their minds and hearts the seeds for forming the demonic stronghold itself.[2] (See Luke 22:53). Around the key leaders and the creative minority, the larger organization, movement, and the political and military structure are built. This human component of the stronghold is given a particular name such as the, "Ku Klux Klan," "Nazi Party," "ISIS," or "The Islamic Republic of Iran." It maintains cohesiveness and dynamism through the following:

1. The inspiration of the ideas and worldview of the foundational deception.
2. The presence of evil spirits and the power of Satan.
3. The "routinization"[3] of the vision through enforced imitation of the ideas and behaviors of the creative minority.
4. Systems of coercion that enforce compliance and eradicate any deviance from the inner and external reality of the stronghold by death, enslavement and intimidation.

Discerning the names that Satan is using to speak to Muslim hearts and minds in order to construct the strongholds is daunting. To those not steeped in Arabic language and history, a term like "Islamic Caliphate" has little meaning or power. However, from within the stronghold, the proclamation of a caliphate releases a vortex of demonic power that draws Muslim "true believers" into the stronghold far beyond the creative minority.

Keep in mind that using the name ISIS or the Islamic State is in order to illustrate the general principles of the formation of that particular category of strongholds based on Islam that share similar purposes of implementing Satan's four purposes. In 2016, ISIS is a major threat, but in the future this could well change and a new name may emerge that will be a more accurate description of the stronghold Satan is using.

Implications for Battle Strategy and Tactics

In this war against Radical Islam, as in any war, clearly naming our enemy is essential for developing a realistic battle plan for victory. This is consistent with Sun Tzu's wisdom, "If you know the enemy and know yourself, you need not fear the result of a hundred battles. If you know yourself but not the enemy, for every victory gained you will also suffer a defeat. If you know neither the enemy nor yourself, you will succumb in every battle."[4] Book I in the series of *A Prayer Strategy for Jesus' Victory over Radical Islam* is based on the capacity to know and to name the enemy.

Having done this in the process of discerning the times, an enemy of great complexity and danger emerges into clear view. This enemy is both spiritual and human, and requires both human and spiritual tactics to defeat it. Avoiding defeat by Radical Islam and gaining the victory over it is neither simple nor assured. It requires great wisdom, which can only be obtained by naming the enemy and then building an effective battle plan. This is the task of the next book in the series.

5. Means of Implementing the Vision

Means of Implementing the Vision

Holy War and subjugation are ways of forcing profession to the creed of Islam. This is evangelism by the sword. The means of genocide of Jews and Christians is the method of fulfilling the apocalyptic visions of ISIS.

These are the methods chosen for fulfilling the vision, specifically, for bringing the world under submission to the creed of Islam and under the rule of Sharia law.

In the case of ISIS and other expressions based on the particular Islamic texts of the Quran and the Hadith crafted by Satan to form the stronghold of Radical Islam, the means chosen are Holy War and subjugation.

Radical Islam of the 21st century is the direct spiritual and ideological successor of the Ottoman Caliphate, which launched the genocide of Armenian, Greek and Assyrian Christians. It is also the successor of al-Husseini and Adolph Hitler who launched a genocide of the Jewish people and the replacement of the Church of Jesus Christ.

These means of genocide and coerced inclusion into the bondage of Islam are the methods chosen by ISIS and other expressions of Radical Islam. This is evangelism by the sword. The means of murder is chosen for all Muslims who have departed from the true faith as defined by the Wahhabi interpretation of the Islamic text. They have become "infidels," "apostates."

These means chosen by ISIS are intended to fulfill its apocalyptic visions of the Caliphate, the coming of the Mahdi, and the establishment of worldwide Islamic hegemony.

6. Means of Enslaving Human Beings Within the Stronghold

Once people become ensnared in a stronghold, Satan uses various means to enslave them and prevent their escape. In the strongholds of Radical Islam, the first means is through a Wahhabi form of Sharia law which is brutally enforced. The threat of death silences any critical thought or attempt to escape from the deceptive bondage of Islam.

> **Means of Enslaving Human Beings within the Stronghold.**
>
> A Wahhabi form of Sharia law which is brutally enforced. The threat of death is used to silence any critical thought or any attempt to escape from the deceptive bondage of Islam.

All societies and movements implement elements of coercion that keep people within the established norms of the movement. These may be peer pressure, shame, intimidation or laws whose violation requires punishment. But the stronghold of Radical Islam, like Nazism, Stalinism and other tyrannical forms of government, has chosen the most extreme form of coercion—death to all those who seek freedom from bondage.

Implications for Battle Strategy and Tactics

The means chosen to implement the vision and to enslave human beings in the stronghold has profound implications for dealing with the human political, cultural and military aspects of the stronghold. This choice of means—which in the case of Radical Islam is genocide and subjugation—must guide all of our strategies and tactics for defeating them. As amply demonstrated by Ambassador Morgenthau and Prime Minister Nevil Chamberlain, well intentioned attempts to seek diplomatic solutions with regimes supported by demonic strongholds proved futile. In the case of Chamberlain, his efforts amounted to appeasement, which actually bought time for the development of Nazism.

Our role model for winning the war over Radical Islam must be Winston Churchill. He had a grim realistic assessment of the nature of Nazism, and an awareness of the means that they had chosen. This led him not only to discern the times, but to name the evil clearly and decisively. This led to the development of an overall strategy for defeating Nazism. He knew that with an enemy which had chosen death as its means and was committed to the destruction of Christian civilization, there could be no appeasement, no negotiation, only a total commitment to total victory over the evil of Nazism. This victorious strategy, based on naming and rightly understanding the enemy, is summed up in Churchill's famous speech of June 22, 1941 when the Nazis invaded the Soviet Union.

London, June 22, 1941

We have but one aim and one single irrevocable purpose. We are resolved to destroy Hitler and every vestige of the Nazi regime. From this nothing will turn us. Nothing. We will never parley; we will never negotiate with Hitler or any of his gag. We shall fight him by land; we shall fight him by sea; we shall fight him in the air, until, with God's help we have rid the earth of his shadow and liberated its peoples from his yoke. Any man or State who fights on against Nazism will have our aid. Any man or State who marches with Hitler is our foe.[5]

In dealing with the stronghold of Radical Islam and developing the strategy for its defeat, we must be led by the same moral clarity as Winston Churchill in defeating Nazism. All our intelligence gained from discerning the times has revealed to us that the strongholds of Radical Islam share the identical satanic goals and means as Nazism. We must develop our strategy for defeating this evil based on this reality rather than on the basis of our hopes for an ideal world.

In the realm of spiritual warfare and intercessory prayer, it will be our task as intercessors to "stand in the gap" like Moses to break through to the heart of the stronghold to expose the means chosen and to take part in preventing their fulfillment. We shall also be called to pray for government and military leaders who name the enemy and develop plans for victory.

7. Ground Given to Satan

Ground Given to Satan
Invoking the power of Satan through Islamic rituals of the Kaaba that originally welcomed evil spirits, and by speaking death curses against Jews and Christians.

The ground is the legal right granted to Satan and demonic powers to gain and to hold a claim on a person's mind and heart. Invoking the power and presence of Satan through Islamic rituals grants this legal right of occupation. Death curses spoken against God's chosen people and redeemed people—Jews and Christians—also invoke the power of Satan who is a "murderer from the beginning." Muhammad did not do away with the pagan rituals of Mecca and the Kaaba that invoked evil spirits, but made them obligatory for all Muslims. Each time Muslims prostrate themselves in rote prayers toward Mecca, they are in fact invoking evil spirits and are opening doors for demonization.

These prayers and rituals include the invocation of a false god named Allah whose attributes, as revealed in the Quran and attested to by his servants and recorded in the Ahadith, are not those of the one true God, the Creator of heaven and earth, revealed in the Torah, the Old and New Testaments, and in Jesus Christ.

When death curses are ritualistically and corporately incanted against God's chosen and redeemed people, they open a door for demons to enter both individual human hearts and corporate organizations by bringing curses down upon themselves (cf. Genesis 12:1-3). So when Muslims chant "death to America" and "death to Israel," that is, to kill Jews and Christians, they are in fact welcoming demonic spirits to enter into their own hearts.

8. Ground Given to Demons

This is similar to the legal right given to Satan to exercise control over a person's mind and heart. This giving ground to demons to harass and to become attached to a person is due to specific sins committed that are not confessed, repented of and forgiven. The Ten Commandments given by Yahweh to Moses provide the universal categories of his law that when trespassed, open the person or a human social organization to the affliction by demonic spirits. This affliction starts from without, but may move into deeper levels of attachment within a person's psyche. In extreme situations, the attachment may reach the level of possession or total control by the demonic spirits. Possession, however, cannot happen to born-again Christians because of the Holy Spirit indwelling them, de facto a shield against compete control. For non-Christians, I believe there is a general protection against the occupation of evil spirits by having been created in the image of God and by having followed their consciences which keeps them within the parameters of God's Law for human life.[6]

Individuals deceived by forms of Islam that Satan has used to construct the strongholds of Radical Islam are especially vulnerable to attachment and possession by evil spirits because Islam is not a religion of grace and forgiveness. Also, the religion has condoned hatred, murder and the sexual abuse of women. Ground to demons has been given through centuries of cursing, oppressing, and murdering God's chosen and redeemed people, Jews and Christians. If the ground is not removed and the demons are welcomed to continue in the present strongholds of Radical Islam because of stratum upon stratum of unconfessed sins against Jews and Christians, then these demons are passed down to future generations.

> **Giving Ground to Demons**
> Through hatred, un-forgiveness and un-repentance of sins against God's chosen and redeemed people, Jews and Christians.

Muhammad's lack of forgiveness is now compounded by today's Islamists refusing to forgive the atrocities committed against Muslims by crusaders and more recent alleged offenses of Westerners against Islam.

Regardless of how justified one's hatred or refusal to forgive may be, it is spiritually necessary to do so. Unforgiveness always opens doors for demons to strengthen their control over human hearts and minds by blocking a person from receiving the Father's forgiveness. Jesus taught, 14"For if you forgive others their sins, your heavenly Father will also forgive you. 15But if you do not forgive others, your Father will not forgive you your sins." (Matthew 6:14-15) This applies to all human beings regardless of their faith because it is based on the way we are created in his image.

Additionally, the commands of Muhammad given in the Quran

and the Ahadith that allows such evil treatment of women, especially captive women, demonstrated in the Armenian genocide and the present actions of ISIS, are direct violations of God's law and thus an invitation to demonic spirits to occupy and possess those who commit these atrocities and condone them. When these evil practices become ingrained in an entire cultural system as they have in Radical Islam, then ground is provided for the demonization and possession of individuals, their culture, and their organizations.

9. The Foundational Deception

The Foundational Deception

In ISIS and Radical Islam, Satan, using the Quran and the Hadith, has woven together a set of doctrines that point by point deny Jesus Christ as divine, that he died bodily on the cross, that he was raised from the dead bodily, and that he is the only way to salvation. Christian teaching on Jesus once refuted, Islamic deception takes root.

The religious, political, and legal system of Islam and the strongholds of ISIS and Radical Islam are built upon this deception. The foundational deception took root first in the heart of Muhammad, was transferred to his companions, and is now thriving in the hearts of the present day leaders and creative minority. This foundational deception provides the conceptual framework which enables the social organization of the stronghold to adhere as one.

Deception is defined as any false ideology or concept concerning the nature of God, human nature, or God's covenant promises and commandments as revealed in the Old and New Testaments. In ISIS and Radical Islam, Satan has used the Quran and the Hadith to weave a set of doctrines that point by point deny and replace Jesus Christ as divine, as actually having died on the cross, as having been raised from the dead, and as the only way to salvation.

This foundational deception provides the legal right for Satan to exercise control over the hearts and minds of all those within the stronghold.

10. Archons, High Level Demonic Spirits.

The archons, or high level demonic spirits, are generally located in the heavenly realm above the earthy human sphere (Ephesians 6:12). Usually archons accomplish their purposes through the stronghold by the demons under their command. There are times, however, when an archon works directly in the stronghold by possessing the leader or the leaders around whom the stronghold has coalesced. Whatever the case, the archon expresses its particular evil attributes through the medium of the demonic/human organization of the stronghold.

In Radical Islam, especially in the present expression of ISIS, these high level demonic spirits are known by their biblical names, Gog (Ezekiel 38, Revelation 20:7-10), Molech (Jeremiah 32:35, Acts 7:43), the Spirit of Lawlessness (2 Thessalonians 2:1-12), The Spirit of the Antichrist (1 John 2:18, 4:3), and the Demonic spirit of the Amalekites (Exodus 17:16). Each of these archons has unique functions and spheres of authority, that together under the coercive rule of Leviathan (who may well be Satan himself) are both building the stronghold of Radical Islam and expressing their natures through it.

Implications for Battle Strategy and Tactics

These building blocks provide the interface between the human and demonic and enable Satan to control human hearts. The tactics for dealing with all of these begin in the realm of the spirit, and require us to engage directly with the high level demonic powers. This will lead us into the tactics of high level spiritual warfare where we will be called to oppose the archon in the authority of the name of Jesus Christ. This complex and controversial sphere of spiritual warfare I lay out.

In addition, this part of the battle is directly connected with our taking part in the great moves of the Holy Spirit that are bringing the gospel of Jesus Christ into the Muslim world. These are the way that God is overcoming the "Foundational Deception" of Islam upon which the entire structure of evil is based. This leads us into the strategies for cooperating with the Holy Spirit in the work of mission and evangelism of Muslims worldwide. The beginning of strongholds is in the human heart, and it is only in the working of the Holy Spirit within the human heart that deceptions from Satan may be replaced by the life giving truths of Jesus Christ.

11. Demonic Cloaking Protects and Holds the Entire Stronghold Together

The cloaking is complex and works both within and outside of the stronghold. Within, it functions like a "strong delusion" in which Satan darkens people's minds to prevent them from seeing. The cloaking is also maintained within the culture of the stronghold by attitudes and prohibitions that prevent any critical thought or criticism of Satan's woven structure of deception. The delusion and prohibitions are reinforced with harsh, institutionalized methods of silencing anyone who violates these taboos.

Outside the stronghold, the cloaking works to prevent the true purposes, goals, means, and actions of the stronghold from being seen and understood by those who are either the intended victims of the stronghold and those who may have the power to expose, destroy, or prevent the stronghold from accomplishing Satan's purposes. Satan utilizes a diverse arsenal to provide the cloaking. Secrecy and distortion of the facts by those within the stronghold keep it hidden. A worldview held by those outside the stronghold that cannot imagine the evil that Satan is intending to work also keeps people blinded.

Demonic Cloaking

Demonic cloaking is essential to the formation of Satan's strongholds, especially in the beginning stages of their construction before they have obtained the earthly power for either self-defense or to impose their view of reality upon others.

Implications for Battle Strategy and Tactics

Having reliable intelligence is essential for cooperating with the Holy Spirit in Jesus' war to defeat Radical Islam. A first task in our warfare is to understand the nature of Satan's cloaking. This will lead us to implement our first prayer strategy, that is, to pray for the Holy Spirit to pierce the cloaking so that we may see clearly Satan's methods and plans. Specifics to come in Book II.

12. The External Human Expression of the Demonic Stronghold

This chart of the demonic stronghold of Radical Islam, and ISIS in particular, depicts the internal human and demonic realities fused together to form the core of the stronghold. Around this core, like an external shell, is the human, political, cultural, and military organizational aspects, together with the many individuals who form the outward and earthly expression of the stronghold.

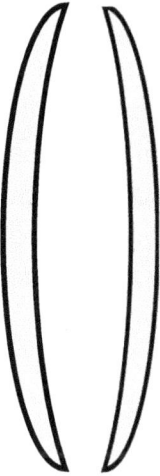

It may help to understand this with the image of the Old Testament model of the human heart, in which the mind, soul, and spirit (this last being the dwelling place of the Holy Spirit in believers) are completely fused with and expressed through the physical biological part of us, our body. So we are both spiritual and material. Likewise, a demonic stronghold has both spiritual as well as material dimensions. Just like our physical bodies, the external physical, human expression provides means for both the spiritual demonic entities as well as our own ideas and visions to be expressed in the physical and human world.

Implications for Battle Strategy and Tactics

When we realize that the stronghold of Radical Islam has its roots in the human heart through deceptions planted by Satan, we are led to the conclusion that only the victory of Jesus Christ over Satan on both fronts—the spiritual and the material—can prevail against the stronghold. God's grand strategy for victory is that those in bondage to Islam may be set free by accepting Jesus Christ as Lord and Savior. Only then can the lies of Satan planted in their hearts through Islam be overturned by the indwelling Holy Spirit who bears witness to the truth. The implication for us is that spiritual warfare and earthly military warfare will be taking place simultaneously in the war to defeat the strongholds of Islam. Tactics and strategies for victory over both the Devil and his Islamic slaves who have declared war on us must be developed which take into account this interwoven demonic/spiritual and human/earthly nature of our adversary.

The keys to defeating Radical Islam and to bringing the Gospel to the entire Muslim world are contained in the intelligence summarized in the map of the particular demonic stronghold of ISIS. This reveals an adversary that is a demonic and human fused structure. This implies that spiritual and earthly means are both required to prevail over it.

It will be left to those in the military, cultural, and political arenas to develop the military, political, and cultural strategies for defeating and destroying the human dimensions of Radical Islam. We Christian intercessors must ask our Father to grant wisdom and success to our governments' coordinated efforts to quench Radical Islam. Further, the Holy Spirit may lead us into another dimension of spiritual warfare, that is, to oppose the evil on spiritual battlefields which undergird the earthly battlefields.

The Next Steps in Defeating Satan's Plans

I began this book by citing the words of Winston Churchill who described the gathering storm of evil about to break loose upon the world. Churchill was writing in retrospect of the years in which the demonic stronghold of Nazism was relentlessly gaining spiritual, political, and military power. The storm broke with the onset of World War II. Churchill knew the consequences of doing nothing to prevent Nazism from reaching its terrible maturity to unleash death and tyranny.

I have completed the mission of this first book. I have given you the results of discerning the times. Satan's plans for the future have been exposed to us through prophetic vision, observing the past, seeing present confirmations, as well as hearing and seeing the visions for that future being cast by the Islamist leaders themselves.

1. Replace God's way of salvation with the deception of Islam.
2. Exterminate Jews and Christians in order to replace Yahweh's Covenants of Salvation for humanity.
3. Stifle the Holy Spirit moving in the house of Islam.
4. Establish a radical Islamic Caliphate from which to wage offensive jihad, accomplish the genocide of Jews and

Christians, and impose Islamic hegemony through Sharia law.

Satan has already started carrying out these four plans through the strongholds based on Islam. The storm clouds are gathering!

This book is occasioned by my encounter with Jesus Christ in which I was caught up into the heavenlies and shown visions of the future that Satan is working through Radical Islam. In that same vision I heard the Lord say, "These are NOT my plans! These are Satan's plans. I am calling you to take part in mobilizing, equipping, and deploying an army of intercessors who can cooperate with me to defeat these strongholds and insure that Satan's plans are not accomplished."

In 2016, when this book is being published, the outcome is all in doubt. Unlike the storm of Nazism, the gathering storm of Radical Islam has not yet broken upon us. There is still time for the full onslaught of evil to be stopped. However, it is not enough to discern the times, to name the enemy. We must now move to the urgent work of developing and implementing the prayer strategies and tactics to overcome these strongholds, thwart Satan's plans and advance the Gospel of Jesus Christ into the Muslim world.

This volume comes to an end here, the next phase, the hard work of prayer, is crucial to undertake. That is contained in Book II *A Prayer Strategy for The Victory of Jesus Christ: Defeating the Demonic Strongholds of ISIS and Radical Islam.*

A Glossary of Selected Islamic Terms*

Allahu Akbar—See Takbir, below.

Dar al-Islam—The house of Islam signifies Muslim lands and peoples around the world.

Dhimmi—A protected second-class citizen living under Muslim rule.

Fiqh—The application of sharia in the lives of Muslims.

Hadith—Collections of traditional sayings and actions of Muhammad. It also functions as an overall term for sunnah, the actions of Muhammad recorded in tradition.

Jihad—Jihad means "struggle." It became to refer to the Muslim doctrine of spiritual warfare. In the Quran, it clearly means holy war.

Quran—The Holy Scriptures of Islam which the angel Gabriel dictated to Muhammad in Arabia (beginning in 610 A.D.)

Ramadan—The Muslim holy month which requires fasting.

Shahada—The proclamation Muslims make, "There is no god but Allah, and Muhammad is his Messenger." If a non-Muslim recites it with true belief and sincerity, it is enough to constitute a conversion to Islam.

Sharia—The most well-known term for Islamic law, that is, how Muslims should live, sharia means literally "path to water."

Shia—One branch of Islam that adheres to the belief that succession of Islamic leaders proceeds from Muhammad's bloodline rather than by election. Shias make up about 15% of Muslims globally. Iranians are predominantly Shia.

Sunnah—The actions of Muhammad according to the traditions of Islam.

Sunni—The majority branch of Islam constituting about 80% of Muslims world-wide. ISIS is Sunni.

Takbir—The Islamic declaration, Allahu Akbar, means Allah is greater. Islamic traditions indicate that Muhammad used it in celebrating and in glorifying Allah. In addition, it was used to intimidate enemies of Islam. It has become very well-known in the West by suicide bombers who shout it before detonating their bombs.

Takfir—The Islamic doctrine of excommunication. Classically, Muslims have sought unity among themselves, dating back to Muhammad. Radical Muslims, however, take advantage of the doctrine in order to justify their attacks on less zealous Muslims.

Ummah—The world-wide population of Muslims.

*With thanks to Nabeel Qureshi's *Answering Jihad, Zondervan, 2016, pages 166-168*

Notes
Author's Notes

[1] "Abbasid Dynasty". *Encyclopædia Britannica. Encyclopædia Britannica Online.* Encyclopædia Britannica Inc., 2016. Web. <http://www.britannica.com/topic/Abbasid-dynasty>.

[2] The Black Banner or Black Standard (راية السوداء rāyat al-sawdā', also known as راية العقاب rāyat al-'uqāb "banner of the eagle" or simply as الراية al-rāya "the banner") is one of the flags flown by Muhammad in Islamic tradition. It was historically used by Abu Muslim in his uprising leading to the Abbasid Revolution in 747 and is therefore associated with the Abbasid Caliphate in particular. It is also a symbol in Islamic eschatology (heralding the advent of the Mahdi), and it has been used in contemporary Islamism and jihadism since the late 1990s.

Wikipedia contributors. "Black Standard." *Wikipedia, The Free*

Encyclopedia. Wikipedia, The Free Encyclopedia, 25 Mar. 2016. Web. <https://en.wikipedia.org/wiki/Black_Standard>.

Chapter 1
The Gathering Storm

[1] *The Holy Bible*. New English Translation. Biblical Studies Press, L.L.C., copyright 1996-2016. Web. <http://netbible.com/>.

I Chronicles 12:32 From Issachar there were 200 leaders and all their relatives at their command—they understood the times and knew what Israel should do.

Matthew 16:2-3 He said, "When evening comes you say, 'It will be fair weather, because the sky is red,' and in the morning, 'It will be stormy today, because the sky is red and darkening.' You know how to judge correctly the appearance of the sky, but you cannot evaluate the signs of the times."

[2] Hickman, Kennedy. "World War II: Munich Agreement." *About Education*. About Education, 27 May 2015. <http://militaryhistory.about.com/od/worldwarii/p/World-War-Ii-Munich-Agreement.htm>.

[3] "Munich Agreement" *Encyclopædia Britannica. Encyclopædia Britannica Online.* Encyclopædia Britannica Inc., 2016. <http://www.britannica.com/EBchecked/topic/397522/Munich-Agreement>.

[4] Grubb, Norman. *Rees Howells: Intercessor*. Fort Washington, PA: CLC Publications, 1983. Pg. 152

[5] Ibid., Pg. 151

[6] Santorum, Rick.
   A. "The Gathering Storm." *National Review*. National Review, Online 6 Oct., 2006. Web. <http://docslide.us/documents/the-gathering-storm-rick-santorum-speech.html>.
   B. For the video speech: Angier, John. "The Gathering Storm of the 21st Century" parts 1-5. Online Video Clip. YouTube. YouTube, 12 Nov.

in 2007. Web. <https://www.youtube.com/watch?v=IQ8ZzEnWqw8>.

[7] Presbyterian-Reformed Ministries International, <www.prmi.org>.
  A. "Discerning the Times" <http://discernwith.us/>.
  B. Doug McMurry's excellent video teaching called "Glory through Time" <http://www.theclearing.us/media/glory-through-time/>.
  C. A video course, "Father, Thy Kingdom Come" is based on Doug McMurry's "Glory Through Time" course, my teaching on Spiritual Warfare in the PRMI Dunamis Project, and the practical experience of dealing with demonic strongholds during the Bush era, in the Church, and in the world. <http://dunamisinstitute.org/register>. This course provides practical teaching on how Satan forms and works through demonic strongholds to accomplish his purposes on earth. We share the strategies and tactics we have learned from the story of Rees Howells dealing with the stronghold of Nazism. We add our own firsthand experience of praying against the strongholds of Radical Islam and Liberal Progressivism in the Presbyterian Church (USA). This is designed to equip PRMI intercessors and spiritual warriors.

Chapter 2
Apocalyptic Visions and the Call to Prayer

[1] The Community of the Cross: A place of Encounter with Jesus Christ for prayer, equipping, and sending, was established in 2003 by Presbyterian Reformed Ministries International.

[2] It is critically important to understand the role of the worldview of Liberal Progressivism in undermining and destroying Western culture and values, most especially in the Christian Church, and our subsequent vulnerability to the assault from Radical Islam. But in order to keep a laser focus on the demonic stronghold of Radical Islam, this other menace will not be the topic of this book's prayer strategy. That will require another careful study and will appear in another publication.

[3] **Ezekiel 3:14-15**.

14 A wind lifted me up and carried me away. I went bitterly, my spirit full of fury, and the hand of the LORD rested powerfully on me. 15 I came to the exiles at Tel Abib, who lived by the Chebar River. I sat dumbfounded among them there, where they were living, for seven days.

[4] In the decision making process of the PRMI Board, leadership teams, and at events of Presbyterian-Reformed Ministries International, we have built in a careful discernment process to keep in step with the guidance of the Holy Spirit and to guard against deception. This process consists of the following:

A. After-Action Reviews: anytime there have been manifestations of the Holy Spirit or we have received guidance from the Holy Spirit calling for action as I have described above.

B. Allowing others to evaluate critically what another has experienced.

C. Asking the Four Discernment Questions:

    i. Does this word or guidance give glory to Jesus Christ in the present and the future?

    ii. Is it consistent with the revelation of God's nature and intentions in the Bible as determined by the Reformed hermeneutic that "Scripture Interprets Scripture?"

    iii. Do other born again Christians share a confirming inner witness of the Holy Spirit?

    iv. Is there objectively verifiable fruit or results within human lives, history, or the physical world demonstrating that God really is at work in this way?

This process of discernment has been applied both to the initial vision calling me to prayer engagement, and throughout the development of this prayer strategy.

[5] Churchill, Winston S. *The Second World War: The Gathering Storm.* Boston: Houghton-Mifflin Co., 1948. Pg. iv-v.

[6] Ibid.

Notes

Chapter 3
The Dangers of Exposing Satan's Plans in Radical Islam

[1] Wilders, Geert. *Marked for Death: Islam's War Against the West and Me.* Washington, DC: Regnery Pub., Inc., 2012.

Chapter 4
The War Declared by Satan and Muhammad

[1] Long, Brad. *The PRMI Dunamis Project, Unit #5: Equipping for Spiritual Warfare and Kingdom Advancement.* Black Mountain, NC: Presbyterian-Reformed Ministries, International, 1999. Pg. 56-62. See also Genesis 1:3, 6.

[2] Ibrahim, Raymond. *Crucified Again: Exposing Islam's New War on Christians.* Washington, DC: Regnery Publishing, Inc., & New York: The Gatestone Inst., 2013. Pg. 19.

[3] *The Qu'ran.* Trans. Sahih International and Mohsin Khan. *The Quranic Arabic Corpus.* Kais Dukes, ed. Copyright 2009-2011. Web. <http://www.corpus.quran.com/translation.jsp?chapter=5&verse=60>.

[4] Roark, Dallas M. "Why Do Muslims Hate the Jews?" *Answering Islam: A Christian-Muslim Dialogue.* 13 Apr. 2016 < http://www.answering-islam.org/authors/roark/hate_jews.html>.

[5] Ibid.

[6] Some apologists for Islam have pointed out the various verses of the Old Testament which also command the people of Israel to take up the sword against the enemies of God. In the Old Testament law, death was the penalty for any number of offenses from adultery to being a wizard. Indeed, some of these passages sound very similar to the Quran. It is true that Satan has at times used these verses, especially from the Old Testament, to build strongholds among Christians to foster hatred and death. These biblical "Sword Verses" however are very different from the Koranic "Sword Verses" on two counts.

First, the Biblical verses are given as specific commands to people at a specific time and place—during the conquest of the Land of Canaan, for example. Unlike the Quran, they are not given as universal commands for all Jews and Christians for all times and places.

The second and most important reason is that Jesus Christ has fulfilled the Old Testament. In Jesus, sinners find grace and mercy as they turn to Him and repent of their sin. Jesus tells us in Luke 6:27-28 (NET), "But I say to you who are listening: Love your enemies, do good to those who hate you, bless those who curse you, pray for those who mistreat you." In Islam as fixated at the 7th century by the Wahhabi interpretative framework, there is no such balancing of God's grace and mercy. As already noted, the "doctrine of abrogation" which Satan has so cleverly built into the Quran itself as Allah's allegedly infallible word, makes it impossible for the Muslim to go back to the earlier parts of Muhammad's life which were more conciliatory.

Allow me a quick digression here; millions of Muslims have rejected the violence of Muhammad's later years, in direct contradiction to this dynamic of abrogation. They are not true Muslims in the eyes of Radical Islamists. If they cling to their belief, the Radicals will ultimately murder them as infidels.

In addition, there are as many verses in the Old Testament that specifically forbid the people of Israel from harming the people of the land "until they have reached the full measure of their sin," in other words, until a specific time in God's plan for the good of the world. When the Israelites harmed the Gibeonites, for example, they committed sin, for which they were required to repent.

[7] *The Qur'an*. Trans. by Saheeh International. Riyadh: Abulqasim Publishing House, 1997.

Surah 9:5

And when the sacred months have passed, then kill the polytheists wherever you find them and capture them and besiege them and sit in wait for them at every place of ambush. But if they should repent, establish prayer, and give zakah, let them [go] on their way. Indeed, Allah is Forgiving and Merciful."

Also see <http://www.answering-islam.org/Silas/swordverse.htm> for commentary.

[8] Ibrahim, *Crucified Again: Exposing Islam's New War on Christians*, pg. 20-21.

[9] Congressman Joe Walsh. "Prime Minister of Israel Benjamin Netanyahu Speech at the Joint Session of Congress-May 24, 2011." Online video clip. *YouTube*. YouTube, 24 May 2011. Web. <https://www.youtube.com/watch?v=0BaMLlnb_KI>.

[10] Washington Post Staff. "The Complete Transcript of Netanyahu's Address to Congress." *The Washington Post*. 3 March 2015. <http://www.washingtonpost.com/blogs/post-politics/wp/2015/03/03/full-text-netanyahus-address-to-congress/>.

Chapter 5
Jesus' Call to Warfare

[1] Sommer, Allison. "What's in a name? A guide to the subtle but serious implications of choosing ISIS, ISIL, Islamic State, or Daesh." *Haaretz* 18 Nov. 2015. Web.<http://www.haaretz.com/blogs/routine-emergencies/.premium-1.615126>.

Chapter 6
Actionable Intel for Spiritual Warriors

[1] **John 15:15**. "I no longer call you slaves, because the slave does not understand what his master is doing. But I have called you friends, because I have revealed to you everything I heard from my Father."

[2] Von Clausewitz, Carl. *On War*. Edited and Translated by Michael Howard and Peter Paret. Princeton, NJ, Princeton University Press, 1976. Pg. 117.

[3] Ibid.

[4] Pipes, Daniel. "*None Dare Call It Treason*...25 Years Later." Review of *None Dare Call It Treason* by John A. Stormer. <u>Orbis</u> Spring 1991. Web.<<u>http://www.danielpipes.org/526/none-dare-call-it-treason-25-years-later</u>>.

[5] Murray, Williamson. "Winston Churchill's Prewar Effort to Increase Military Spending." *History Net* 12 June 2016 <<u>http://www.historynet.com/winston-churchills-prewar-effort-to-increase-military-spending.htm</u>>.

[6] The inability to see evil and accept evil is profoundly relevant to today's Radical Islam. From the article:

> Conquest dedicated his later years at Stanford's Hoover Institution to plumbing delusion, which he defined as "massive reality denial," or why Russia had so many apologists and sympathizers. He blamed the persistence of destructive beliefs on the bottomless human capacity for self-deception...Conquest added that the lessons of the bloody 20th century "have not yet been learned, or not adequately so." Many today across the world still offer solace to dictators and mass murderers for various reasons, so Conquest's insights into human deception remain and will always be relevant.

Editorial. "The Triumph of Robert Conquest." *The Wall Street Journal* 5 Aug. 2015. Web. <<u>http://www.wsj.com/articles/the-triumph-of-robert-conquest-1438814435</u>>.

[7] Spencer, Robert. *Jihad Watch*. Free Speech Defense, 2016. Web. <<u>www.jihadwatch.org</u>>

[8] Ibrahim, Raymond. *Raymond Ibrahim*. Free Speech Defense, 2016. Web. <<u>www.raymondibrahim.com</u>>

[9] Contributor. *The Heritage Foundation*. The Heritage Foundation, 2016. Web. <<u>www.heritage.org</u>>.

[10] Horowitz, David. *The David Horowitz Freedom Center.* Nation Builder, 2016. Web. <<u>www.horowitzfreedomcenter.org</u>>.

[11] Kasperowicz, Pete. *The Blaze.* The Blaze, 2016. Web.

.

[12] The Answering Islam Team. *Answering Islam.* Answering Islam, Web. <www.answering-islam.org>

[13] Intrater, Asher. *Revive Israel.* Tikkun International, 2015. Web. <www.reviveisrael.org>.

[14] Wood, Graeme. "What ISIS Really Wants." *The Atlantic.* Mar. 2015. Web. <http://www.theatlantic.com/features/archive/2015/02/what-isis-really-wants/384980/>

Chapter 7
Exposing Satan's Plans in Islam

[1] Asher Intrater is the founder of Revive Israel. <http://reviveisrael.org/>.

[2] Intrater, Asher. *Who Ate Lunch with Abraham: The Appearances of God in the Form of a Man in the Hebrew Scriptures.* Frederick, MD: Revive Israel Media, 2011. Pg. 21. <www.reviveisrael.org>.

[3] Garrison, David. *"A Wind in the House of Islam: How God is Drawing Muslims around the World to Faith in Jesus Christ.* Monument, CO: WIGTake Resources LLC, 2014.

[4] **Acts 4:11-12** "This Jesus is the stone that was rejected by you, the builders, that has become the cornerstone. **12** And there is salvation in no one else, for there is no other name under heaven given among people by which we must be saved."

[5] Silas. "The Punishment for Apostasy from Islam." *Answering Islam: A Christian-Muslim Dialogue* 24 Jan. 2007. Web. <http://www.answering-islam.org/Silas/apostasy.htm>.

[6] In this article there is an excellent discussion of the nature of the Caliphate: Wood, "What ISIS Really Wants," *The Atlantic* <http://www.theatlantic.com/features/archive/2015/02/what-isis-really-wants/384980/>.

[7] A law enforcement bulletin obtained by FoxNews.com warned that

Islamic State fighters have increased calls for "lone wolves" to attack U.S. soldiers in America in recent months, citing one tweet that called for jihadists to find service members' addresses online and then "show up and slaughter them."

Winter, Jana. "Law Enforcement Bulletin Warned of ISIS Urging Jihad Attacks on US Soil." *Fox News* 18 Sep. 2014. Web. <http://www.foxnews.com/world/2014/09/17/law-enforcement-bulletin-warned-isis-urging-jihad-attacks-on-us-soil/>.

[8] Segall, Michael, & Joshua Teitelbaum. *The Iranian Leadership's Continuing Declarations of Intent to Destroy Israel 2009-2012.* Jerusalem: Jerusalem Center for Public Affairs, המרכז הירושלמי לענייני ציבור ומדינה (ע"ר), ©2012. <http://jcpa.org/wp-content/uploads/2012/05/IransIntent2012b.pdf>.

[9] Franklin, Lawrence A. "Iran's Quds Day: Death to America, Death to Israel." *Gatestone Institute International Policy Council.* Gatestone Institute, 14 Jul. 2015. Web. <http://www.gatestoneinstitute.org/6160/iran-quds-day-death-america-israel>.

[10] Shoebat, Walid. "ISIS Sends Out This Message To All Christians: 'You Will Soon See An Ocean Of Blood For All The Nations Of The Cross.'" *The Shoebat Foundation.* The Shoebat Foundation, 15 Feb 2015. Web. <http://shoebat.com/2015/02/15/isis-sends-message-christians-will-soon-see-ocean-blood-nation-cross/>.

[11] Beck, Glenn. "New ISIS Video Lays Out End Times War Plan, Rich with Symbolism." *Glenn Beck.* Glenn Beck, 29 Nov. 2015. Web. <http://www.glennbeck.com/2015/11/29/new-isis-video-lays-out-end-times-war-plan-rich-with-symbolism/>.

[12] Ibid.

[13] Rosenberg, Joel C. "What is Apocalyptic Islam, and Why is it So Dangerous? The Research Behind My Remarks to the Jerusalem Leaders Summit." *Joel C. Rosenberg's Blog.* Joel C. Rosenberg, 5 Nov. 2015. Web. <https://flashtrafficblog.wordpress.com/

2015/11/05/what-is-apocalyptic-islam-and-why-is-it-so-dangerous-the-research-behind-my-remarks-to-the-jerusalem-leaders-summit/>.

[14] Wood, "What ISIS Really Wants,"
<http://www.theatlantic.com/features/archive/2015/02/what-isis-really-wants/384980/>.

[15] The Jerusalem Leaders Summit took place November 3-4, 2015, at the Inbal Jerusalem Hotel, Jerusalem, Israel.
<http://jerusalemleaderssummit.org/>.

[16] Rosenberg, "What is Apocalyptic Islam, and Why is it So Dangerous?"
<https://flashtrafficblog.wordpress.com/2015/11/05/what-is-apocalyptic-islam-and-why-is-it-so-dangerous-the-research-behind-my-remarks-to-the-jerusalem-leaders-summit/>.

Chapter 8
Confirming Satan's Four Schemes

[1] For more systematic teaching on this important topic that provides the basis of discernment, see the following: The Dunamis Project Manual 5, *In the Spirit's Power: Cooperating with the Holy Spirit*, Chapter 5.
Long, Zeb Bradford. *In the Spirit's Power: Cooperating with the Holy Spirit*. Ed. Cindy Strickler. Black Mountain, NC: Presbyterian-Reformed Ministries International, Black Mountain NC, 2006.

[2] Mills, DiAnn, & Abraham Nhial. *Lost Boy No More: A True Story of Survival and Salvation*. Nashville, TN, B&K Publishing Group, 2004. Pg. 83-85.

[3] Morey, Robert A. *The Islamic Invasion: Confronting the World's Fastest Growing Religion*. Eugene, OR: Harvest House Publishers, 1992. Pg. 152-153.

[4] Durie, Mark. "Isa, the Muslim Jesus." *Answering Islam: A Christian-Muslim Dialogue*. Answering Islam. Web. <http://www.answering-islam.org/authors/durie/islamic_jesus.html>.

[5] Ibid.

6 These are listed as the thirty-point program for the "National Reich Church".

Shirer, William L. *The Rise and Fall of the Third Reich: A History of Nazi Germany*. New York: Simon and Schuster, 1960. Pg. 240.

7 Otis, George Jr. *The Last of the Giants: Lifting the Veil on Islam and the End Times*. Grand Rapids, MI: Chosen Books, Baker Book House Co., 1991. Pg. 214-215.

8 Just to name a few resources on the role of Islam at the End Times:

Tom. "Tag: Islam Matches All Biblical Criteria for the End Times Beast Empire, The Antichrist: Part I." *Always Proven True: Biblical Accuracy*. Tom, 9 Sep. 2012. Web. <http://alwaysproventrue.com/tag/islam-matches-all-biblical-criteria-for-the-end-times-beast-empire/>.

9 Gingrich, Newt, & Callista Gingrich. *America at Risk*. Citizens United Productions, 2010. Web. <http://www.americaatrisk.com/>.

10 Santorum, "The Gathering Storm." *The National Review* <http://www.nationalreview.com/article/219058/gathering-storm-nro-primary-document>.

11 Team B II. *Shariah the Threat*. Center for Security Policy. Web. 27 May 2016. <www.shariahthethreat.org>.

12 Bolte, Kim. "Obsession: Radical Islam's War Against the West (2007)." Online video clip. *YouTube*. YouTube, 8 Jun. 2011. Web. < https://www.youtube.com/watch?v=-t2gzOCSHRk>.

13 Davis, Gregory M. & Bryan Daly. *Islam: What the West Needs to Know*. Quixotic Media, LLC, 2007. Web. <http://www.whatthewestneedstoknow.com/>.

14 Jewish Pulse Radio. "FITNA – Geert Wilders' Unedited Film." Online video clip. *Vimeo*. Vimeo, 6 Mar. 2011. Web. <https://vimeo.com/20710133>.

15 Rosenberg, Joel C. "Fact Sheet: The Islamic State's Apocalyptic Beliefs." *Tyndale Websites*. Joel C. Rosenberg, 4 Sep. 2015. Web.

<http://sites.tyndale.com/joelrosenberg/files/2015/09/RESEARCH-ApocalypticBeliefs-ISIS.pdf>.

[16] Wikipedia contributors. "Fatawā of Osama bin Laden." *Wikipedia, The Free Encyclopedia*. Wikipedia, The Free Encyclopedia, 6 Mar. 2016. Web. <https://en.wikipedia.org/wiki/Fataw%C4%81_of_Osama_bin_Laden>.

[17] Lieberman, Joseph. "A Global War on Radical Islam." *The Wall Street Journal* 12 Jan. 2015. Web. <http://www.wsj.com/articles/joseph-lieberman-a-global-war-on-radical-islam-1421106699>.

[18] I recommend the following for understanding the history:

Hanson, Victor Davis. *Carnage and Culture*. New York: Anchor Books, Random House, Inc., 2001. (For understanding how Islam's advance into the West was defeated read the chapters on Poitiers, October 11, 732 and Lepanto, October 7, 1571.)

Stark, Rodney. *God's Battalions: The Case for the Crusades*. New York: HarperCollins Publishers, 2009.

Spencer, Robert. *The Politically Incorrect Guide to Islam (And the Crusades)*. Washington, DC: Regnery Publishing, Inc., 2005.

Werfel, Franz. *The Forty Days of Musa Dagh*. New York: The Modern Library, Random House, Inc., 1934. (This is an historical novel about the Armenian Genocide perpetrated by the Ottoman Turks.)

   For the present facts go to:

Steyn, Mark. *America Alone: The End of the World as we Know It*. Washington, DC: Regnery Publishing, Inc., 2006.

Ibrahim, *Crucified Again: Exposing Islam's New War on Christians*.

[19] Reilly, Robert R. "Exterminating Christians in the Middle East." *The Wall Street Journal* 20 Aug. 2015. Web. <http://www.wsj.com/articles/exterminating-christians-in-the-middle-east-1440112782>.

[20] Netanyahu, Benjamin. "Netanyahu to Congress: 'We Are Better Off'

Without the Emerging US Deal with Iran'." *The National Journal* 3
Mar. 2015. Web. <http://www.nationaljournal.com/congress/here-
s-what-benjamin-netanyahu-wants-congress-to-know-20150303>.

Chapter 9
The Gathering of the Archons

[1] Calvin, John. *Institutes of the Christian Religion*. Edited by John T.
McNeill, Translated by Ford Lewis Battles. London: The Westminster
Press, 1960. Pg. 171-172

[2] See the PRMI Dunamis Project, Unit # 5, *Equipping for Spiritual Warfare
and Kingdom Advancement*. I have also done a number of online courses
and videos on the topic. Check out the web pages <www.prmi.org> and
<www.dunamisinstitite.org>.
Long, *The Dunamis Project: Equipping for Spiritual Warfare and Kingdom
Advancement,* pg. 325.

[3] Ibid. Pg. 325.

[4] Αρχας

[5] Κοσμοκρατορας

[6] Otis, *The Last of the Giants: Lifting the Veil on Islam and the End Times,*
pg. 212-213.

[7] "The Shahada--لا إله إلا الله محمد رسول الله lā 'ilāha 'illā-llāh, muḥammadur-
rasūlu-llāh There is no god but God. Muhammad is the messenger of
God."
Wikipedia contributors. "Shahada." *Wikipedia, The Free Encyclopedia.*
Wikipedia, The Free Encyclopedia, 13 Apr. 2016. Web.
<https://cn.wikipedia.org/wiki/Shahada>.

[8] There are, of course, other strongholds in the world where the archon
Gog is gaining power and influence, as in North Korea, China and Russia.
There is also evidence of this demon gaining power wherever socialism
(collectivism) takes hold and moves toward totalitarian government.
This is presently happening in the USA with the coercion to conformity

of the left's moral and political agenda. See *The Road to Serfdom* by F.A Hayek as warnings of liberalism's tendency toward tyranny.

[9] The Islamic version of Jesus Christ, however, is completely opposed to the true Jesus Christ as revealed to us in the Bible and the universal creeds of the Church. Indeed, the Islamic Jesus Christ is actually the anti-Christ revealed in the Bible. See http://www.answering-islam.org/Authors/JR/Future/ch06_the_muslim_jesus.htm for evidence of this.

Richardson, Joel. *Will Islam be Our Future? A Study of Biblical and Islamic Eschatology*. Answering Islam: A Christian-Muslim Dialogue: Copyright held by Joel Richardson. Web. <http://www.answering-islam.org/Authors/JR/Future/ch06_the_muslim_jesus.htm>.

[10] McCants, quoting from the *Hadith Sunan Abi Dawud,* uses the term "God." In the original it is Allah. From our biblical understanding, the God of Judaism and Christianity as revealed in the Bible is not the same god as Allah revealed in the Quran and the Hadith. So anytime Muslims say the name of their deity, we need to use their own name: Allah.

McCants, William. *The ISIS Apocalypse: The History, Strategy, And Doomsday Vision of the Islamic State*. New York: St. Martin's Press, 2015.

[11] Ibid. Pg. 175.

[12] For penetrating discernment of the apocalyptic vision that is driving ISIS, see the article in *The Atlantic*, "What ISIS Really Wants:" The Islamic State is no mere collection of psychopaths. It is a religious group with carefully considered beliefs, among them that it is a key agent of the coming apocalypse. Here's what that means for its strategy—and for how to stop it." This is what many—such as Robert Spenser of Jihad Watch—have been saying all along. This article has gotten attention because it was published in *The Atlantic*.

Wood, "What ISIS Really Wants," <http://www.theatlantic.com/features/archive/2015/02/what-isis-really-wants/384980/>.

13 Hillman, Os. *Seven Cultural Mountains.* Marketplace Leaders Ministries, 2007. Web. <http://www.7culturalmountains.org/>.

14 In this prayer strategy there is not the space to build our argument for the existence or nature of the demonic stronghold of liberal progressivism nor to confirm its collusion with the stronghold of Radical Islam from within Western culture and especially from within the church. However, I am convinced from all the evidence that this stronghold does exist and that Satan is actively working through it to destroy the Judeo-Christian basis of Western cultural and political institutions that sustain our liberty and freedoms. This stronghold is also very much at work within the mainline protestant denominations in Canada, the UK, and the USA, removing the authority of the Bible as the Word of God and Jesus Christ as the only way of salvation, and thus destroying the Church of Jesus Christ from within. Satan's plans—which are rapidly coming to fruition in Europe—are to remove the Church as the only bulwark against both the spiritual and political tyranny of Islam, and to nullify the reaction against Islam by some form of fascism.

Chapter 10
How Satan Works On Earth

1 I am using this example of the Taliban attack on fellow Muslims because it demonstrates the true nature of Radical Islam free from the smoke screen of the Palestinian-Israeli conflict.

2 Dawar, Safdar, Qasim Nauman, & Saeed Shah. "Taliban Militants Attack Pakistan School." *The Wall Street Journal* 17 Dec. 2014. Web. <http://www.wsj.com/articles/taliban-militants-attack-pakistan-school-1418716418?KEYWORDS=Taliban+Massacre+Students>.

3 "Allahu akbar (Arabic: الله أكبر) is an Islamic phrase, called Takbir in Arabic, meaning 'God is greater' or 'God is [the] greatest'".

Wikipedia contributors. "Allahu Akbar (disambiguation)." *Wikipedia, The Free Encyclopedia.* Wikipedia, The Free Encyclopedia, 27 Dec. 2015. Web.

Notes

<http://en.wikipedia.org/wiki/Allahu_Akbar_%28disambiguation%29>.

[4] Dawar, Qasim, & Saeed, "Taliban Militants Attack Pakistan School," <http://www.wsj.com/articles/taliban-militants-attack-pakistan-school-1418716418?KEYWORDS=Taliban+Massacre+Students>.

[5] Birrell, Ian, Steph Cockroft, Imtiaz Hussain, Aamir Iqbal, Aoun Sahi, & Thornhill, Ted. "Was Pakistan School Massacre in Revenge for Malala's Nobel Prize? Children forced to watch their teacher being burned alive as Taliban murder 132 children." *MailOnline* 16 Dec. 2014. Web. <http://www.dailymail.co.uk/news/article-2875729/Up-20-dead-500-children-teachers-taken-hostage-Taliban-gunmen-storm-military-run-school-Pakistan.html>.

[6] Spencer, Robert. "The Real Meaning of 'Allahu Akbar'." *Jihad Watch* 7 Jan. 2011. Web. <http://www.jihadwatch.org/2011/01/the-real-meaning-of-allahu-akbar>.

[7] Birrell, Cockroft, Hussain, Iqbal, Sahi, & Thornhill. "Was Pakistan School Massacre in Revenge for Malala's Nobel Prize?" <http://www.dailymail.co.uk/news/article-2875729/Up-20-dead-500-children-teachers-taken-hostage-Taliban-gunmen-storm-military-run-school-Pakistan.html>.

[8] Dawar, Qasim, & Saeed, "Taliban Militants Attack Pakistan School," <http://www.wsj.com/articles/taliban-militants-attack-pakistan-school-1418716418?KEYWORDS=Taliban+Massacre+Students>.

[9] CNN Wires. "Nobel Laureate Wiesel: Hamas Must Stop Using Children as Human Shields." *Fox2 Now*, 3 Aug. 2014. Web. <http://fox2now.com/2014/08/03/nobel-laureate-wiesel-hamas-must-stop-using-children-as-human-shields/>.

[10] "Moloch, also known as Molech, Molekh, Molok, Molek, Melek, Molock, Moloc, Melech, Milcom, or Molcom."
Wikipedia contributors. "Moloch." *Wikipedia, The Free Encyclopedia.* Wikipedia, The Free Encyclopedia, 28 Mar. 2016. Web.

<(https://en.wikipedia.org/wiki/Moloch>.

For Biblical references with these various names, see Leviticus 18:21, 1 Kings 11:33, Zephaniah 1:5, Amos 5:26, and Acts 7:43. It is my contention, which we shall return to later, that in the demonic stronghold of Radical Islam, the same four high level demonic powers have joined forces that were also present in the 1930s and 1940s in the building of Nazism.

11 The Pakistani Taliban, formed in 2007, is closely linked to al Qaeda. It was inspired by the Afghan Taliban and pays homage to that group's leader Mullah Muhammad Omar as its spiritual leader. Both groups often use the same sanctuaries on both sides of the Afghan-Pakistan border, but the Pakistani Taliban operates independently.

Dawar, Qasim, & Saeed, "Taliban Militants Attack Pakistan School," <http://www.wsj.com/articles/taliban-militants-attack-pakistan-school-1418716418?KEYWORDS=Taliban+Massacre+Students>.

12 Staff Writer. "Pakistani Taliban Vow Support for ISIS Fighters." *Al Arabiya News English*. 5 Oct. 2014. Web. <http://english.alarabiya.net/en/News/middle-east/2014/10/05/Pakistan-Taliban-pledges-support-to-ISIS-.html>.

Chapter 11
Forming the Core of the Stronghold
Satan's Deception of the Visionary Leader

1 NET Bible note on 2 Corinthians 10:4: "Ultimately, Paul is referring here to the false arguments of his opponents, calling them figuratively 'strongholds'. This Greek word (ὀχύρωμα, ochurōma) is used only here in the NT."

The Holy Bible, New English Translation. <http://netbible.com/>.

2 This is well documented in Russell Kirk's book, The *Roots of American Order,* and in David Barton's work in Wall Builders such as his video series entitled "America's Godly Heritage".

Kirk, Russell. *The Roots of American Order.* Wilmington, DE: ISI Books, 2003.

Notes

Curtis, Linda. "America's Godly Heritage Series". Online video clip. *YouTube*. YouTube, 3-4 Jul. 2011. Web. <https://www.youtube.com/watch?v=pme3o0WimkU&list=PL9A80 02C80FA935C5&index=1>.

3 United States. Office of the Press Secretary. "Islam is Peace, Says President." Pres. George W. Bush. 17 Sep. 2001. <http://georgewbush-whitehouse.archives.gov/news/releases/2001/09/20010917-11.html>.

4 Qureshi, Nabeel. *Seeking Allah, Finding Jesus: A Devout Muslim Encounters Christianity*. Grand Rapids, MI: Zondervan, 2014.

5 Wikipedia contributors. "Mirza Ghulam Ahmad." *Wikipedia, The Free Encyclopedia*. Wikipedia, The Free Encyclopedia, 13 Apr. 2016. Web. <https://en.wikipedia.org/wiki/Mirza_Ghulam_Ahmad>.

6   Some years later, a prominent Muslim leader and scholar, Ahmed Raza Khan, was to travel to the Hejaz to collect the opinions of the religious scholars of Mecca and Medina. He compiled these opinions in his work *Hussam ul Harmain (The sword of two sanctuaries on the slaughter-point of blasphemy and falsehood)*; in it, Ghulam Ahmad was again labeled an apostate. The unanimous consensus of about thirty-four religious scholars was that Ghulam Ahmad's beliefs were blasphemous and tantamount to apostasy and that he must be punished by imprisonment and, if necessary, by execution.

Ibid.

7 BBC News. "Who are the Ahmadi?" *BBC News.co.uk*. 28 May 2010. <http://news.bbc.co.uk/2/hi/8711026.stm>.

8   Henri Bergson, in full Henri-Louis Bergson (born Oct. 18, 1859, Paris, France—died Jan. 4, 1941, Paris), French philosopher, the first to elaborate what came to be called a process philosophy, which rejected static values in favor of values of motion, change, and evolution. He was also a master literary stylist, of both academic and popular appeal, and was awarded the Nobel Prize for Literature in

1927.

"Henri Bergson". *Encyclopedia Britannica. Encyclopedia Britannica Online.* Encyclopedia Britannica Inc., 2016. Web. <http://www.britannica.com/biography/Henri-Bergson>.

A personal note about Bergson: His work has been profoundly important for me as I have struggled to understand the dynamic of how human beings have been enabled to shape reality by having been called as co-creators with God. Bergson had a profound influence on the American psychologist William James who for me practically explained the ideas of the role of the mystic creator in his great book, *Varieties of Religious Experience.* Bergson and his philosophy were profoundly important in building the basis of our present war with Radical Islam which has declared war on Jews, Christians, and Western culture. That Bergson who is Jewish is a co-warrior with us in our present battle is evidenced in his own faith and battle against Nazism. He acknowledged in his will of 1937, "My reflections have led me closer and closer to Catholicism, in which I see the complete fulfillment of Judaism." Yet, although declaring his "moral adherence to Catholicism," he never went beyond that. In explanation, he wrote: "I would have become a convert, had I not foreseen for years a formidable wave of anti-Semitism about to break upon the world. I wanted to remain among those who tomorrow were to be persecuted." To confirm this conviction, only a few weeks before his death, he arose from his sickbed and stood in line in order to register as a Jew, in accord with the law just imposed by the Vichy government and from which he refused the exemption that had been offered him. (http://www.britannica.com/biography/Henri-Bergson)

[9] Toynbee, Arnold J. *A Study of History*, Abridgement of Volumes I-VI by D.C. Somervell. New York: Oxford University Press, 1947. Pg. 212-213.

[10] Long, Zeb Bradford. *Passage Through the Wilderness: A Journey of the Soul.* Grand Rapids, MI: Chosen Books, 1998.

Long, Brad, & Doug McMurry. *Prayer That Shapes the Future: How to*

Pray with Power and Authority. Grand Rapids, MI: Zondervan, 1999.

[11] All that follows about the life of Muhammad is based upon Islamic sources themselves. Regardless of whether these are reports of actual facts or myths created by others, they point to the working of Satan in implanting his deceptions which provide the heart of powerful strongholds for attacking the Church of Jesus Christ.

Frankly, after a review of Robert Spencer's book *Did Mohammad Exist? And Inquiry into Islam's Obscure Origins (ISI Books 2012)* I have to wonder if there is much historical basis at all in these stories of Muhammad that were told many decades and in some cases hundreds of years after he was supposed to have lived. The process of the formation of the Quran as well as of the Hadith lends itself to both human distortions as well as demonic deception.

[12] Ibn Ishaq, Sira. *The Life of Muhammad*. Trans. A. Guillaume. Oxford: Oxford University Press, 1955. Pg. 106.

[13] This *Life of Muhammad* is especially helpful in providing insight into the beginnings of Islam. The thesis of the book is given as follows:

> The book thus presents in English "The Life of Muhammad." Professor Guillaume's translation of the *Sira of Ibn Ishaq* is now reissued. The translator used Ibn Hisham's abridgement and also included many additions and variants found in the writings of early authors. The book thus presents in English practically all that is known of the life of the Prophet.
> <http://ukcatalogue.oup.com/product/9780196360331.do>.

Ibid.

[14] Gairdner, W.H.T. *The Reproach of Islam*. 4th ed. London: Young People's Missionary Movement (Foreign Mission Committee of the Church of Scotland), 1911. Pg. 158. <http://www.answeringislam.org/Authors/JR/Future/ch11_the_dark_nature.htm>.

[15] Ibn Ishaq, *The Life of Muhammad*, pg. 105-107.

[16] Ibid. Pg. 106.

[17] Al-Bukhari, Muhammad. *The Translation of the Meanings of Sahih Al Bukhari Arabic English*. Trans. Muhammad Muhsin Khan. Vol. 6. Cairo: Press of Mustafa Al-Babi Al-Halabi, 1959. Book 60, Number 478. <http://www.answering-islam.org/Authors/JR/Future/ch11_the_dark_nature.htm>.

[18] "Yet they turn away from him and say: 'Tutored (by others), a man possessed!'" - **Surah 44:14 (Yusuf Ali)**

"And say: 'What! Shall we give up our gods for the sake of a poet possessed?'" - **Surah 37:36 (Yusuf Ali)**

Apparently it was even necessary that Allah come to Muhammad's defense and respond to his critics within the Quran itself:

"No, your compatriot [Muhammad] is not mad. He saw him [Gabriel] on the clear horizon. He does not grudge the secrets of the unseen, nor is this the utterance of an accursed devil." - **Surah 81:22-25**

"It [the Quran] is no poet's speech: scant is your faith! It is no soothsayer's divination: how little you reflect! It is revelation from the Lord of the Universe." - **Surah 69:41, 42**

Al-Bukhari, *The Translation of the Meanings of Sahih Al Bukhari Arabic English*, Vol. 7, Book 71, Number 660. <http://www.answering-islam.org/Authors/JR/Future/ch11_the_dark_nature.htm>.

[19] Ibid.

[20] Ibid.

[21] Ibn Ishaq, *The Life of Muhammad*, pg. 107.

[22] Ibid. Pg. 107.

[23] Ibid. Pg. 107.

[24] Long & McMurry, *Prayer That Shapes the Future: How to Pray with Power and Authority*, pg. 49-50.

[25] Silas. "The Pagan Sources of Islam." *Answering Islam: A Christian-Muslim Dialogue*. Answering Islam. Web. <http://www.answering-islam.org/Silas/pagansources.htm>.

[26] Ibn Ishaq, *The Life of Muhammad*, pg. 107.

Notes

[27] For documentation and evidence of rituals and practices of Islam that provide the means for continued demonization for all who practice them see:

Otis, *The Last of the Giants: Lifting the Veil on Islam and the End Times*, pg. 62-67.

Otis Jr., George. *The Twilight Labyrinth: Why Does Spiritual Darkness Linger Where It Does?* Grand Rapids, MI: Chosen Books, 1997. Pg. 202, 207, 221-222.

[28] Otis, *The Twilight Labyrinth: Why Does Spiritual Darkness Linger Where It Does?* Pg. 218.

[29] Katz, Jochen. "Answering Islam and the 'Allah is a pre-islamic moon-god' hypothesis." *Answering Islam.* Answering Islam, 2 Nov. 2006. Web. <http://www.answering-islam.org/Responses/Saifullah/moonotheism.htm>.

[30] Shamoun, Sam. "Is Allah the God of the Bible?" *Answering Islam.* Answering Islam, Web. <http://www.answering-islam.org/Shamoun/god.htm>.

[31] Otis, *The Twilight Labyrinth: Why Does Spiritual Darkness Linger Where It Does?* Pg. 221.

[32] Durie, "Isa, the Muslim Jesus." <http://www.answering-islam.org/authors/durie/islamic_jesus.html>.

[33] FunkensteinJr. "George W. Bush Predicts ISIS in 2007." Online Video Clip. *YouTube.* YouTube, 5 Sept. 2014. Web. <https://www.youtube.com/watch?v=84ukJlcpqEY>.

Homeland Security. "Bush in 2007 Delivered Eerily Accurate Warning about Iraq Unrest." *Fox News.* 11 Sept. 2014. Web. <http://www.foxnews.com/politics/2014/09/11/bush-in-2007-delivered-eerily-accurate-warning-about-iraq-unrest.html>.

Paulin, David. "George Bush's Prediction of the Iraq Meltdown." *Frontpage Magazine.* 19 June, 2014. <http://www.frontpagemag.com/fpm/234365/george-bushs-prediction-iraq-meltdown-david-paulin>.

Chapter 12
Forming the Core of the Stronghold
The Creative Minority

[1] I have written about this process in the book I coauthored with Doug McMurry entitled, *Prayer That Shapes the Future.*
Long & McMurry, *Prayer That Shapes the Future: How to Pray with Power and Authority.*

[2] 2 Corinthians 10:4 (NET).

[3] For a more complete explanation of how these mental structures are formed and the process of demonization, see *Let Jesus Heal Your Hidden Wounds: Cooperating with the Holy Spirit in Healing Ministry* by Brad Long and Cindy Strickler. Chapters 11 through 15 provide the theoretical basis for the formation of "vortex memories" and how these allow for evil spirits to enter into and control a person.
Long, Brad, & Cindy Strickler. *Let Jesus Heal Your Hidden Wounds: Cooperating with the Holy Spirit in Healing Ministry.* Grand Rapids, MI: Chosen Books, 2001.

[4] I get the term "creative minority" from Toynbee's *A Study of History* (pg. 214-215). According to Toynbee they play a role similar to the mystic in enabling the growth of a civilization.
Toynbee, *A Study of History.*

[5] The biblical term for such an organization is an "exousia" (*Strong's Concordance*, ἐξουσία, 1849.) The definition of exousia is (a) power, authority, weight, especially: moral authority, influence, (b) in a quasi-personal sense, derived from later Judaism, of a spiritual power, and hence of an earthly power.
Strong, James. "Exousia." *Strong's Exhaustive Concordance.*
StudyBible.info. Web. 20 Apr. 2016.
<http://studybible.info/strongs/G1849>.
This is used to describe the authority that an individual may exercise in

order to fulfill his role as a witness to Jesus Christ. For example, "Jesus called the twelve and began to send them out two by two. He gave them authority over the unclean spirits." **(Mark 6:7)** This authority is exousia. Here, however, I am using the term in the way that St. Paul does to define a demonic organization that has authority. These references are as follows:

Ephesians 2:2 describes the "ruler of the kingdom [exousia] of the air, the spirit who is now at work in those who are disobedient."

Ephesians 3:10–11 says, "[God's] intent was that now, through the church, the manifold wisdom of God should be made known to the rulers and authorities in the heavenly realms, according to his eternal purpose that he accomplished in Christ Jesus our Lord." (The church of Jesus Christ is also an "exousia" in that it has authority and power which is greater than Satan's exousia.)

Ephesians 6:12 tells us that we struggle against those powers or authorities. That is why God also has given us spiritual armor for the battle so that we can be strong in the Lord and His mighty power.

Colossians 1:13–14 encourages, "For he has rescued us from the dominion [exousia] of darkness and brought us into the kingdom of the Son he loves, in whom we have redemption, the forgiveness of sins."

Colossians 2:15 tells us that Christ has "disarmed the powers and authorities [exousia]" and "made a public spectacle of them, triumphing over them by the cross." We battle a defeated foe because we serve the One who has authority over all. (See also 1 Corinthians 15:20–28 and 1 Peter 3:21b–22.)

In this study I found the entry http://www.gotquestions.org/exousia-meaning.html to be most helpful for defining the various biblical usages of *exousia*.

"What is the Meaning of Exousia in the Bible?" *Got Questions.* Got Questions Ministries, Web. 20 Apr. 2016. <http://www.gotquestions.org/exousia-meaning.html>.

[6] This is the baptism with the Holy Spirit which Jesus promises his

disciples in Acts 1:4-8.

[7] This term is from Eric Hoffer's 1951 book *The True Believer: Thoughts on the Nature of Mass Movements.*

Hoffer, Eric. *The True Believer: Thoughts on the Nature of Mass Movements.* New York: Harper & Row, 1951.

[8] I have been profoundly helped in understanding this complex process of the formation of strongholds that are intermingled spiritual and human realities by the two following sources:

a. Berger, Peter L., & Thomas Luckmann. *The Social Construction of Reality: A Treatise in the Sociology of Knowledge.* Garden City, NY: Doubleday & Company, 1966.

Section II, "Society as Objective Reality", elucidates the principles of how a social structure such as the Islamic State with its own social and spiritual reality may be formed.

b. Toynbee, *A Study of History*, pg. 214-230.

Toynbee explains the role of the mystic with a vision of reality. He gives a number of examples which include both Jesus and Muhammad. He also includes Machiavelli so that we may see that "mystic" is not just a matter of religious experience. He notes that an essential aspect for visionaries who shape reality whether political or religious is the dynamic of withdrawal when they receive the vision and then return to implement it.

[9] In the history of any movement for good or for evil, this dynamic is at work. An instance is the withdrawal of George Washington and his army after a series of defeats to Valley Forge in the harsh winter of 1777-78. This was a time of terrible refinement of the army that gave them the resolve and the cohesion to return to the engagement to turn defeat into victory. The same dynamic was at work in the formation of a stronghold of great evil: the "Long March" of 1934-35 made by Communist Chinese forces that led to Mao Zedong coming to power. History is replete with such examples.

[10] Toynbee, *A Study of History*, pg. 227.

Notes

[11] Ibid. Pg. 228.

[12] The term aṣ-ṣaḥābah (Arabic: الصحابة meaning "the companions", from the verb صَحِبَ meaning "accompany", "keep company with", "associate with") refers to the companions, disciples, scribes and family of the Islamic prophet Muhammad. This form is definite plural; the indefinite singular is masculine sahabi (ṣaḥābī), feminine sahabia (ṣaḥābīyah).

Later scholars accepted their testimony of the words and deeds of Muhammad, the occasions on which the Quran was revealed and various important matters of Islamic history and practice. The testimony of the companions, as it was passed down through chains of trusted narrators (isnads) was the basis of the developing Islamic tradition. From the traditions (hadith) of the life of Muhammad and his companions are drawn the Muslim way of life (sunnah), the code of conduct (sharia) it requires, and the jurisprudence (fiqh) by which Muslim communities should be regulated. The two largest Islamic denominations, the Sunni and Shia, take different approaches in weighing the value of the companions' testimony, have different hadith collections and, as a result, have different views about the Sahabah.

Wikipedia contributors. "Sahabah." *Wikipedia, The Free Encyclopedia.* Wikipedia, The Free Encyclopedia, 18 Apr. 2016. Web. <https://en.wikipedia.org/wiki/Sahabah>.

[13] "The Life of Muhammad: An Inconvenient Truth." *The Religion of Peace.* The Religion of Peace. Web. <http://www.thereligionofpeace.com/pages/history.htm>.

"The Myths of Muhammad." *The Religion of Peace.* The Religion of Peace. Web <http://www.thereligionofpeace.com/pages/muhammad/index.aspx>.

[14] Silas. "The Verse of the Sword: Surah 9:5 and Jihad." *Answering Islam: A Christian-Muslim Dialogue.* Answering Islam. Web.

<http://www.answering-islam.org/Silas/swordverse.htm>.

15 Fatoohi, Louay. "Myths About 'The Verse of the Sword.'" *Qur'anic Studies*. Qur'anic Studies, 23 Mar. 2014. Web. <http://www.quranicstudies.com/law/myths-about-the-verse-of-the-sword/>.

16 Kessler, Glenn. "Spinning Obama's Reference to Islamic State as a 'JV Team.'" *The Washington Post* 3 Sept. 2014. Web. <http://www.washingtonpost.com/blogs/fact-checker/wp/2014/09/03/spinning-obamas-reference-to-isis-as-a-jv-team/>.

17 Bartiromo, Maria. "'Every Day We Wait, They Grow Stronger': McKeon Calls for More Aggressive Action Against ISIS." *Fox News*. 14 Sept. 2014. Web. <http://insider.foxnews.com/2014/09/14/every-day-we-wait-they-grow-stronger-mckeon-calls-more-aggressive-action-against-isis>.

18 McCants, *The ISIS Apocalypse: The History, Strategy, and Doomsday Vision of the Islamic State*, pg. 174.

19 Tran, Mark, & Matthew Weaver. "Isis Announces Islamic Caliphate in Area Straddling Iraq and Syria." *The Guardian*. 30 June 2014. Web. <http://www.theguardian.com/world/2014/jun/30/isis-announces-islamic-caliphate-iraq-syria>.

Chapter 13
The Means Chosen to Implement the Vision

1 Hall, Anna. "Time for Acknowledgement: Christian-Run Native Boarding Schools Left Legacy of Destruction." *Sojourners* 16 Dec. 2013. Web. <https://sojo.net/articles/time-acknowledgement-christian-run-native-american-boarding-schools-left-legacy-destruction>.

2 Wikipedia contributors. "Martin Luther and antisemitism." *Wikipedia, The Free Encyclopedia*. Wikipedia, The Free Encyclopedia, 24 Jan.

Notes

2016. Web.
   <http://en.wikipedia.org/wiki/Martin_Luther_and_antisemitism>.

3 Ibid.

4 Ibid.

5 Bainton, Roland H. *Here I Stand: A life of Martin Luther*. New York &
   Nashville: Abingdon-Cokesbury Press, 1950. Pg. 379-380.

6 Ibid. Pg. 379.

7 Shirer, *The Rise and Fall of the Third Reich: A History of Nazi Germany*,
   pg. 236.

8 Goldhagen, Daniel Jonah. *Hitler's Willing Executioners: Ordinary
   Germans and the Holocaust*. New York: Alfred a. Knopf, 1997.

Walker, Jim. "Martin Luther's Dirty Little Book: *On the Jews and Their
   Lies*." *No Beliefs.com* 20 Nov. 2005. Web.
   <http://www.nobeliefs.com/luther.htm>.

9 For a comparison of the means that Jesus Christ chose and required his
disciples to follow and those of Muhammad, I recommend reading the
articles in *Answering Islam* by James M. Arlandson, Ph.D. These present a
well-researched comparison:

Arlandson, James M. "The Mission of Muhammad and the Sword."
   Answering Islam: A Christian-Muslim Dialogue. Answering Islam 24
   July 2012. Web. <http://www.answering-
   islam.org/authors/arlandson/sword/>.

10 Ali, Ayaan Hirsi. "Why Islam Needs a Reformation." *The Wall Street
   Journal* 20 March 2015. Web. <http://www.wsj.com/articles/a-
   reformation-for-islam-1426859626>.

11 Raymond Ibraham and, I am certain, Robert Spencer would both argue
that this return to the 7th century Medina period of Islam is the Islamic
Reformation.

Ibrahim, Raymond. "Islam's 'Reformation' is Already Here—and It's
   Called 'ISIS'." *Jihad Watch*. Jihad Watch, 12 May 2015. Web.
   <https://www.jihadwatch.org/2015/05/raymond-ibrahim-islams-
   reformation-is-already-here-and-its-called-isis>.

12 Ali, "Why Islam Needs a Reformation,"
<http://www.wsj.com/articles/a-reformation-for-islam-1426859626>.

13 Lewis, Bernard. *The Crisis of Islam: Holy War and Unholy Terror*. New York: Random House Inc., 2003. Pg. 104-105.

14 The story of how Saudi Arabia is complicit in extending the fundamentalist version of Islam taught by Muhammad ibn Abd al-Wahhab is told by Dr. Sebastian Gorka in his book, *Defeating Jihad: The Winnable War.*

Gorka, Sebastian. *Defeating Jihad: The Winnable War*. Washington, DC: Regnery Publishing, 2016. Pg. 81-84.

15 Ibrahim, *Crucified Again: Exposing Islam's New War on Christians*, pg. 20.

16 Ibid. Pg. 179.

17 Ibid. Pg. 181.

18 Ibid. Pg. 182.

19 Ibid. Pg. 95.

20 Ibid. Pg. 96.

21 Ibrahim is quoting from the great Islamic scholar, Majid Khadduri and the book, *War and Peace in the Law of Islam.*
Ibid. Pg. 97.

22 Ibid. Pg. 98.

Chapter 14
Preparing to Commit Genocide
First Stream—Islam Growing a Culture of Hate

1 Al-Azhar University (ahz-har; Arabic:)الشريف(جامعة الأزهر Jāmi'at al-Azhar (al-Sharīf), IPA: [ˈɡæmˤet elˈʔazhɑɾ eʃʃæˈriːf], "the (honorable) Azhar University") is a university in Cairo, Egypt, founded in 970 or 972 by the Fatimids as a centre of Islamic learning. Its students studied the Qur'an and Islamic law in detail, along with logic,

Notes

grammar, rhetoric, and how to calculate the lunar phases of the moon. It is associated with Al-Azhar Mosque in Islamic Cairo. The university's mission includes the propagation of Islamic religion and culture. To this end, its Islamic scholars (ulamas) render edicts (fatwas) on disputes submitted to them from all over the Sunni Islamic world regarding proper conduct for Muslim individuals and societies. Al-Azhar also trains Egyptian government-appointed preachers in proselytization (da'wa).

Wikipedia contributors. "Al-Azhar University." *Wikipedia, The Free Encyclopedia*. Wikipedia, The Free Encyclopedia, 9 Apr. 2016. Web. < http://en.wikipedia.org/wiki/Al-Azhar_University>.

2   The Ministry of Awqaf of Egypt (Arabic: وزارة الأوقاف) is one of eighteen ministries in the Egyptian government and is in charge of religious endowments. Religious endowments, awqaf, are similar to common law trusts where the trustee is the mosque or individual in charge of the waqf and the beneficiary is usually the community as a whole. Examples of waqfs are of a plot of land, a market, a hospital, or any other building that would aid the community.

Wikipedia contributors. "Ministry of Awqaf (Egypt)." *Wikipedia, The Free Encyclopedia*. Wikipedia, The Free Encyclopedia, 5 Feb. 2016. Web. <http://en.wikipedia.org/wiki/Ministry_of_Awqaf_%28Egypt%29>.

3   Ulama ("Ulamā", singular عالِم 'Ālim, "scholar"), also spelled ulema, alimah (female) and "uluma", in contemporary usage by Muslims refers to the religious elite of scholars at the top of the sectarian hierarchy. They mainly specialize in fiqh (Islamic jurisprudence) and are considered the arbiters of sharia law by mainstream sects; however, their authority is not universally accepted (See Controversial Aspects).

Wikipedia contributors. "Ulama." *Wikipedia, The Free Encyclopedia*. Wikipedia, The Free Encyclopedia, 2 Apr. 2016. Web. <http://en.wikipedia.org/wiki/Ulama>.

4 Translator's word: "Note: It is unclear if in the last instance of umma Sisi

- 280 -

is referring to Egypt 'the nation' or if he is using it in the pan-Islamic sense as he did initially to refer to the entire Islamic world."

Ibrahim, Raymond. "Egypt's Sisi: Islamic 'Thinking' Is 'Antagonizing the Entire World.'" *Raymond Ibrahim*. Raymond Ibrahim, 1 Jan. 2015. Web. <http://www.raymondibrahim.com/2015/01/01/egypts-sisi-islamic-thinking-is-antagonizing-the-entire-world/>.

[5] Ibid.

[6] This was in the Saturday/Sunday, January 31-Februrary 1, 2015 issue of the Wall Street Journal by Jonathan Sacks. The print version is entitled, "Ever Again (with the N crossed out)" the Online Title is "THE SATURDAY ESSAY The Return of Anti-Semitism: Seventy years after the liberation of Auschwitz, violence and hatred against Jews is on the rise, especially in the Middle East and among Muslims in Europe."

Sacks, Jonathan. "The Return of Anti-Semitism." *The Wall Street Journal* 30 Jan. 2015. Web. <http://www.wsj.com/articles/the-return-of-anti-semitism-1422638910?KEYWORDS=Jonathan+Sacks>.

[7] Stephens, Bret. "Palestine: The Psychotic Stage: The truth about why Palestinians have been seized by their present blood lust." *The Wall Street Journal* 12 Oct. 12, 2015. Web. < 7:34 p.m. ET <http://www.wsj.com/articles/palestine-the-psychotic-stage-1444692875?alg=y>.

[8] Ibrahim, *Crucified Again: Exposing Islam's New War on Christians*, pg. 157.

Chapter 15
Preparing to Commit Genocide
Second Stream—Uniting Islamism with German Occultism

[1] Sass, Erik. "WWI Centennial:[1] The Young Turks Plot Armenian Genocide." *Mental Floss* 15 Feb. 2015. Web. <http://mentalfloss.com/article/61674/wwi-centennial-young-turks-plot-armenian-genocide>.

Notes

[2] Rubin, Barry, & Wolfgang G. Schwanitz. *Nazis, Islamists, and the Making of the Modern Middle East*. New Haven & London: Yale University Press, 2014. Pg. 24.

[3] Ibid. Pg. 12.

[4] Wikipedia contributors. "Max von Oppenheim." *Wikipedia, The Free Encyclopedia*. Wikipedia, The Free Encyclopedia, 3 Mar. 2016. Web. <https://en.wikipedia.org/wiki/Max_von_Oppenheim>.

[5] "Mehmed V". *Encyclopedia Britannica. Encyclopedia Britannica Online*. Encyclopedia Britannica Inc., 2016. Web. <http://www.britannica.com/biography/Mehmed-V>.

[6] Rubin & Schwanitz, *Nazis, Islamists, and the Making of the Modern Middle East*, pg. 13.

[7] Ibid pg. 34.

[8] Morgenthau, Henry I. *Ambassador Morgenthau's Story*. Garden City, NY: Doubleday, Page, & Co., 1918. From Online edition *Great War Primary Documents Archive* Chapter XIV. 19 Apr. 2016. <http://www.gwpda.org/wwi-www/morgenthau/Morgen14.htm>.

[9] Rubin & Schwanitz, *Nazis, Islamists, and the Making of the Modern Middle East*, pg. 36.

[10] Wikipedia contributors. "Henry Morgenthau, Sr." *Wikipedia, The Free Encyclopedia*. Wikipedia, The Free Encyclopedia, 27 Feb. 2016. Web. <https://en.wikipedia.org/wiki/Henry_Morgenthau,_Sr.>.

[11] Ibid

[12] Rubin & Schwanitz, *Nazis, Islamists, and the Making of the Modern Middle East*, pg. 53.

[13] Wikipedia contributors. "Armenian Genocide." *Wikipedia, The Free Encyclopedia*. Wikipedia, The Free Encyclopedia, 17 Apr. 2016. Web. <https://en.wikipedia.org/wiki/Armenian_Genocide>.

[14] Ibrahim, Raymond. "The Islamic Genocide of Christians: Past and Present." *Raymond Ibrahim*. Raymond Ibrahim, 26 Apr. 2015. Web. <http://www.raymondibrahim.com/muslim-persecution-of-

christians/the-islamic-genocide-of-christians-past-and-present/>.

[15] Schultz, Marisa. "ISIS Savages Behead Four Children: Christian
Leader." *The New York Post* 12 Dec. 2014. Web.
<http://nypost.com/2014/12/12/christian-leader-isis-savages-
behead-four-children/>.

[16] Zuhlsdorf, John. "Muslims are crucifying Christians who refuse to
convert to the Religion of Peace." *Fr. Z's Blog* Posted on 4 Aug. 2014.
Web. <http://wdtprs.com/blog/2014/08/muslims-are-crucifying-
christians-who-refuse-to-convert-to-the-religion-of-peace/>.

These persecutions are also definitively documented by Raymond
Ibrahim in his well-researched book, *Crucified Again: Exposing Islam's
New War on Christians.* The following pages are witness to hundreds of
modern-day examples of Christian persecution that conform perfectly to
Quran 9:29, *The Conditions of Omar*, and, in a word, to Sharia—the "way"
of Islam.
Ibrahim, *Crucified Again: Exposing Islam's New War on Christians*, pg. 30.

[17] Shirer, *The Rise and Fall of the Third Reich: A History of Nazi Germany*,
pg. 106.

[18] Rubin & Schwanitz, *Nazis, Islamists, and the Making of the Modern
Middle East*, pg. 43.

Chapter 16
Preparing to Commit Genocide
The Third Stream—al-Husseini's Link with Adolph Hitler

[1] Satan was very busy in the fertile soil of the interwar period marked by
massive social and economic change. This is the period in which the
strongholds of Stalinist Communism as well as Japanese Imperialism
were all being formed as the means of genocide and tyranny both aimed
at destroying Christians and the Church. During this time the rise of
theological liberalism in Christianity and Judaism led to a departure
from orthodox Christian and Jewish Bible/Torah based faith. This
liberalism was accompanied throughout the Western world with a surge

Notes

of occult practices and spiritualism that welcomed a demonic invasion. These movements at the end of the 20th and beginning of the 21st centuries have formed Satan's "fifth column" to destroy the Judeo-Christian faith and values foundations of the West from within. As intercessors we will be engaged with this movement, but that will require another prayer strategy.

[2] I have seen the name as al-Husseini but also as al-Husaini. When quoting a source, I have used the spelling that they used. In my own writing, I have used "al-Husseini".

[3] The meticulous search done by Barry Rubin and Wolfgang Schwanitz on the relationship between German ideology, Islam, and their connection to the Armenian Genocide, the Holocaust, and today's Jihadists provides the historical basis for the thesis of this book. This thesis is that the present day demonic stronghold of Radical Islam is Satan's means of bringing a global genocide of Jews and Christians. Without this foundation in historical facts which actually connects the dots that I had already discovered on my own, I would not have had the confirmation and confidence to go public with this discernment of Satan's terrible plans in Radical Islam.

Rubin &Schwanitz, *Nazis, Islamists, and the Making of the Modern Middle East.*

[4] Ibid. Pg. 63.

[5] Ibid. Pg. 66.

[6] Ibid. Pg. 67-68.

[7] Ibid. Pg. 91-92.

[8] Ibid. Pg. 160.

[9] Ibid. Pg. 93-94.

[10] I have been looking for an English translation of al-Husseini's appeal so I can check these facts. All that I have been able to find is "Amin al-Husaini, 'Islam-Judentum: Aufruf des Großmuftis an die islamische Welt 1937," in Muhammad Sabri, Islam-Judentum-Bolschewismus (Berlin: Juncker & Dünnhaupt, 1938).'" Pg. 22–32. This is cited by Rubin and

Schwantz.

Rubin & Schwanitz, *Nazis, Islamists, and the Making of the Modern Middle East*, pg. 63.

[11] Ibid. Pg. 94-95.

[12] Ibid. Pg. 95.

[13] Ibid. Pg. 95.

[14] "...Hajj Amin al-Husaini, who was an officer of the Ottoman Empire who participated in the Armenian genocide..."

Geller, Pamela. "Obama, Tell the Truth About the Armenian Genocide." Newsmax 8 Mar. 2010. Web. <http://www.newsmax.com/PamelaGeller/bloomberg-soda-tax-schools/2010/03/08/id/351987/>.

[15] Lutzer, Erwin W. *Hitler's Cross: The Revealing Story of How the Cross of Christ was Used as a Symbol of the Nazi Agenda.* Chicago: Moody Publishers, 1995. Pg. 67-69.

[16] John 19:33-37. (NET)

[17] Lutzer, *Hitler's Cross: The Revealing Story of How the Cross of Christ was Used as a Symbol of the Nazi Agenda*, pg. 74.

[18] Ravenscroft, Trevor. *The Spear of Destiny: The Occult Power Behind the Spear Which Pierced the Side of Christ.* York Beach, ME: Samuel Weiser, Inc., 1982. Pg. 64.

[19] Ibid. Pg. 64.

[20] Stein is one of the chief characters in Trevor Ravenscroft's books, *The Spear of Destiny* and *The Cup of Destiny*. Though Ravenscroft claimed that he had been a pupil of Stein's, investigative reporter Eric Wynants discovered the Stein/Ravenscroft connection was a complete fabrication while interviewing Ravenscroft for an article in 1982.

Wikipedia contributors. "Walter Johannes Stein." *Wikipedia, The Free Encyclopedia*. Wikipedia, The Free Encyclopedia, 15 Feb. 2016. Web. <https://en.wikipedia.org/wiki/Walter_Johannes_Stein>.

According to Wynants, Ravenscroft admitted during their interview that he had never actually met W.J. Stein, but "talked to him only via a medium."

MacMellan, Alec, *The Secret of the Spear: The Mystery of the Spear of Longinus*. London: Souvenir Press, Ltd., 2004. Pg. 116. <https://en.wikipedia.org/wiki/Walter_Johannes_Stein>.

[21] Lutzer is quoting from Hermann Rauschning's *The Voice of Destruction*. I have included the full text of Rauschning as Lutzer left out a key line about how one could confirm Hitler's hatred through his rages.

Lutzer, *Hitler's Cross: The Revealing Story of How the Cross of Christ was Used as a Symbol of the Nazi Agenda*, pg. 68.

Rauschning, Hermann. *The Voice of Destruction*. New York: G. Putnam's Sons, 1940. Pg. 262.

[22] Lutzer, *Hitler's Cross: The Revealing Story of How the Cross of Christ was Used as a Symbol of the Nazi Agenda*, pg. 68.

[23] Rubin & Schwanitz, *Nazis, Islamists, and the Making of the Modern Middle East*, pg. 175.

[24] Ibid. Pg. 161.

[25] Hitler's words and William Shirer's reflections.

If the international Jewish financiers...should again succeed in plunging the nations into a world war the result will be...the annihilation of the Jewish race throughout Europe." This was a prophecy, he said, and he repeated it five times, verbatim, in subsequent public utterances.

Shirer, *The Rise and Fall of the Third Reich: A History of Nazi Germany*, pg. 964.

[26] Ibid. Pg. 964-965.

[27] ISLAM=NAZISM. "Islam and the Nazis." Online video clip. *YouTube*. YouTube, 31 Mar. 2008. Web. <https://www.youtube.com/watch?v=dxCzwz7zTco>.

[28] This way of Satan working through human beings agreeing together to do great evil is comparable to the way the Holy Spirit is able to work

through human beings who agree together about doing something in the name of Jesus. "Again, I tell you the truth, if two of you on earth agree about whatever you ask, my Father in heaven will do it for you. **20** For where two or three are assembled in my name, I am there among them." (Matthew 18:19-20 NET)

[29] Rubin & Schwanitz, *Nazis, Islamists, and the Making of the Modern Middle East*, pg. 162.

[30] On January 20, 1942, 15 high-ranking Nazi Party and German government officials gathered at a villa in the Berlin suburb of Wannsee to discuss and coordinate the implementation of what they called the "Final Solution of the Jewish Question."

United States Holocaust Memorial Museum. "Wannsee Conference and the Final Solution." *Holocaust Encyclopedia*. Web. 19 Apr. 2016. <http://www.ushmm.org/wlc/en/article.php?ModuleId=10005477>.

[31] Shirer, *The Rise and Fall of the Third Reich: A History of Nazi Germany*, pg. 958

[32] Ibid. Pg. 958.

[33] Ibid. Pg. 965.

[34] Ibid. Pg. 163.

[35] Administrator. "Hitler and the Mufti: The Muslim Love Affair with the Nazis." *The Muslim Issue*. 4 Aug. 2012. Web. <https://themuslimissue.wordpress.com/2012/08/04/hitler-and-the-muslim-mufti/>.

[36] Glick, Caroline. "CRAZY LIKE A FOX: What Netanyahu's "gaffe" about the Mufti and the Holocaust accomplished." *Frontpage* 23 Oct., 2015. Web. <http://www.frontpagemag.com/fpm/260546/crazy-fox-caroline-glick>.

[37] This link between Nazism and Islamic terrorism is a documented historical fact. If you want to explore that history, do a search on the Internet. There are a large number of links. There is also an excellent book by Chuck Morse, *The Nazi Connection to Islamic Terrorism: Adolf*

Hitler and Haj Amin al-Husaini (Paperback). You can find this and other books at:
<http://www.amazon.com/s/ref=ntt_athr_dp_sr_1?_encoding=UTF8&so rt=relevancerank&search-alias=books&field-author=Chuck%20Morse>.

[38] Lutzer, *Hitler's Cross: The Revealing Story of How the Cross of Christ was Used as a Symbol of the Nazi Agenda*, pg. 76.

[39] Ibid. Pg. 76.

Chapter 17
Demonic Cloaking

[1]   At the end of World War II, General Eisenhower made a decision to personally visit as many Nazi concentration camps as he could. His reason? He wanted to document the camps and their appalling conditions.

Anticipating a time when Nazi atrocities might be denied, General Eisenhower also ordered the filming and photographing of camps as they were liberated. Members of the U.S. Army Signal Corps recorded approximately 80,000 feet of moving film, together with still photographs... It didn't take long for Eisenhower's concerns to materialize. Despite his presence in many photographs, Holocaust deniers persist to this day.

Bos, Carole D. "Eisenhower's Proof." *Holocaust Evidence.* Awesome Stories.com 01 Mar. 2006. Web. <https://www.awesomestories.com/asset/view/EISENHOWER-S-PROOF-Holocaust-Evidence>.

[2] Wikipedia contributors. "Timeline of al-Qaeda attacks." *Wikipedia, The Free Encyclopedia*. Wikipedia, The Free Encyclopedia, 11 May. 2016. Web. <https://en.wikipedia.org/wiki/Timeline_of_al-Qaeda_attacks>.

[3] From an intercessor in Canada who requests to be unnamed.

[4] MacAskill, Ewen, & Chris McGreal. "Israel Should Be Wiped Off Map, Says Iran's President." *The Guardian* 26 Oct. 2005. Web.

<http://www.theguardian.com/world/2005/oct/27/israel.iran>.

[5] Shoebat, "ISIS Sends Out this Message to All Christians: 'You Will Soon See an Ocean of Blood for All the Nations of the Cross.'" <http://www.godismysalvation.com/t17795-isis-sends-out-this-message-to-all-christians-you-will-soon-see-an-ocean-of-blood-for-all-the-nations-of-the-cross>.

[6] Carlson, Gretchen. "New ISIS Video: 'We Will Raise Black Flag Over White House.'" *Fox News* 8 Aug. 2014. Web. <http://insider.foxnews.com/2014/08/08/new-isis-video-%E2%80%98we-will-raise-black-flag-over-white-house%E2%80%99>.

[7] Rossomando, John. "ISIS Threatens to Commit Another Holocaust Against Jews." *The Algemeiner Beta* 8 July 2014. Web. <http://www.algemeiner.com/2014/07/08/isis-threatens-to-commit-another-holocaust-against-jews/#>.

[8] Walker, Christopher. "The West's Failure of Imagination: The democratic world won the Cold War but has underestimated the tenacity of the new threats to freedom." *The Wall Street Journal* 3 Aug. 3, 2015. Web. <http://www.wsj.com/articles/the-wests-failure-of-imagination-1438642772>.

[9] Shirer, *The Rise and Fall of the Third Reich: A History of Nazi Germany*, pg. 81.

[10] "Abbasid Dynasty". *Encyclopædia Britannica*. <http://www.britannica.com/topic/Abbasid-dynasty>.

[11] The Black Banner or Black Standard (راية السوداء rāyat al-sawdā' , also known as راية العقاب rāyat al-'uqāb "banner of the eagle" or simply as الراية al-rāya "the banner") is one of the flags flown by Muhammad in Islamic tradition. It was historically used by Abu Muslim in his uprising leading to the Abbasid Revolution in 747 and is therefore associated with the Abbasid Caliphate in particular. It is also a symbol in Islamic eschatology (heralding the advent of the Mahdi),[and it has been used in contemporary Islamism and jihadism since

the late 1990s.

"Black Standard." *Wikipedia, The Free Encyclopedia.*
   <https://en.wikipedia.org/wiki/Black_Standard>.

[12] Mr. Nawaz is the founding chairman of Quilliam,
(http://www.quilliamfoundation.org/.) a London-based counter-extremism organization, and the author of "Radical: My Journey Out of Islamist Extremism."

Nawaz, Majid. "How to Beat Islamic State." *The Wall Street Journal* 11
   Dec. 2015. Web. <http://www.wsj.com/articles/how-to-beat-
   islamic-state-1449850833>.

[13] Ibid.

[14] CNN staff. "Transcript: President Obama's Speech on Combating ISIS
   and Terrorism." *CNN Politics* 10 Sep. 2014. Web.
   <http://www.cnn.com/2014/09/10/politics/transcript-obama-
   syria-isis-speech/index.html?hpt=po_c1>.

[15] United States. "President Obama: 'We Will Degrade and Ultimately
   Destroy ISIL.'" By David Hudson. *The White House* 10 Sep. 2014. Web.
   <https://www.whitehouse.gov/blog/2014/09/10/president-
   obama-we-will-degrade-and-ultimately-destroy-isil>.

[16] "Useful Idiots" is a pejorative term that was used by the Soviets to
   describe Soviet sympathizers in Western countries and in the United
   States in particular. It is thought that the Soviet leader Lenin was the
   first to use the term and it was used by the Soviets for many years to
   ridicule misguided Americans who were willing to take the
   Soviet/Marxist side against their own country.
   Roebling, Paul. "Why are Liberals Called Useful Idiots?" *Paul
   Roebling: My Writing* 2012. Web.
   <https://www.sites.google.com/site/paulroebling/home/why-are-
   liberals-called-useful-idiots>.

[17] Fox News Staff. "State Department Spokeswoman Floats Jobs as
   Answer to ISIS." *Fox News* 17 Feb. 2015. Web.
   <http://www.foxnews.com/politics/2015/02/17/state-

department-spokeswoman-floats-jobs-as-answer-to-isis/>.

[18] Wood, "What ISIS Really Wants," <http://www.theatlantic.com/features/archive/2015/02/what-isis-really-wants/384980/>.

[19] Isikoff, Michael. "FBI Director Comey: San Bernardino Shooting Now a 'Federal Terrorism Investigation.'" *Yahoo News* 4 Dec. 2015. Web. <http://news.yahoo.com/fbi-director-comey-san-bernardino-shooting-now-federal-terrorism-investigation-232722009.html>.

[20] McGurn, William. "The Liberal Theology of Gun Control: Guns are what you talk about to avoid having to talk about Islamist terrorism." *The Wall Street Journal* 7 Dec. 2015. Web. <http://www.wsj.com/articles/the-liberal-theology-of-gun-control-1449533861>.

Chapter 18
A Map of the Strongholds Created from Islam

[1] I have been profoundly helped in understanding this complex process of the formation of strongholds that are intermingled spiritual and human realities by the two following sources:

Toynbee, *A Study of History*, pg. 214-217.

Toynbee explains the role of the mystic with a vision of reality. A "creative minority" forms around the mystic, and it is through them that the vision actualized in human society.

Berger & Luckmann, *The Social Construction of Reality: A Treatise in the Sociology of Knowledge*.

Section II, "Society as Objective Reality," elucidates the principles of how a social structure such as the Islamic State with its own social and spiritual reality may be formed.

[2] The Lord Jesus points to what we may call demonic kairos moments or a demonic moment of opportunity while he is being arrested. "Day after day when I was with you in the temple courts, you did not arrest me. But this is your hour, and that of the power of darkness!" (Luke

22:53 NET) "Hour" here is for "hour" or "season" and not "kairos," but it is clearly the opportunity when the conditions were right for the Devil to work within human history.

3 The "routinization of charisma" is Max Weber's term for how charismatic, prophetic leadership becomes structured, organized, and made transferable to others.

Wikipedia contributors. "Charismatic authority." *Wikipedia, The Free Encyclopedia*. Wikipedia, The Free Encyclopedia, 11 Mar. 2016. Web.<https://en.wikipedia.org/wiki/Charismatic authority>.

4 Contributors. "Sun Tzu>Quotes>Quotable Quote." Quotable Quotes. *Good Reads*. Web. 20 Apr. 2016. http://www.goodreads.com/quotes/17976-if-you-know-the-enemy-and-know-yourself-you-need.

5 Churchill, Winston. "Minister Winston Churchill's Broadcast on the Soviet-German War." The BBC, 22 Jun. 1941. Radio. http://www.ibiblio.org/pha/policy/1941/410622d.html.

6 This statement is based on my experience of working with non-Christians in China, Taiwan, Korea, and Africa who--while involved in non-Christian religions including Islam—were neither possessed nor, in many cases, occupied by demons. They were people whom the Bible would call "God fearers" and were like Cornelius in Acts 10. They were also those whom Paul talks about in Romans 2:13-16 (NET). I must also affirm that in many more cases when those outside of the Christian faith—including Muslims—came to faith in Jesus Christ, their conversions were accompanied by the casting out of demons who had gotten attached to them through both their unconfessed sins of violating the Ten Commandments and/or participating in non-Christian beliefs and practices.

Presbyterian-Reformed Ministries International

PRMI was founded in 1966 to pray and work for the spiritual renewal of Presbyterian and Reformed churches. Over the past 50 years, we have grown to include parts of the Body of Christ in many nations, and continue to have a distinctive role in the world wide movement of the Holy Spirit advancing the Gospel of Jesus Christ for the fulfillment of the Great Commission. www.prmi.org

Dunamis Institute
Equipping the Church for the Advancement of the Kingdom of Jesus Christ Worldwide

The Dunamis Institute is the teaching ministry of PRMI. It equips Christians to cooperate with the Holy Spirit in ministry, missions and evangelism, growing the Church and advancing the Kingdom of God. Free online video courses available, www.DunamisInstitute.org

Other books available by this author related to mobilizing prayer

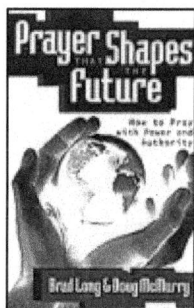

Prayer that Shapes the Future: How to Pray with Power and Authority

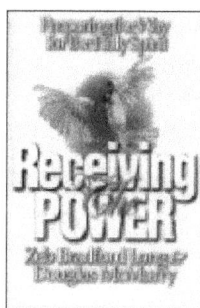

Receiving the Power: Preparing the Way for the Holy Spirit

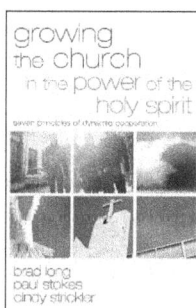

Growing the Church in the Power of the Holy Spirit: The Two Foundations and Seven Dynamics

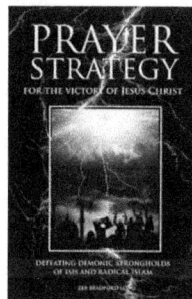

Prayer Strategy For the Victory of Jesus Christ: *Defeating the Demonic Strongholds of ISIS and Radical Islam*

Order books online at www.prmi.org/resources

the Dunamis project

"But you will receive power when the Holy Spirit has come upon you, and you will be my witnesses in Jerusalem, and in all Judea and Samaria, and to the farthest parts of the earth." Acts 1:8

Learn how to cooperate with the Holy Spirit to be an effective witness to Jesus Christ by effectively engaging in ministries of prayer, healing, spiritual warfare, and evangelism for growing the Church and advancing the Kingdom of God.

Dunamis can help you deepen your walk with the Lord and prepare you for effective ministry wherever the Lord has called you. "Dunamis" is the Greek term for "power."

With the Dunamis teaching, you'll discover

- Solid biblical theology about the person and work of the Holy Spirit in the life of the believer.
- Teaching forged from the Scriptures, proven in ministry, and informed by 200 years of renewal and revival movements.
- Your spiritual gifts and how to use them effectively in the Kingdom of God.
- How to recognize God's guidance for ministry in a given moment through the experience based lab times and review debriefings.

The Dunamis Project consists of six units each taught over five days six months apart in the same location. Each event consists of intensive biblical teaching and practical application in the context of prayer and worship. These events are designed to enable every believer to grow in their faith, personal relationship with God and participation in the ministry of the Holy Spirit.

For more information, go to www.dunamisinstitute.org/dp

Equipping Projects are offered in English, Spanish, Korean, Japanese, Chinese, and other languages in the United States, Central and South America, Canada, the United Kingdom, South Korea, and other locations